IN THE SHADOW OF EXTINCTION

R.D.S. Jenkinson and D.D. Gilbertson

IN THE SHADOW OF EXTINCTION:

A Quaternary Archaeology and Palaeoecology of the Lake, Fissures and Smaller Caves at Creswell Crags SSSI.

by

D.D. Gilbertson and R.D.S. Jenkinson

with contributions by
Ann Blackham, D. Bramwell, D.J. Briggs, K.M. Cartledge, G.M. Coles, Christine Griffin, Jennifer Hillam, C.O. Hunt, F.B. Pyatt, Dorothy Row, R. Row, C. Samson, R.E. Stebbings, Sheila Sutherland, Carolyn Watts.

Department of Prehistory and Archaeology
University of Sheffield
Sheffield S10 2TN
Publisher: John R. Collis
Editor: Robin Gould-Zvelebil
Illustrator and Cover Design: Shaun Kavanaugh, Peter Dennis
Typist: Val Kinsler

Nottingham and Derby;
Nottinghamshire and Derbyshire County Councils
Printed by: H. Charlesworth and Co. Ltd.
Huddersfield, England.

ISBN 0 906090 21 0

CONTENTS

LIST OF FIGURES

LIST OF TABLES

CONTRIBUTORS

Ann Blackham B.Sc.	*Department of Biology, Kings Lynn Technical College, Norfolk.*
Dr. D. Bramwell	*Department of Prehistory and Archaeology, University of Sheffield.*
Dr. D.J. Briggs	*Department of Geography, University of Sheffield.*
Kathryn M. Cartledge B.A., M.A.	*Department of Prehistory and Archaeology, University of Sheffield.*
G.M. Coles, B.A.	*Department of Prehistory and Archaeology, University of Sheffield.*
Dr. D.D. Gilbertson M.I.Env.Sci., F.G.S.	*Department of Prehistory and Archaeology, University of Sheffield.*
Christine M. Griffin, B.Sc.	*Department of Prehistory and Archaeology, University of Sheffield.*
Jennifer A. Hillam, B.Sc.	*Dendrochronology Laboratory, Department of Prehistory andArchaeology, University of Sheffield.*
Dr. C.O. Hunt	*Department of Prehistory and Archaeology, University of Sheffield.*
Dr. R.D.S. Jenkinson	*Creswell Crags Visitor Centre, Welbeck, Worksop, Notts.*
M. Norris	*Creswell Crags Visitor Centre, Welbeck, Worksop, Notts.*
Dr. F.B. Pyatt M.I. Biol., M.I. Env. Sci.	*Department of Life Sciences, Trent Env. Sci. Polytechnic, Nottingham.*
D. Row	*Creswell Crags Visitor Centre, Welbeck, Worksop, Notts.*
R. Row	*Creswell Crags Visitor Centre, Welbeck, Worksop, Notts.*
Dr. C. Samson	*Department of Anthropology, University of Sydney, N.S.W., Australia (formerly Department of Prehistory and Archaeology,University of Sheffield).*
Dr. R.E. Stebbings	*Institute of Terrestrial Ecology, Natural Environment Research Council, Abbots Ripton, Huntingdonshire.*
Sheila Sutherland, B.A.	*Department of Prehistory and Archaeology, University of Sheffield.*
Carolyn Watts, B.Sc., M.A.	*Department of Anthropology, University of Sydney, N.S.W., Australia (formerly Department of Prehistory and Archaeology,University of Sheffield).*

ACKNOWLEDGEMENTS

This volume represents the first results of the current research programme at Creswell Crags. These studies owe much to the support of Nottinghamshire and Derbyshire County Councils. The Science and Engineering Research Councils, in collaboration with both County Councils, have generously awarded SERC/CASE post-graduate scholarships to C.M. Griffin and G. Coles for research at Creswell. Access to some of the sites mentioned in this report was freely granted by Welbeck Estates Limited, Steetley Minerals Limited, and Steetley Refractories Limited. Steetley Minerals Limited and the National Coal Board both generously loaned specialist equipment to aid exploration and excavation. All of the case studies reported here would not have been completed without the enthusiasm and generous volunteer help from many local amateur archaeologists and local natural history and archaeology societies—the Hunter Archaeological Society (Dog Hole Fissure study), the Sherwood Archaeological Society (Dog Hole Fissure and the molluscan study of the Crags lake), and the Creswell Archaeological and Natural History Society (Steetley Cave and lake study). We would like to thank the following for their continued support, especially for excavation and post-excavation work: B. Adams, M. Bannister, L. Calow, B. Chambers, P. Finch, J. Haynes, N. Heywood, D. Row and R. Row.

PREFACE

This book describes and interprets the archaeology and ecological history of important sites at the Creswell Crags S.S.S.I. This site is world famous for its archaeological and palaeontological remains, especially those which accumulated in the period 100,000 to 7,000 years ago. This was a time of notably different climate to that of the area today. For example, approximately 20,000 years ago, Creswell Crags was no more than 40kms from a vast ice sheet extending down the east coast of Britain to Norfolk from its sources in upland Britain and Scandinavia. Hyaenas, mammoths, woolly rhino and sabre-toothed cats roamed open, largely treeless, landscapes. The beginning and end of this period were essentially similar in climate to that of today. The landscape was forested, and the wildlife dominated by woodland animals. In this scene of remarkable landscape change, people would occasionally visit and live in the Creswell Caves. The evidence is to be found in the finds of human bones, their hearths, and the implements that they made.

Throughout this period life at Creswell Crags has been in the shadow of extinction. Life was threatened by the severity of the arctic climates which have prevailed, by the rates of climatic change which occurred on several occasions, and by the increasing technical and hunting skills of prehistoric people at the Crags. Some humble animal groups—such as many molluscan species—survived. Other species—such as the oaks, elms and ashes which characterise the present woodland—relocated in refuges in Mediterranean lands, and recolonised Britain 10,000 to 5,000 years ago. Fate was more unkind to the hyaenas, mammoths, sabre toothed cats, and the northern lynx of the cover illustration. These species became extinct. Their fossil bones occur in the cave sediments at Creswell. With luck, studies of their remains and their associated sediments will indicate how and why they became extinct in Britain. In recent years the existence of both the caves and their archaeological resources have been threatened and it has become a major task to protect them and their contents from the same unhappy fate as befell so many of the more spectacular, previous occupants.

The sites and themes described in this book have not been discussed in depth before. They are different to the more familiar topics with which archaeologists commonly associate the Crags. The extensive use of illustrations and non-technical text will aid the amateur archaeologist wishing to understand recent work at Creswell, and the natural historian wanting to understand the evolution of the modern flora and fauna of the area.

This volume is the first in a series of major reports on Creswell Crags. The second will deal with recent studies of the famous Robin Hood's Cave; the third will describe current research in Pin Hole Cave.

The Creswell Crags Visitor Centre maintains a wide range of visual aids, facsimiles, exhibits and supporting 'popular' and 'technical' literature to help interpretation of this major site. Visitors to the centre have access to lectures, field guides and tours, as well as the exhibitions and re-enactments of early human history in the caves.

PART I INTRODUCTION

CHAPTER 1: THE LEGACY OF CRESWELL CRAGS

CONTENTS

THE ARCHAEOLOGY AND GEOLOGY OF CRESWELL CRAGS

The complimentary colour postcard enclosed shows a George Stubbs' painting entitled *Two Gentlemen Going Shooting, with a view of Creswell Crags* of AD 1770 (Yale University Centre for British Art: Catalogue number B 1976.7.85). The painting shows a large mill pond and accompanying thatched cottages of a hamlet with a watermill at the western end of the Gorge. The sluice and mill-run in the foreground lead to the area of the present gorge. The cliffs are rather stylised but are recognisable. Trees, copses and woods abound. The dalmations are ready to gather the prey once rifle loading has been finished. Stubbs used the Crags Gorge as a background for many of his animal paintings. These pictures provide the oldest pictorial evidence of the appearance, life and times of the Crags.

Although there are no clear records, the settlement of Creswell, of which the watermill and hamlet were part, appears to have developed around AD 1175 when Thomas de Cuckney endowed the Abbey of Welbeck (Thomson 1938). Further descriptive documentary records of Creswell are common until the period 1535 to 1846, when it was part of the Welbeck Abbey.

Stubbs' *Two Gentlemen* must have had to walk or ride to hunt their prey in the wooded gorge, because in 1821 Laird in his *Description of the County of Nottingham* describes the Gorge as impassable for carriages.

In 1854 further cottages associated with the mill were built to accommodate quarrymen employed at the recently opened Creswell quarry shown on *Figure 1*. One of these housed Richard Tebbet, a quarry supervisor, who found the first fossil bones in the caves at Creswell. During the 1870's the mill declined. The landowner—the Duke of Portland—demolished the hamlet and drained the millpond shown on the postcard.

Downstream of the former mill the land was deliberately flooded by the construction of a dam at the western end of the gorge, to produce the present Crags Pond—a duck shooting lake for the Duke's enjoyment. In the 1960's the appearance of the northern side of the gorge was altered drastically during the installation of the main sewer from Creswell alongside the lake. The duck shoot pond itself was also infilling rapidly with sediment and was dredged in 1982 to meet the requirements of the lease.

But this picture of change in a microcosm of rural England does not go back far enough in time to reach the more distant periods of prehistory for which the evidence from the Creswell Crags caves is world famous. Many of the caves have produced intriguing fossil remains of mammoths, woolly rhinoceros, hyaenas, bears, lions, northern lynx (cover picture) and other animals which are now extinct.

Change, loss, death, decay and extinction are recurrent themes in the archaeology and geology of Creswell Crags. The shadow of extinction was cast by the prevalence of severe arctic climates, rapid climatic shifts, and the activities of people hunting or competing with animals.

The extinction of the northern lynx in Britain may have been accelerated by the clearance of its forest habitat by early agriculturalists. More recent agricultural developments and industrialisation have threatened many other species. Only a few years ago, it looked as if the Crags gorge and several of its famous, archaeologically rich caves were also going to be destroyed by the pressures of the late twentieth century.

This book describes and interprets the results of archaeological and palaeoecological studies carried out over the past five years on some of the smaller, often overlooked, sites at Creswell which provide interesting new evidence of ancient life and environments at Creswell. In the second part of the book, these new data are combined with a re-evaluation of earlier studies to identify the history of faunal migration, colonisation, death, decay and extinction experienced at Creswell Crags over the past 100,000 years.

THE ARCHAEOLOGICAL SIGNIFICANCE OF CRESWELL CRAGS

The great archaeological and geological significance of Creswell Crags is best appreciated when seen against our knowledge of:
1) the great changes of climate and environments experienced in the British Isles over the past two million years; and 2) the development of our understanding of the antiquity of man, and the various motives and methods of a very long list of archaeologists and geologists who have tackled this problem at Creswell Crags over the past 120 years.

We are still living in a great Ice Age. Glaciers and ice sheets still cover substantial areas of the earth's surface. It was only slightly over 10,000 years ago that the last glaciers and ice sheets in the mountains of the British Isles melted away. The present period of time represents an interglacial—a warmer, more temperate stage, between much colder episodes. The date for the onset of the next major cooling lies at an unknown period—far into the future. The history of the past two million years of the Quaternary Period, characterised by major climatic and environmental changes, is becoming increasingly well known. This period has seen enormous changes in climate:

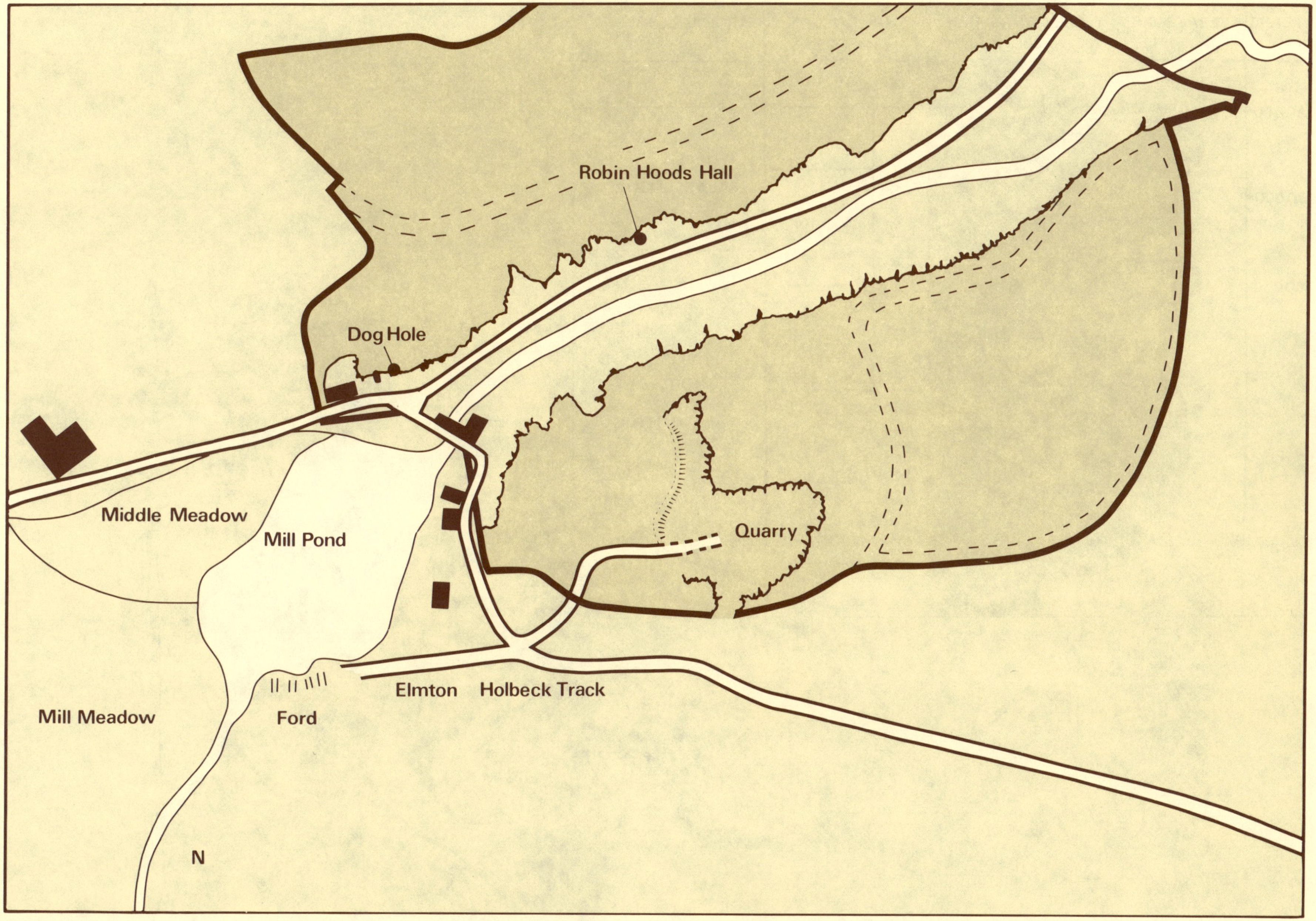

Figure 1. Reconstruction showing the appearance of Creswell Crags during the eighteenth and nineteenth centuries.

Figure 2. The last 100,000 years of Creswell's history.

- the spread and decline of vast ice masses;
- substantial falls and recoveries of ocean levels as ocean water nourished the former ice sheet growth with precipitation;
- radical changes of geography consequent upon sea level change, with the British Isles being repeatedly connected with, and then separated from, the European mainland;
- major changes in the distribution of plants, animals and soils;
- the development of the hominids and the eventual emergence of our own species, *Homo sapiens sapiens* and his cultural and technological progress;
- widespread migrations, colonisations and extinctions as a response to all these factors.

The Last 100,000 Years

In this text we deal with the last 100,000 years of this enormously complicated but fascinating story. The general pattern of events in the Creswell area is summarised graphically in *Figure 2*. Deposits covering this period are fairly well represented at Creswell, despite the depredations of nineteenth century scientists who often "quarried" with scant regard for science.

At the start of this episode, the British Isles were experiencing the temperate climate of the Ipswichian interglacial stage: named after deposits of this period which are located near Ipswich. Deciduous woodland covered the landscape and warmth-loving animals such as lion, hippopotamus, bison and red deer, roamed the land around Creswell.

A deterioration of climate set in with coniferous forest spreading down from the north to replace the temperate woodlands. Heath became more and more common, the soils increasingly acidic and podsolic.

The 'warm' interglacial was replaced by the generally cold to very cold conditions of the Devensian cold-stage which commenced *c*. 70–80,000 years ago. Periods of extreme cold occurred, with Britain covered in treeless arctic/sub-arctic tundra and steppe. Ice sheets fed by precipitation developed, ocean levels declined and Ireland and Great Britain became part of the European mainland (*Figure 3*). The warmth-loving plants and animals were now surviving in refuges far to the south in Mediterranean lands. The generally bitter cold was occasionally broken by milder episodes called interstadials. During the Chelford interstadial the landscape of much of the lowland of Britain was covered in dense spruce-pine coniferous forest similar to that which covers southern Finland today. Deposits of this age are exposed in gravel workings at Chelford in Cheshire. Other milder periods were more complex. During parts of the later Upton Warren interstadial, summer temperatures were not far below those prevailing nowadays in the English midlands; although winters were much colder. The climate was more continental than occurs today in essentially oceanic Britain.

Vast changes in the character of the British landscape occurred in the period 26,000–14,000 years ago, before the present (i.e. BP). Ice sheets and glaciers spread into the lowlands from source areas in the Lake District, northern Britain and Scandinavia to coalesce and form a major ice sheet. One branch occupied the present North Sea Basin. It reached as far south as the Norfolk coast, abutting the eastern margin of the Lincolnshire Wolds, and extending north to Harrogate. West of the Pennines its margin is defined by lines joining Wolverhampton to Newport, Monmouthshire, and across to Pembrokeshire.

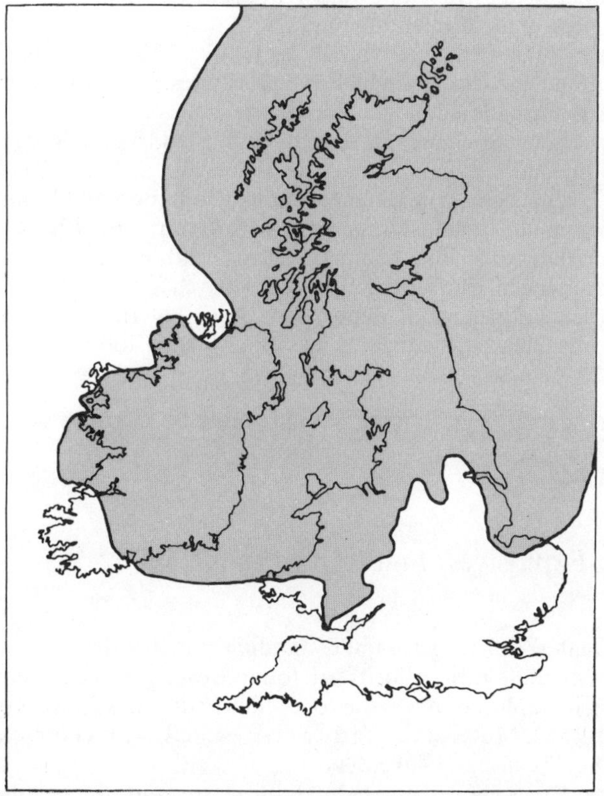

Figure 3. Reconstruction of Devensian Britain showing the extent of ice sheets.

The decay and retreat of this ice sheet were complex phenomena. At its most rapid, melting water flooded back into the oceans at such a rate that ocean level rose by well over one metre every hundred years. Occasionally warmer episodes recurred—the Lake Windermere interstadial 13–11,000 years ago witnessed the replacement of open tundra with Birch woodland. A brief, colder, snap 11,000–10,000 years ago saw a temporary resurgence of glaciers in highland Britain. However, by 10,000 years ago the climate was again warming very rapidly, and the British Isles were left ice-free.

The most recent 10,000 years, known in Britain as the Flandrian warm stage, have been far warmer, with climates in the Creswell Caves essentially similar to that of today. One after another, our forest trees—Birch, Pine, Elm, Oak, Alder, Lime, Ash and Beech—from their associated animals returned to Britain from the glacial refuges. This return migration continued until the flooding of the North Sea and Channel in the early and mid-Flandrian terminated the last land links with the European mainland.

Subsequently, forest clearance by early agriculturalists commencing about 5,000 years ago, initiated the changes which eventually resulted in the essentially open, impoverished, man-made landscapes of today.

Throughout the Ipswichian, Devensian and Flandrian, the caves have been occupied only intermittently by prehistoric people and animals. The evidence from the Creswell Caves for this colossal environmental change, and human and animal occupation, is some of the most important known in the British Isles and Europe. A full understanding of the complex events and changes in environmental conditions experienced during the last 100,000 years has been very difficult to achieve, complete sequences of deposits representing this period are extremely rare. However at Creswell, sequences spanning this period have been located.

THE LEGACY OF TWELVE DECADES OF EXCAVATION

1862–1900: Explosives, Finds and Frauds

Perhaps the greatest difficulty for understanding sites like the Creswell caves where large amounts of these rare deposits are found, results from the manner in which they have been explored over the one hundred years since they were first investigated in 1862. Much of this early work resulted in the complete "extinction" of vital evidence, bones and cave deposits.

Many sites at Creswell were discovered during the mid-nineteenth century when research into prehistory was in its infancy. Many excavators were not too careful and usually their overriding concern was to dig out evidence of prehistoric man.

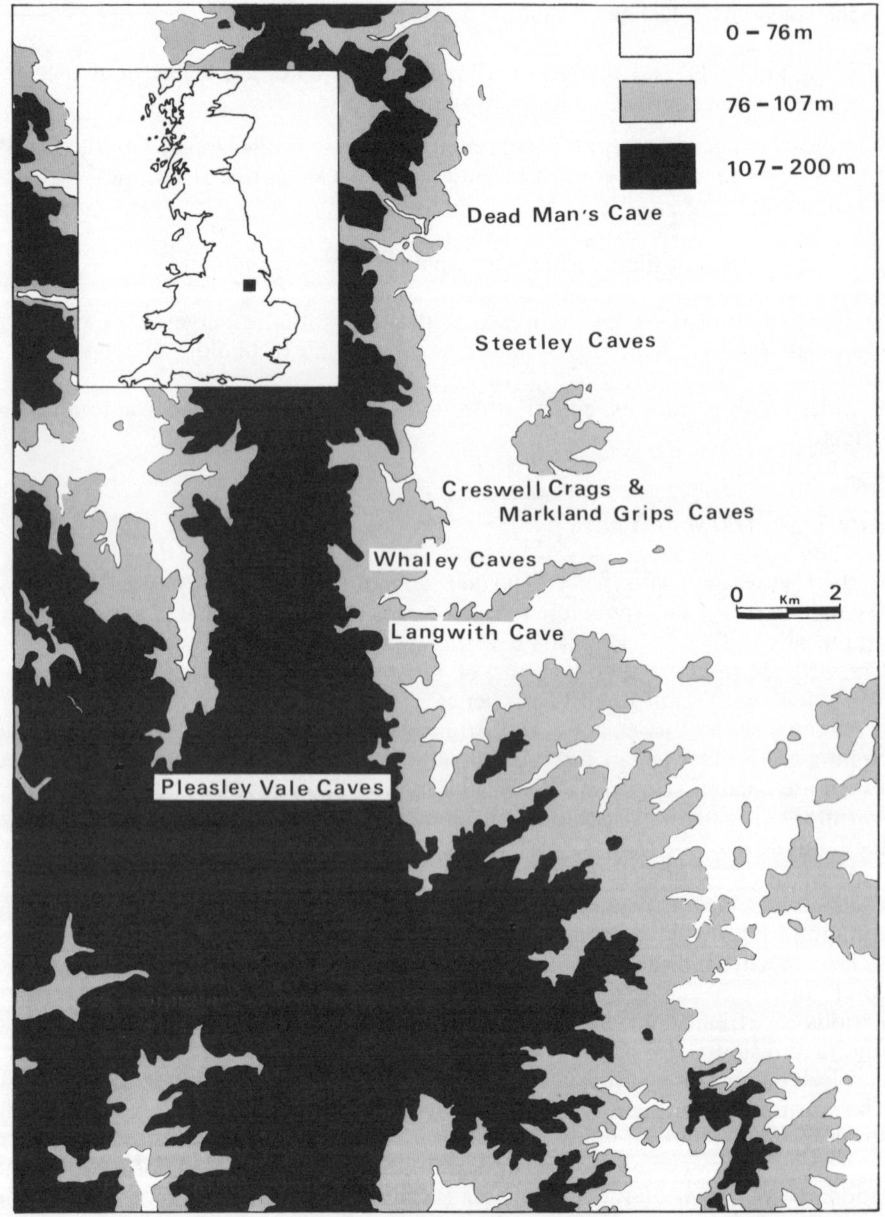

Figure 4. The distribution of caves and rock shelters in the area around Creswell Crags.

Due to the hard nature of the deposits, explosives were sometimes employed. Use of this method and the haste with which many deposits were dug out allowed little control over the recording of complex variation in the cave sediments. The haste to find prehistoric artefacts was at the expense of virtually all other forms of prehistoric information preserved within many of these caves.

The first archaeological discovery was made in 1862 when workmen uncovered a cave containing Pleistocene bones within Pleasley Vale Gorge (Anon 1862), the location of which is shown in *Figure 4*. This discovery aroused the interest of a local doctor, Dr. Ransom, who discovered a further cave, named Yew Tree Cave. In 1865, this produced one of the first evidences of fossil Lynx (*Felis lynx*) known from Britain (Ransom 1866).

Following these early discoveries of the 1860's, there was a lull in cave exploration within the Creswell area and it was not until 1873 that the next discovery was made. In 1873, Mr. R. Tebbet, the Creswell Crags Quarry Supervisor, observed 'fossil bones' eroding from the rear of a cattle byre then occupying the mouth of Church Hole Cave within the Creswell Gorge (*Figure 5*). Tebbet enthusiastically reported his find to the local priest, the Reverend Magens Mello, who visited the site himself in 1874. He was intrigued by the archaeological potential not only of Church Hole Cave, but also the further caves he noticed on his visit. News of the discovery travelled fast, particularly to Thomas Heath, the Curator of the Derby Museum. Both Mello and Heath made simultaneous applications to the Duke of Portland, the owner of Creswell Gorge, for permission to excavate. Both decided to pool their resources and mounted a joint exploration with Heath supervising the actual excavations and record keeping. Neither had previous experience of identifying faunal material and they consequently enlisted the help of Professor George Busk at the Institute of Geological Sciences, who undertook to report on the mammal fauna of Pin Hole Cave (Mello's fissure A).

Operations commenced late in 1874 at Pin Hole Cave and was followed soon after by trial explorations in Church Hole Cave. The results at Church Hole Cave were disappointing, so in 1876 operations were concentrated at both Church Hole Cave and Robin Hood's Cave (Mello 1875, Boyd Dawkins 1876). By 1876 the explorations had attracted considerable attention, not least on the part of William Boyd Dawkins, a paragon of Victorian science and Curator of the University Museum at the Victoria University of Manchester. Boyd Dawkins had published a preliminary account in *Pall Mall* magazine (1875) long before his involvement with the excavations, a development which at once placed him in a difficult position with Mello and Heath. The Reverend Mello was quick to patch over any jealousies and was delighted when Dawkins' circle of friends also joined the work. This was particularly the case with Richard Tiddeman who had made similar discoveries in North Yorkshire and had travelled from Yorkshire to help with the work. Heath, who was undertaking most of the actual work and recording, felt aggrieved and the seeds were sown for the ensuing clash of personalities which greatly affected the progress of excavations.

Arguments reached a head during the final stages of excavations in Robin Hood's Cave, particularly after the spectacular finds of the horse head engraving (*Figure 6*) and the canine tip of dirk toothed cat—one of the sabre-toothed cats. Heath believed both of these remarkable finds to be planted forgeries. He observed drily that both had been found in an 'unusual week' by Mello and Dawkins, and

"a week when both were present and at the same time".

These archaeologists had a bad habit of avoiding the more arduous and demanding aspects of field work. This was clear from the few written descriptions of their work. The outcome of the rather drawn out arguments was the eventual ostracising of Heath from the Victorian scientific and archaeological community in early 1877. Heath (1880) resorted to private publication of the results of the work taken from his notebooks, which he refused to hand over to Mello. Mello and Dawkins published their own account based on Mello's memory and a small quantity of Dawkins' diary notes (1875), a very unsatisfactory and unnecessary state of affairs.

Mello and Dawkins continued their exploration at Mother Grundy's Parlour, in a search for an interglacial deposit, the presence of which was suggested by the finding of a Hippopotamus tooth which appeared at a London auction and which was said to be from the cave. These excavations at Mother Grundy's Parlour marked the end of the work of Mello and Dawkins at Creswell for the time being, but the exploration and ensuing public arguments had attracted to the site the attention of both scholars and public.

During the next twenty years this attraction manifested itself at Creswell with the occurrence of many small unorganised excavations aimed chiefly at specimen collecting, usually for financial reward. Most, if not all, of these activities are unpublished and are only known today from the occasional "journalistic reports" which occurred from time to time in the local newspaper.

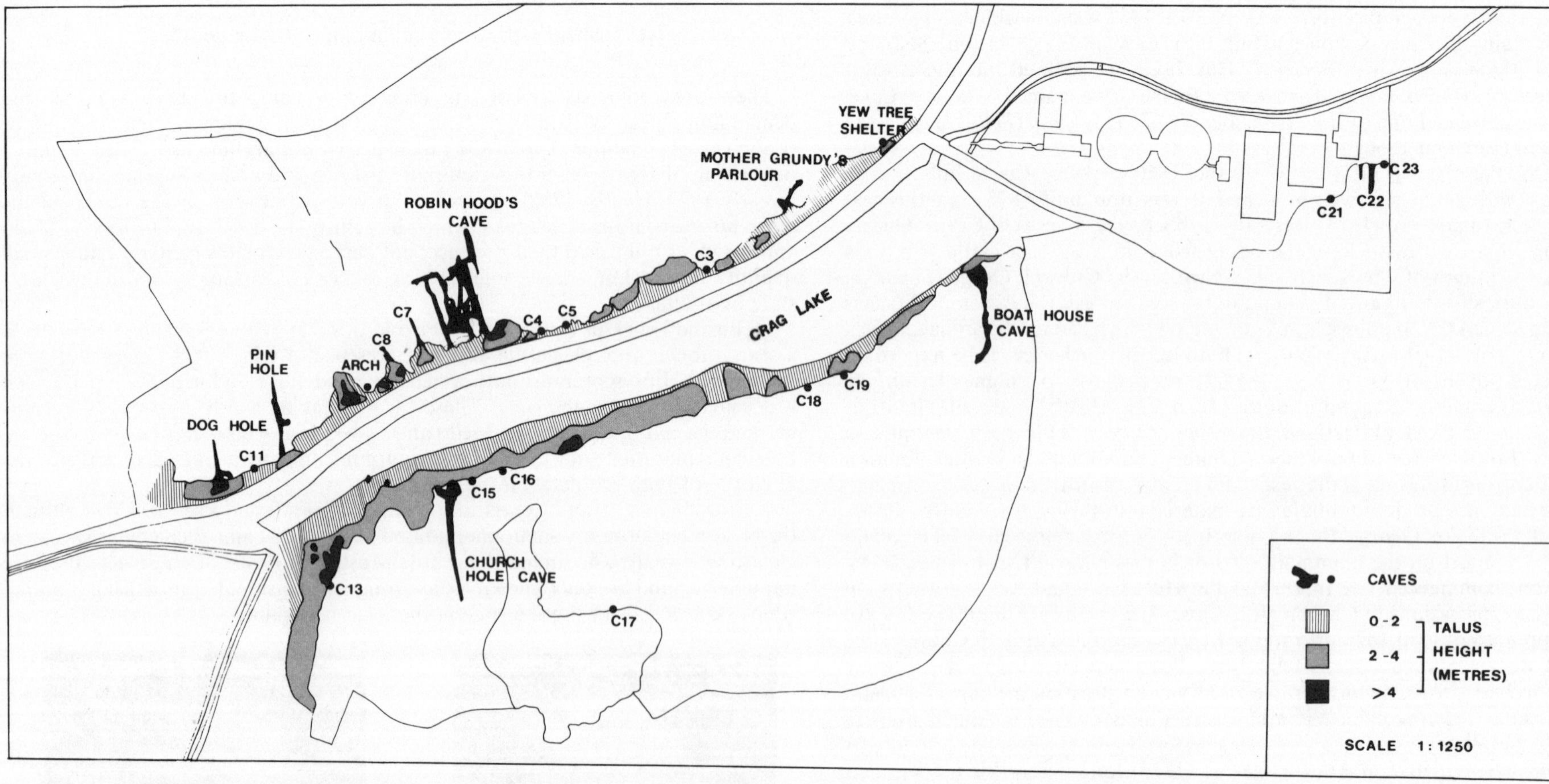

Figure 5. The distribution of caves and rock shelters at Creswell Crags.

Formal excavations started again in 1888 when the retired Scottish antiquarian, Dr. Robert Laing, commenced excavations at Dog Hole Cave on the northeastern outcrop at Creswell and at Robin Hood's Cave. The excavations were unfortunately never formally published by Laing, who died during the excavations, after no fewer than twelve years activity on the site. Both artefactual material and any written records of the excavation—if they ever existed—disappeared at the time of Laing's death. Indeed this excavation of Dog Hole Cave was unknown until the present work at Dog Hole Fissure revealed the history of the adjacent cave. Even so, the only indications of the importance of the cave and its location occur in the report of a tour made by a local society and apparently conducted by Laing which was published in abbreviated form in the *Transactions of the East Derbyshire Field Club* (Burr 1910). The whole episode was a sad waste of time and, more important, destroyed irreplaceable deposits for all time.

In 1894 two Cambridge geologists, W.L.H. Duckworth and F.E. Swainson working at the Sedgwick Museum, undertook a small excavation in a fissure on the north face of Creswell Crags (*Cave C8, Figure 5*). The excavation produced a small collection of bone material associated with some flint tools. Thankfully these geologists published their results of a first season's work (Duckworth and Swainson 1895). This suggested the potential of further work at the site, which unfortunately does not seem to have been undertaken.

By the end of the century the pace of exploration had slackened. The excitement generated by the great "excavations" of the 1870's had subsided. The enormous amounts of arduous work that had taken place over the years had demonstrated the wealth of human occupation within the Creswell caves. Despite the backdrops of allegations of fraud, Boyd Dawkins had, by the end of the century, incorporated much of the Creswell work into a major publication dealing with the early human occupation of Britain (Dawkins 1910). He was also responsible for a detailed series of monographs published by the Palaeontographical Society, describing Pleistocene animal remains in Britain (Dawkins and Sandford 1865, 1872).

Today there are major difficulties interpreting many of the nineteenth century discoveries. Despite the arduous and difficult nature of cave excavations, the failure of these early researchers to recover, in a stratified context, the large numbers of smaller animal bones evident today on their spoil heaps, is inexcusable. Their work presents us with a highly biased collection of prehistoric artefacts and fossil bones. Similarly, scant regard was given to the finer points of cave stratigraphies. Examination of their published accounts demonstrates the appalling speed with which these deposits were removed. Most of the archaeological deposits in Church Hole Cave were removed during eight hours work. The work at Robin Hood's Cave was more pedestrian, taking just over a month to empty one of the largest caves in Northern Britain!

In this setting, where the excavation organisers only occasionally visited the sites while work was in progress, it is necessary to regard many of their observations as quite unreliable.

1900–1925: Continued Allegations and Recriminations

By 1900, the prevalent view of Creswell Crags was that archaeologically it had been "worked out" and that little was left to warrant the attentions of archaeologists and geologists. However, further discoveries were in the offing. In 1909 the Reverend E. Mullins, priest to the village of Langwith Bassett, was told of a cave immediately behind his church which had recently been discovered by two schoolboys. Mullins commenced excavations and reported the discovery to (now "Sir") William Boyd Dawkins. Dawkins however did not become involved with the work although he maintained contact by corresponding with Mullins who due to his style of excavations rapidly became referred to by Dawkins (1910) as "meddler Mullins".

In fact, Mullins received a good deal of assistance from W.J. Sollas, a capable man, later to achieve great eminence as an archaeologist. At the time, Sollas was writing the first edition of his book, *Ancient Hunters and their Modern Representatives* (1915). On the basis of conversations with Mullins, Sollas included in this publication details of what he believed to be the Creswell "forgeries" (the horse head engraving in particular, *Figure 6*). By the time of this publication, Heath's (1880) view that the dirk toothed cat canine was deliberately "planted" in the excavations had by now gained wide acceptance. In contrast, the horse engraving described by Dawkins (1876) was largely held to be genuine by Sollas (1915) who stated that his information came from a reliable source who had in fact worked on the excavations in the 1870's. Smith-Woodward (1924), a noted surgeon, famous for his involvement in the "Piltdown Man" discoveries, promptly wrote to Dawkins informing him of the accusation by Sollas, an accusation which Dawkins strenuously denied (1924).

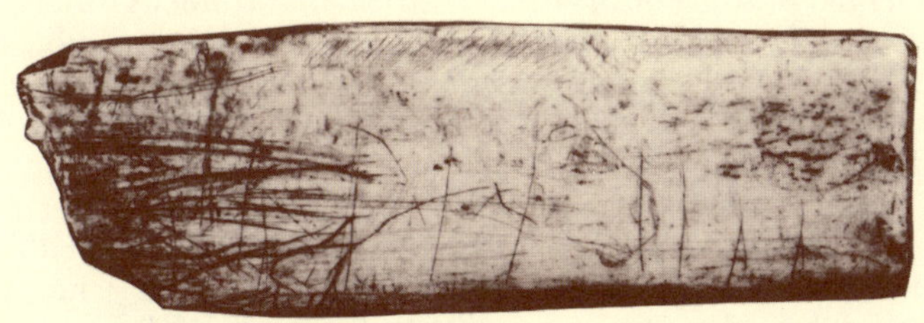

Figure 6. Engraving of a horse's head found by nineteenth century excavators in Robin Hood's Cave.

The whole episode was witnessed and later reported by the highly competent J.W. Jackson, who was at that time Boyd Dawkins' young assistant at the Manchester Museum. In later years Jackson held that the engraving was a genuine find while the dirk toothed cat canine was definitely a "plant".

In fact in his final year Jackson claimed to know the identity of the perpetrator of this fraud although he was loathe to impart this information to the present authors (Jackson pers. comm. 1979). Cave excavation at Langwith Basset by Garrod (1926) marked the end of an era of archaeological work in the Creswell area.

1925–1958: The Controversial Leslie Armstrong

When attention was redirected to Creswell and its surrounding sites in the 1920's, the participants were archaeologists rather than clergymen and gentlemen geologists. The mood had changed. The British Association for the Advancement of Science, on Boyd Dawkins' advice, appointed a *Committee for the Archaeological Exploration of Derbyshire Caves.* It was presided over by Sir William Boyd Dawkins!

Albert Leslie Armstrong was appointed as field archaeologist and J.W. Jackson as palaeontologist. Armstrong lived in Warrington, Cheshire, working full time as an Inspector of Taxes for the Inland Revenue. After a short stay at Bowden Hall, the home of Sir William Boyd Dawkins, he was transferred to the Sheffield office of the Inland Revenue. He soon made the acquaintance of Dr. Arthur Court, a noted local figure and doctor; J.B. Himsworth, a well-known Sheffield silversmith; and J. Hanbury, a Derby-based geologist. Armstrong, in his fifties, and the youngest of his "team", dominated Derbyshire cave archaeology during the period from the 1920's until his death in 1958. He died on a Johannesburg railway station platform, following a strenuous lecture tour of Rhodesia and South Africa.

Armstrong's activities started at Creswell in 1921, when he made a reconnaissance of the gorge (Armstrong 1923). During this early period he was excited by the further potential of some of the caves, particularly Mother Grundy's Parlour and Pin Hole Caves. In the latter case he rightly, as it turned out, reasoned that the termination of the 1875 excavations was not in fact the end of the cave, but was simply a narrowing of it and that in all probability it expanded at a greater distance from the entrance.

Armstrong's tenacity during excavation of the Creswell Caves, particularly at Mother Grundy's Parlour and Pin Hole, is remarkable. Early in the day, he regularly cycled from Sheffield, returning in the evening with a heavy load of "finds". Many of his excavations were carried out in candlelight and under extremely arduous, damp conditions. Despite these problems he managed to conduct an excavation on two Pleistocene sites which was unrivalled for its technical quality during the period 1930–50. His sieving techniques, success at recovering very small fossils, his novel recording methods and the accuracy of his observation still make the results of his work of great relevance today. The Pin Hole excavation dominated Armstrong's activities throughout this period. But as work continued on the site, exploratory trenches were cut into many other sites at Creswell Crags, at the nearby Markland and Hollinhill Grips, the Whaley Valley and Burnt Cinders Grips. The excavations were joined periodically by Dorothy Garrod, later Professor of Archaeology at Oxford. Particularly important were the 1924–25 excavations at Mother Grundy's Parlour.

The spate of work which marked these years came to an abrupt end in 1958 with Armstrong's death, when he was in the midst of excavating Ash Tree Cave in the Burnt Cinders Grips. Work continued at this cave with the help of the Hunter Society (of which both Himsworth and Dr. Court were prominent members) and under the supervision of Dr. Derek Riley.

1959–1983: Towards a Modern Synthesis

In the summer of 1959, the late Dr. C.B.M. McBurney commenced an excavation in the platform of Mother Grundy's Parlour as part of a systematic programme of investigations into British caves, sponsored by the Prehistoric Society. Soon after, he joined the continuing excavations at Ash Tree Cave, now under the supervision of Mr. Stanley West. The excavations by McBurney in Mother Grundy's Parlour have not been published. This is a great pity.

During the 1960's, the late Jeffrey Radley of Sheffield City Museum undertook fieldwork and excavation within the nearby Whaley Valley. His attention soon turned to the Creswell sites, particularly to Mother Grundy's Parlour, and application was made to the Duke of Portland for permission to excavate. Permission was refused on the basis of advice tendered to the Duke and because of growing concern about the preservation of the Creswell sites on the part of both the landowners and the Nottinghamshire and Derbyshire County Councils (McBurney 1962).

Also during the late 1960's , excavations were undertaken at Dead Man's Cave, North Anston (White 1970, Mellars 1969), Lob Wells Shelter and Thorpe Common Shelter (*Figure 4*) (White, personal communication). This excavation produced the first indications of small Upper Palaeolithic occupation sites outside the Creswell Gorge. The first comprehensive synthesis of the Creswell sites was produced by John Campbell in his Doctoral dissertation on the British Upper Palaeolithic, submitted to Oxford University in 1971. As part of a larger programme of excavations on British Upper Palaeolithic sites, areas of Mother Grundy's Parlour and Robin Hood's Cave were excavated. Excavations were also undertaken at Holly Shelter (*Figure 4*) which proved sterile. Campbell's (1977) results are widely known and form the basis of the present-day division of the British Upper Palaeolithic into an Earlier and a Later sequence which is summarised in *Figure 2.*

Simon Collcutt (1975), a student of Campbell's at Edinburgh, reported further work at Creswell undertaken in 1974 in those areas of potential outlined by Campbell. He made a general study, dealing with the chronology as well as stratigraphy of various Creswell sites. Excavations were undertaken by Collcutt at Mother Grundy's Parlour, Pin Hole Cave, Dog Hole Cave, Boat House Cave and samples were taken from the travertine levels of Church Hole Cave in an attempt to rationalise the stratigraphy of the Creswell caves.

Since 1975 the Creswell gorge has been managed jointly by Nottinghamshire and Derbyshire County Councils. The site was designated a Conservation Area and opened to the public as a Country Park.

Coinciding with this development, the local authorities have sponsored a new research project. Initially this was intended to evaluate the archaeological status of finds from the Creswell Caves and to improve the visiting public's enjoyment of this important site. The results of this work were reported by Jenkinson (1984).

It is obvious that despite an enormous amount of exploration work within the Creswell Caves over the past twelve decades, our understanding of many aspects of prehistoric life is very limited. The application of archaeological or scientific techniques in isolation from each other in the 60's and 70's meant that our understanding of prehistoric situations did improve, but it was within rather narrow parameters. The human occupation of the Creswell Caves, for instance, is often presented only in terms of stone tool technologies and their change through time. Animal populations are very crudely equated only with their preference for cold or warm stage environments. Few attempts have been made to integrate knowledge of their ecology, life styles, habitats and environments into a wider picture of prehistory.

During the last five years, Nottinghamshire and Derbyshire County Councils, and the University of Sheffield, have sponsored a research project which aims to foster multi-disciplinary studies of the prehistory of Creswell Caves. It is hoped that this volume, the first results of this approach, will considerably enhance our understanding of the past and present life and times of Creswell Crags.

R.D.S. Jenkinson and D.D. Gilbertson. The Legacy of Creswell Crags. Chapter 1 in Jenkinson, R.D.S. and Gilbertson, D.D. 1984 *In the Shadow of Extinction: A Quaternary Archaeology and Palaeoecology of the Lake, Fissures and Smaller Caves at Creswell Crags S.S.S.I.* Sheffield: Department of Prehistory and Archaeology, University of Sheffield. Pp. 1 to 11.

Part II RECENT RESEARCH

CHAPTER 2: CRESWELL CRAGS: TOWARDS A NATURAL HISTORY

with A.M. Blackham, D.J. Briggs, K.M. Cartledge, G.M. Coles, C.M. Griffin, J.A. Hillam, C.O. Hunt, M. Norris, F.B. Pyatt, D. Row and R. Row

CONTENTS

The ecology and the history of human settlement and environment changes of the Crags Lake and Gorge are of considerable importance for a comprehensive understanding of Creswell Crags. The modern ecological information provides baseline data which aid the reconstruction and interpretation of past environments. Archaeological and palaeoecological studies of the lake sediments reveal details of woodworking, buildings, settlement and land use from before Tudor times to the present. The impact of pollution over a long history of coal mining nearby is clear in sedimentological studies, plant and faunal extinctions and colonisation.

INTRODUCTION

Throughout this book we make frequent use of the study of plant and animal remains in lake sediments and cave sediments to reconstruct the nature of past environments and to identify the forces responsible for patterns of migration, colonisation and extinction recorded within those sediments. The agents of change might be climatic shifts causing the climate of the area to exceed the tolerance limits of the plants or animal species involved, causing them to become extinct. Alternatively, other species or vegetation types which served as a food source or habitat for a further species might have shifted, thus causing a local extinction of the dependent species. Extinction or faunal changes may also have been caused by human predation.

Paul Martin's (1967) controversial Pleistocene "overkill" hypothesis states that in late Pleistocene Europe, hunting may have been the cause of the widespread extinction of the many large vertebrate species which occurred at that time. There is good evidence of prehistoric hunting from Creswell for the Mesolithic period. After this period, widespread deforestation and habitat change caused by prehistoric farmers and their descendants have caused many species to become extinct. These activities have, however, favoured the spread and establishment of other species better adapted for life in association with humans.

The successful use of palaeontological evidence to elucidate these patterns and agents of change consequently must depend upon our understanding of the modern ecological associations and tolerances of the plant and animal species concerned.

Nowadays there is a comparative wealth of information on the modern ecology of plants, ground vertebrates, birds and molluscs—the groups yielding fossils studied in this book. However there is often a dearth of detailed information on the species-associations or microhabitat preferences in the Creswell region, where the soils and landforms are developed upon Magnesian limestone. In particular, there are no data on the processes and patterns of transportation of organisms, alive or dead, by animal or geomorphic processes which help determine the character of the fossil assemblages found by archaeologists and geologists. Data on such taphonomic processes are particularly important for studies of molluscs and vertebrates, whose remains are especially abundant in archaeological sites. Such data are essential for a satisfactory understanding of the variations in species content and frequency at the micro-spatial scales recorded here. The following section is a summary of the available relevant modern ecological and taphonomic data. A fuller account of the *Natural History of Creswell Crags* is in preparation.

THE NATURAL HISTORY OF CRESWELL CRAGS

The following habitats are found at Creswell Crags:

1) the cliff top woodland
2) the cliffs and rock faces of the gorge walls
3) screes and talus
4) grassland and marsh, and occasional walls
5) stream and lake

Botany

The plants occurring at the Crags are listed in *Table 1*. The details of their frequency are given in *Figure 7*, which illustrates the percentage cover of each species noted in 1m^2 quadrats on Transect Q across the gorge from Dog Hole Fissure (*Figure 5*).

The woodland is dominated by Wych elm, Common oak and Ash, with Alder, Yew, Holly, Blackthorn, Wild Cherry, Hawthorn and Mountain Ash common in the understory. Introduced species and "garden escapes" are frequent. Sycamore and Sweet chestnut are common together with brambles, the Gingko, the Spurge and Portugese laurels, Privet and the interesting Duke of Argyll's Tea Plant. The woodland has a fairly rich ground flora with numerous shade tolerant species. The flora is fairly typical of that remaining on the alkaline, lime rich soils of the Magnesian Limestone. The Lime tree (*Tilia* spp) is not common in the area today.

Table 1. Frequency of plant species in the Creswell Crags gorge.

Trees	South Cliff	South Scree	Gorge Floor	Stream	North Scree	North Cliff	Woodland
Wych Elm *(Ulmus glabra)*		X	X		X		X
Spurge Laurel *(Daphne laureola)*							X
Silver Birch *(Betula pendula)*			X				
Alder *(Alnus glutinosa)*			X				
Hazel *(Corylus avellana)*			X			X	
Sweet Chestnut *(Castanea sativa)*							X
Common Oak *(Quercus robur)*			X			X	
Crack Willow *(Salix fragilis)*			X	X			
Ash *(Fraxinus excelsior)*			X		X		X
Duke of Argyll's Tea Plant *(Lycium halimifolium)*							
Privet *(Ligustrum vulgare)*							X
Elder *(Sambucus nigra)*			X				
Portugese Laurel *(Prunus lusitanica)*							X
Gingko *(Gingko biloba)*							X
Spindle Tree *(Euonymus europaeus)*					X		
Scots Pine *(Pinus sylvestris)*							X
Yew *(Taxus baccata)*	X					X	
Sycamore *(Acer pseudoplatanus)*							X
Holly *(Ilex aquifolium)*							X
Gorse *(Ulex europaeus)*	X					X	
Raspberry *(Rubus idaeus)*							X
Blackberry *(Rubus fruticosus)*		X			X		X
Dog Rose *(Rosa canina)*			X				
Blackthorn *(Prunus spinosa)*			X				X
Wild Cherry *(Prunus avium)*							X
Hawthorn *(Crataegus monogyna)*	X		X				X
Mountain Ash *(Sorbus aucuparia)*							X
Crab Apple *(Malus sylvestris)*			X				
Gooseberry *(Ribes uva-crispa)*		X					

Grasses and Sedges

Grasses and Sedges	South Cliff	South Scree	Gorge Floor	Stream	North Scree	North Cliff	Woodland
Bulrush *(Typha latifolia)*				X			
Carnation Sedge *(Carex flacca)*						X	
Sheep's Fescue *(Festuca ovina)*			X				
Annual Meadow Grass *(Poa annua)*		X	X		X		
Couch Grass *(Agropyron repens)*		X	X		X		

Ferns

Ferns	South Cliff	South Scree	Gorge Floor	Stream	North Scree	North Cliff	Woodland
Bracken *(Pteridium aquilinum)*						X	
Hart's Tongue Fern *(Phyllitis scolopendrum)*		X					
Black Spleenwort *(Asplenium adiantium-nigrum)*		X					
Maiden Hair Spleenwort *(Asplenium trichomanes)*		X					
Wall Rue *(Asplenium ruta-muraria)*			X				
Common Polypody *(Polpodium vulgare)*		X					

Mosses

Mosses	South Cliff	South Scree	Gorge Floor	Stream	North Scree	North Cliff	Woodland
Common Moss *(Tortula ruralis)*		X	X		X		
Water Moss *(Fontinalis antipyretica)*				X			
Water Moss *(Tortula latifolia)*				X			

Flowering Plants

Flowering Plants	South Cliff	South Scree	Gorge Floor	Stream	North Scree	North Cliff	Woodland
Marsh Marigold *(Caltha palustris)*				X			
Meadow Buttercup *(Ranunculus acris)*			X				X
Creeping Buttercup *(Ranunculus repens)*		X	X		X		X
Bulbous Buttercup *(Ranunculus bulbosus)*			X				X
Lesser Celandine *(Ranunculus ficaria)*			X				X
Charlock *(Sinapis arvensis)*			X				
Shepherd's Purse *(Capsella bursa-pastoris)*		X	X		X		X
Large Bittercress *(Cardamine amara)*			X				
Hairy Bittercress *(Cardamine hirsuta)*		X	X		X		
Hairy Rock Cress *(Arabis hirsuta)*		X	X		X		
Hedge Garlic *(Alliaria petiolata)*		X	X		X		X
Common Dog Violet *(Viola riviniana)*			X				X
Pale Wood Violet *(Viola reichenbachiana)*							X
Tutsan *(Hypericum androsaemum)*			X				
Rockrose *(Helianthemum nummularium)*						X	
Red Campion *(Silene dioica)*			X				X
White Campion *(Silene alba)*			X				X
Pink Campion *(Silene dioica Xalba)*			X				
Common Mouse Eared Chickweed *(Cerastium fontanum)*		X	X		X		X
Chickweed *(Stellaria media)*			X				
Greater Stitchwort *(Stellaria holostea)*			X				X
Lesser Stitchwort *(Stellaria graminea)*			X				X
Three-veined Sandwort *(Moehringia trinervia)*						X	
Common Mallow *(Malva sylvestris)*			X		X		
Herb Robert *(Geranium robertianum)*	X	X	X		X	X	X
White Clover *(Trifolium repens)*			X				
Red Clover *(Trifolium pratense)*			X				
Bird's Foot Trefoil *(Lotus corniculatus)*			X		X	X	
Tufted Vetch *(Vicia cracca)*			X		X		X
Bush Vetch *(Vicia sepium)*			X				
Meadow Vetchling *(Lathyrus pratensis)*			X				X
Meadow Sweet *(Filipendula ulmaria)*				X			

Flowering Plants	South Cliff	South Scree	Gorge Floor	Stream	North Scree	North Cliff	Woodland
Wild Strawberry *(Fragaria vesca)*							X
Wood Avens *(Geum urbanum)*			X		X		X
Common Agrimony *(Agrimonia eupatoria)*							X
Biting Stonecrop *(Sedum acre)*			X		X		
Meadow Saxifrage *(Saxifraga granulata)*						X	
Great Hairy Willow Herb *(Epilobium hirsutum)*			X	X			X
Lesser Willow Herb *(Epilobium parviflorum)*			X	X			
Broad-leaved Willowherb *(Epilobium montanum)*					X		
Dull-leaved Willowherb *(Epilobium obscurum)*				X			
Marsh Willowherb *(Epilobium palustre)*				X			
Rosebay Willowherb *(Chamaenerion angustifolium)*		X	X		X		
Enchanter's Nightshade *(Circaea lutetiana)*			X				X
Ivy *(Hedera helix)*	X	X			X	X	X
Rough Chervil *(Chaerophyllum temulentum)*			X				
Cow Parsley *(Anthriscus sylvestris)*			X				
Upright Hedge Parsley *(Torilis japonica)*			X				
Hogweed *(Heracleum sphondylium)*		X	X		X		X
Dog's Mercury *(Mercurialis perennis)*		X					X
Red Hen *(Polygonum persicaria)*						X	
Sheep's Sorrel *(Rumex acetosella)*			X				
Sorrel *(Rumex acetosa)*			X				
Broad-leaved Dock *(Rumex obtusifolius)*			X			X	
Sharp Dock *(Rumex conglomeratus)*			X				
Pellitory of the Wall *(Parietaria judaica)*	X					X	
Stinging Nettle *(Urtica dioica)*		X	X		X		X
Cowslip *(Primula veris)*	X						
Primrose *(Primula vulgaris)*	X						
Comfrey *(Symphytum officinale)*			X				
Water Forget-me-not *(Myosotis scorpioides)*				X			
Wood Forget-me-not *(Myosotis sylvatica)*							X
Field Forget-me-not *(Myosotis arvensis)*			X				
Early Forget-me-not *(Myosotis ramosissima)*		X	X				
Small Bindweed *(Convolvulus arvensis)*			X				
Figwort *(Scrophularia nodosa)*				X			
Musk *(Mimulus guttatus)*				X			
Foxglove *(Digitalis purpurea)*	X	X					
Germander Speedwell *(Veronica chamaedrys)*			X				X
Common Calamint *(Calamintha sylvatica)*			X				
Wild Thyme *(Thymus serpyllum)*						X	
Wild Basil *(Clinopodium vulgare)*			X				
Hedge Woundwort *(Stachys sylvatica)*		X	X		X		X

Flowering Plants	South Cliff	South Scree	Gorge Floor	Stream	North Scree	North Cliff	Woodland
Yellow Archangel *(Lamiastrum galeobdolon)*		X	X		X		X
Red Dead Nettle *(Lamium purpureum)*			X			X	
White Dead Nettle *(Lamium album)*		X	X		X		
Catmint *(Nepeta cataria)*				X			
Ground Ivy *(Glechoma hederacea)*	X	X	X		X		X
Bugle *(Ajuga reptans)*			X				X
Great Plantain *(Plantago major)*			X				
Ribwort Plantain *(Plantago lanceolata)*			X				X
Broad-leaved Bellflower *(Campanula latifolia)*		X					
Harebell *(Campanula rotundifolia)*	X	X					
Crosswort *(Galium cruciata)*		X	X		X		X
Goosegrass *(Galium aparine)*		X	X		X		X
Moschatel *(Adoxa moschatellina)*		X					
Common Ragwort *(Senecio jacobaea)*	X	X	X		X	X	
Groundsel *(Senecio vulgaris)*	X	X	X		X	X	X
Coltsfoot *(Tussilago farfara)*					X		X
Daisy *(Bellis perennis)*		X	X		X		X
Mugwort *(Artemisia vulgaris)*		X	X		X		
Burdock *(Arctium minus)*		X	X		X		
Spear Thistle *(Cirsium vulgare)*		X	X				X
Creeping Thistle *(Cirsium arvense)*		X	X		X		X
Knapweed *(Centaurea nigra)*			X				
Nipplewort *(Lapsana communis)*		X	X		X		X
Wall Lettuce *(Mycelis muralis)*			X				
Field Thistle *(Sonchus arvensis)*			X				
Mouse-eared Hawkweed *(Hieraceum pilosella)*		X			X		
Hawkweeds *(Hieracium agg.)*			X				
Dandelion *(Taraxacum officinale)*		X	X		X		X
Water Plantain *(Alisma plantago-aquatica)*				X			
Broad-leaved Pondweed *(Potamogeton natans)*				X			
Bluebell *(Endymion non-scriptus)*			X				X
Field Garlic *(Allium oleraceum)*		X	X				X
Cuckoo Pint *(Arum maculatum)*							X
Duckweed *(Lemna minor)*				X			
Canadian Pondweed *(Elodea canadensis)*				X			

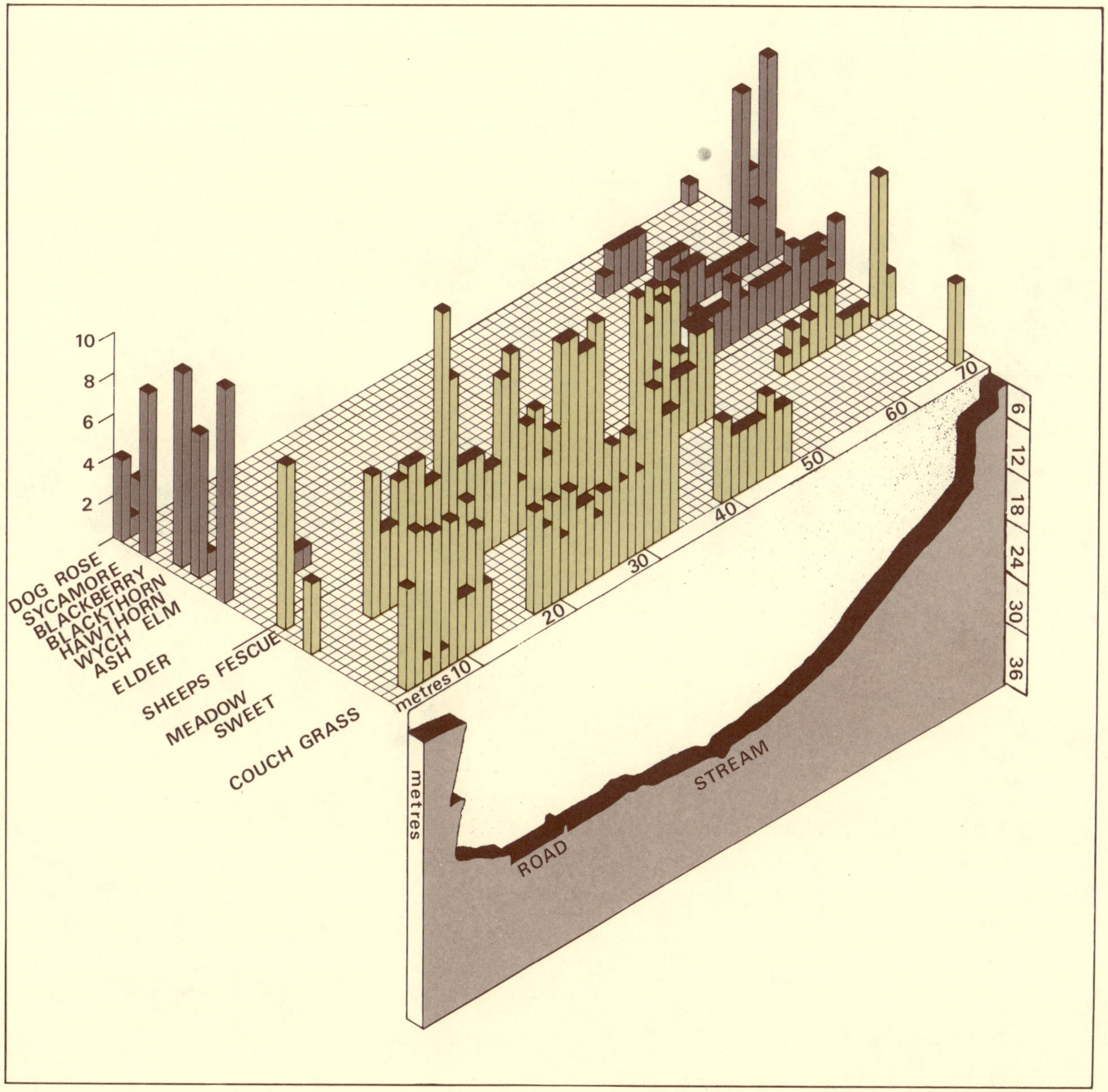

Figure 7. The frequency and dominance of plant species along Transect Q across Creswell Crags Gorge.

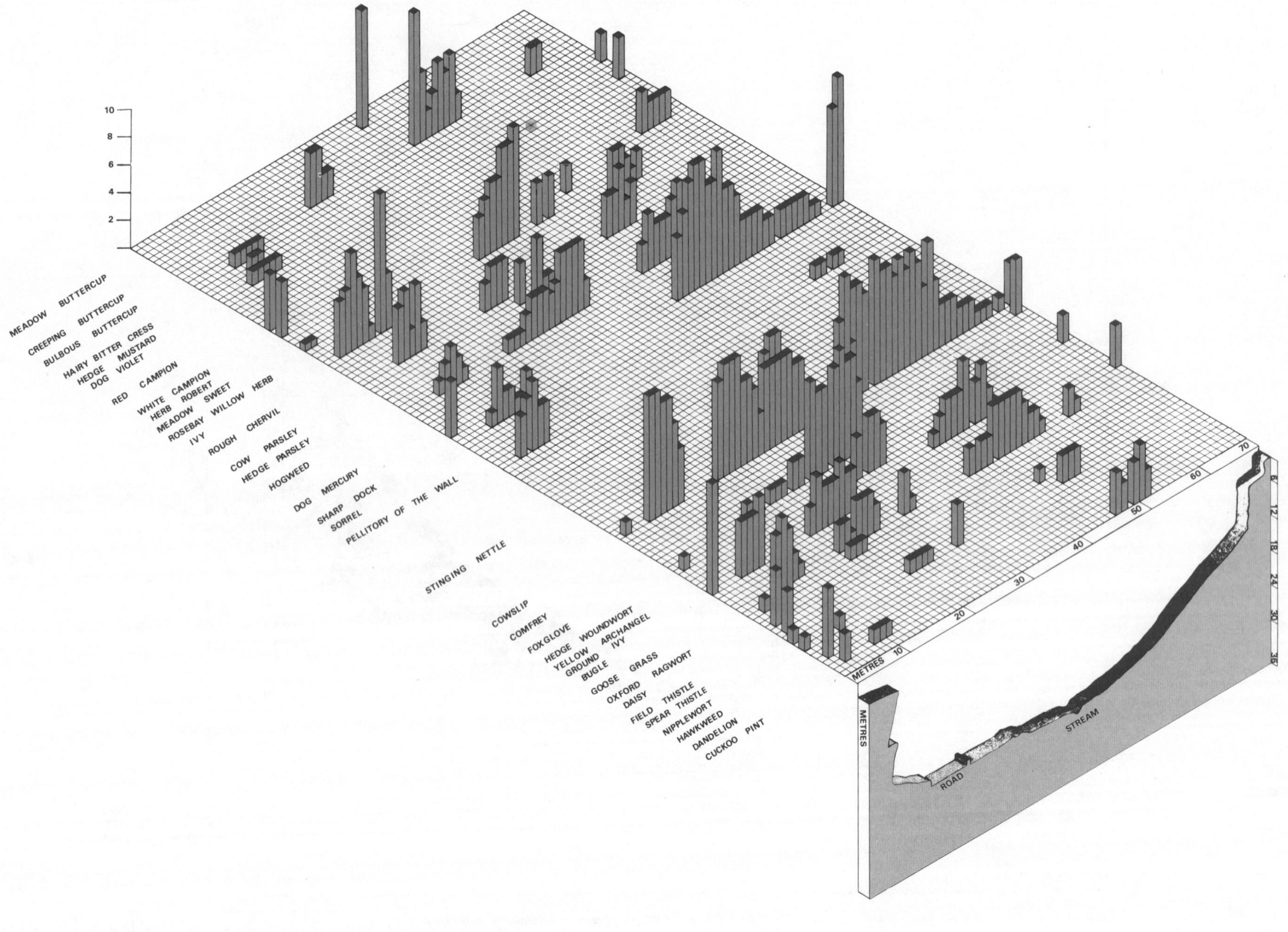
10
8
6
4
2
MEADOW BUTTERCUP
CREEPING BUTTERCUP
BULBOUS BUTTERCUP
HAIRY BITTER CRESS
HEDGE MUSTARD
DOG VIOLET
RED CAMPION
WHITE CAMPION
HERB ROBERT
MEADOW SWEET
ROSEBAY WILLOW HERB
IVY
ROUGH CHERVIL
COW PARSLEY
HEDGE PARSLEY
HOGWEED
DOG MERCURY
SHARP DOCK
SORREL
PELLITORY OF THE WALL
STINGING NETTLE
COWSLIP
COMFREY
FOXGLOVE
HEDGE WOUNDWORT
YELLOW ARCHANGEL
GROUND IVY
BUGLE
GOOSE GRASS
OXFORD RAGWORT
DAISY
FIELD THISTLE
SPEAR THISTLE
NIPPLEWORT
HAWKWEED
DANDELION
CUCKOO PINT
METRES
10
20
30
40
50
60
70
METRES
6
12
18
24
30
36
ROAD
STREAM

The rock faces and screes are frequently overhung by woodlands. The screes of the southern cliff support numerous ferns and shade tolerant herbs. The flora of the sunnier, south-facing northern side is even more diverse. Ash, Hazel, Elm, Yew, Gorse and the Spindle tree occur on this northern side. Nettles thrive on nitrogen and phosphorus rich soils developed upon the bone-rich tips and waste of earlier archaeological excavations. The flora of the cave entrances is gradually increasing in diversity as fern species in particular colonise the entrances in response to the removal of the cave mouth covers in 1976.

The pasture and marshes of the gorge floor contain a rich variety of plants including both open ground species such as the Plantains as well as more shade tolerant species. Several tree species occur in this area, much of which is flood prone. Not unexpectedly, Willows and Alder are common with their roots in the lake and stream margins. Silver birch, Hazel, Oak, Ash, Dogrose and Blackthorn also occur.

The Crack willow occurs in the wettest of soils. Otherwise the flora of the stream and lake is not regarded as notably rich. There are two reasons for this: first, the difficulty of studying the deeper water and marsh habitats and second, the presence of introduced acid mine wastes in the marsh soils and sediments infilling much of the gorge floor and probably bringing about the local extinction of the more sensitive aquatic species.

Invertebrates—Molluscs

Molluscs are the most intensively studied animal taxon at Creswell Crags. They are of particular importance for several reasons. First they occur as fossils in the archaeological deposits at Creswell Crags. At times, the shells can be very numerous indeed. Second, they indicate the character of both the immediate and more regional environments. Third, they can provide evidence on the antiquity of the archaeological deposits and on the nature of the taphonomic processes, i.e. derivation, redeposition and weathering, affecting the accumulation and preservation of the terrestrial and freshwater molluscan faunas contained within these sediments. Finally, molluscan palaeoecological studies are relatively infrequent away from coastal dune systems and the chalklands and river terraces of southern Britain (summarised in Kerney 1977a). Cave and fissure sequences (such as Dog Hole Fissure) have only rarely been investigated by this method (e.g. Evans and Jones 1973, Kerney 1976c, Williams and Williams 1966) which makes the Creswell sites all the more interesting.

Although there is now a comparative wealth of data on the modern ecology of British non-marine Mollusca (see Kerney 1976a, 1977b, Evans 1972, Kerney and Cameron 1979), there is little detailed information on the molluscan species associations or microhabitat preferences in this region where the landforms and soils are developed upon the Magnesian Limestone. There are no previous data on the processes and patterns of molluscan transportation, live or dead, by animal or geomorphic processes (i.e. taphonomy) which affect the resulting fossil assemblage at Creswell. Unfortunately, most molluscan species do not have 'common names'. It is necessary to remember the Latin binomial.

Comparative data on contemporary molluscan associations, habitat preferences and transport are currently being obtained by study of a series of transects across the gorge. Study of Transect Q (*Figures 8 and 9*) is complete and especially relevant to the Dog Hole Fissure study reported in this book (*Chapter 3*), because it is both very close to the site and passes through similar modern fissure traps on the gorge walls. With the exception of deeper water lacustrine habitats, it traverses all other habitat types in the area—woodland, rock cliffs, ledges, scree, wet and dry grassland, marsh and stream.

Transect Q Molluscs were sampled in $0.25 \times 0.25m^2$ quadrats at 1m intervals either by washing and collection from rock faces, or after washing the 1–2mm of surface sediment layer through a 2 phi sieve. Each valve of a lamellibranch was recorded separately. Comparative data were also obtained on slope, aspect, soil, pH, and vegetation cover. The molluscan and environmental data are given in *Table 2* and *Figures 8 and 9*. 3669 molluscs were separated and identified belonging to forty-six taxa by Ms. Carolyn Watts.

Molluscan Ecology at Creswell Crags

The comparative distributional data indicates several interesting points relevant to the palaeoecological study of the archaeological cave and fissure deposits at Creswell. Several groups of land Mollusca are particularly interesting.

Aegopinella pura, Aegopinella nitidula and *Discus rotundatus*, together with other members of the molluscan community, are found beneath the woodland at the cliff top sites—Q 1/2 and Q 67–68. However, many of these species also occur with *Oxychilus* sp. in the screes of the gorge side. *Oxychilus, Vitrea* and possibly *Discus rotundatus* can eat live or dead animal matter, in addition to vegetable matter in this environment (see Evans and Jones 1973 for discussion) enabling them to survive in the interstices of scree and rubble habitats.

Other taxa such as the Clausiliidae (normally associated with shade in woodlands), also occur in this damp, shaded scree-microhabitat. *Vallonia costata*, usually associated with open, drier grassland, similarly occurs in the scree, conforming with previous observations of its living on the broadly similar habitats offered by stone walls and slightly more unstable environments such as those places strongly influenced by man (Evans and Jones 1973).

Many species often regarded as able to withstand a wide variety of ecological conditions—the so-called 'Catholic' terrestrial species, demonstrate this tolerance in the transect, e.g. *Cochlicopa lubrica* and *Euconulus fulvus*.

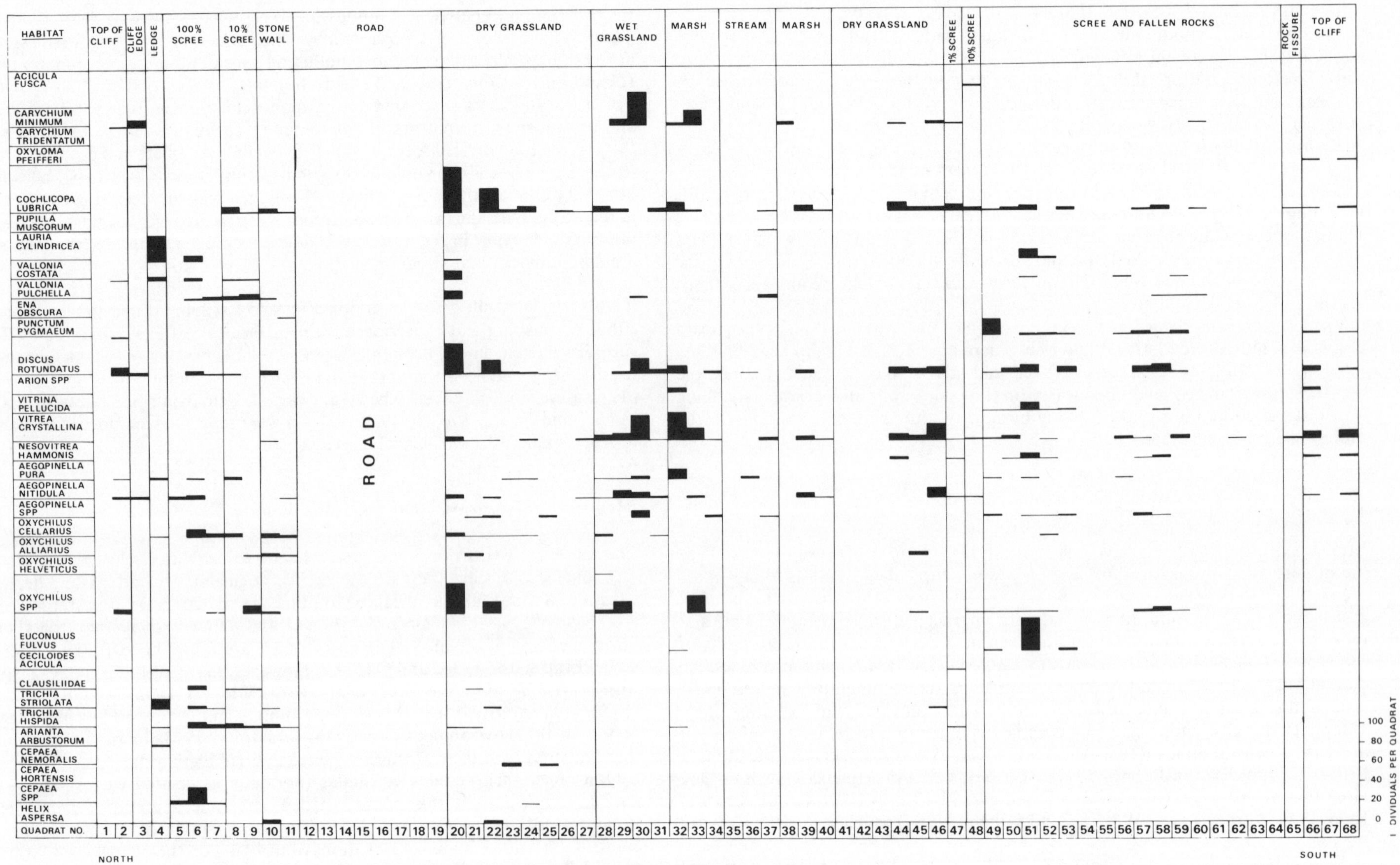

Figure 8. Distribution of terrestrial molluscs and habitats along Transect Q across Creswell Crags Gorge.

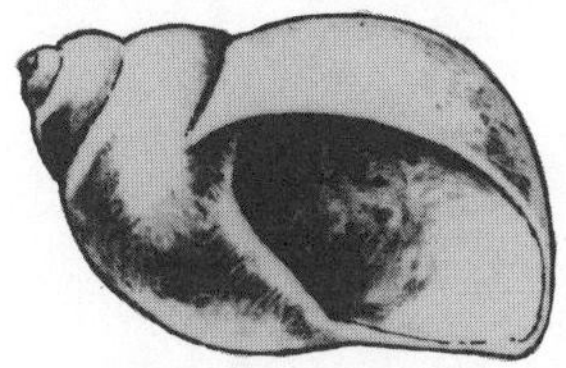

Lymnaea peregra (Müller)

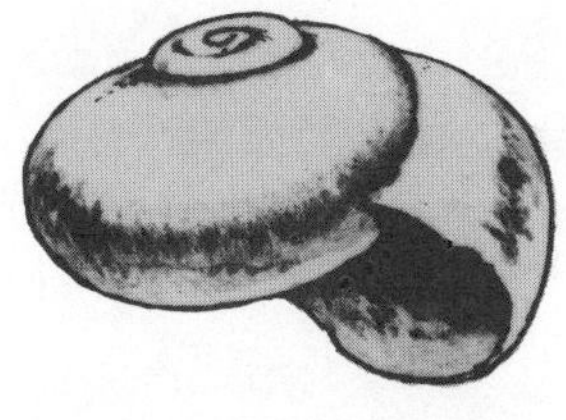

Valvata piscinalis (Müller)

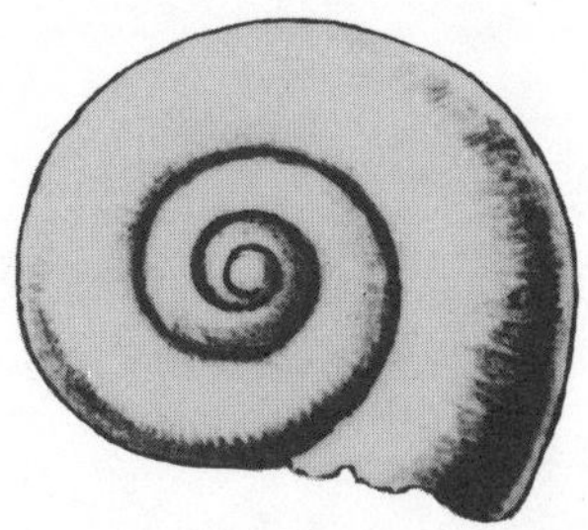

Oxychilus cellarius (Müller)

Discus rotundatus (Müller)

The fissure trap (Q 65) site with its relatively poor, inorganic, in-fill sediments is occupied by a poor fauna—the tolerant *Cochlicopa*, the tolerant but carnivorous *Vitrea crystallina*, and shade demanding Clausiliidae.

The single dead specimen of *Pupilla muscorum*, (a taxon commonly associated with drier, exposed habitats such as grasslands or sand dunes) found in the stream area, probably derives from a colony as yet unlocated on the drier grasslands upslope. This taxon is also frequently found in the past Quaternary cold stage, wet floodplain and valley floor environments in Britain (see Kerney 1977a for summary).

The remarkable distributions of empty shells and valves of *freshwater* taxa, as shown in *Figure 9*, are of particular importance. Specimens occur in significant numbers in fully terrestrial environments well beyond the marsh and stream habitat in which they lived. With the exception of *Ancylus fluviatilis*, their frequency and proportion in surface samples at their life habitats in the stream or marshes are not dissimilar to those where 'dead' specimens were found—at the cliff edge (Q 3) and scree sites (Q 52–54). Shells of the freshwater snail *Potamopyrgus* were even found in the rock fissure (Q 65).

The only mechanism which might bring about this distribution appears to be transport of shells in sediment on birds' feet, or in animals' guts. The high numbers of freshwater shells on the favoured perching and defaecation sites on the cliff edge and scree (Q 3/4) are particularly notable. The apparently lower propensity of *Ancylus fluviatilis*, the river limpet, to be redistributed may be the result of its favouring more cobbly, rocky stream beds, characterised by shallow rapid flow, rather than the quieter, plant-rich muddy waters favoured by grazing bird populations of the area. Transport by birds has long been recognised as a major agent for dispersal of molluscs (Boycott 1934). Its significance in the formation of Quaternary fossil assemblages has recently been re-emphasised by Mellet (1974), Mayhew (1977) and Stuart (1980), who pointed out that up to 30% of the small vertebrate fauna in the Quaternary fluvial deposits may be directly attributable to bird derivation and transportation.

Potamopyrgus jenkinsi (*Figure 8*) is a nineteenth century, fully aquatic accidental introduction to the British Isles. It appears to have originated in New Zealand, and was first noted in Britain in salt and brackish water at major British ports. From here it invaded British freshwater habitats to become the commonest snail in many British streams. The precise date of its arrival at Creswell is unclear. The present consensus is that it would have colonised the area just before the start of the present century.

Table 2. Frequency of mollusc species recovered from Transect Q

LAND MOLLUSCA	SPECIES																												
	1	2	3	4	5	6	7	8	9	10	11	12	13	14	15	16	17	18	19	20	21	22	23	24	25	26	27	28	29
Acicula fusca (Montagu)	-	-	-	-	-	-	-	-	-	-	-	-	-	-	-	-	-	-	-	-	-	-	-	-	-	-	-	-	-
Carychium minimum (Müller)	-	1	8	-	-	-	-	-	-	-	-	-	-	-	-	-	-	-	-	-	-	-	-	-	-	-	-	-	6
Carychium tridentatum (Risso)	-	-	-	1	-	-	-	-	-	-	-	-	-	-	-	-	-	-	-	-	-	-	-	-	-	-	-	-	-
Oxyloma pfeifferi (Rossmassler)	-	-	1	-	-	-	-	-	-	-	-	-	-	-	-	-	-	-	-	-	-	-	-	-	-	-	-	-	-
Cochlicopa lubrica (Müller)	-	-	-	-	-	-	-	8	1	5	1	-	-	-	-	-	-	-	-	47	-	25	3	6	-	2	1	6	3
Pupilla muscorum (L)	-	-	-	-	-	-	-	-	-	-	-	-	-	-	-	-	-	-	-	-	-	-	-	-	-	-	-	-	-
Lauria cylindracea (Da Costa)	-	-	-	27	-	6	-	-	-	-	-	-	-	-	-	-	-	-	-	1	-	-	-	-	-	-	-	-	-
Vallonia costata (Müller)	-	1	-	4	-	5	3	6	7	2	-	-	-	-	-	-	-	-	-	17	-	-	-	-	-	-	-	-	-
Vallonia pulchella (Müller)	-	-	-	-	-	-	-	-	-	-	-	-	-	-	-	-	-	-	-	-	-	-	-	-	-	-	-	-	-
Ena obscura (Müller)	-	-	-	-	-	-	-	-	-	-	1	-	-	-	-	-	-	-	-	-	-	-	-	-	-	-	-	-	-
Punctum pygmaeum (Draparnaud)	-	1	-	-	-	-	-	-	-	-	-	-	-	-	-	-	-	-	-	-	-	-	-	-	-	-	-	-	-
Discus rotundatus (Müller)	-	8	2	-	-	4	1	1	-	4	-	-	-	-	-	-	-	-	-	32	1	15	2	2	1	-	-	-	2
Arion sp.	-	-	-	-	-	-	-	-	-	-	-	-	-	-	-	-	-	-	-	1	-	-	-	-	-	-	-	-	-
Vitrina pellucida (Müller)	-	-	-	-	-	-	-	-	-	-	-	-	-	-	-	-	-	-	-	-	-	-	-	-	-	-	-	-	-
Vitrea crystallina (Müller)	-	-	-	-	-	-	-	-	-	1	-	-	-	-	-	-	-	-	-	5	1	1	-	2	-	-	2	6	7
Nesovitrea hammonis (Ström)	-	-	-	-	-	-	-	-	-	-	-	-	-	-	-	-	-	-	-	-	-	-	-	-	-	-	-	-	-
Aegopinella pura (Alder)	-	1	-	2	-	2	-	3	-	-	-	-	-	-	-	-	-	-	-	-	-	-	1	1	-	-	-	1	1
Aegopinella nitidula (Draparnaud)	-	2	2	-	3	4	-	-	-	-	1	-	-	-	-	-	-	-	-	4	-	1	-	-	-	-	1	1	8
Aegopinella sp.	-	-	-	-	-	-	-	-	4	-	-	-	-	-	-	-	-	-	-	-	1	2	-	-	-	-	-	-	-
Oxychilus draparnaldi (Beck)	-	-	-	-	-	-	-	-	-	-	-	-	-	-	-	-	-	-	-	-	-	-	-	-	2?	-	-	-	-
Oxychilus cellarius (Müller)	-	-	-	1	-	8	4	4	-	4	2	-	-	-	-	-	-	-	-	4	1	1	1	1	-	-	-	2	-
Oxychilus alliarius (Müller)	-	-	-	-	-	-	-	-	1?	3?	1?	-	-	-	-	-	-	-	-	-	2?	-	-	-	-	-	-	-	-
Oxychilus helveticus (Blum)	-	-	-	-	-	-	-	-	-	-	-	-	-	-	-	-	-	-	-	-	-	-	-	-	-	-	-	1?	-
Oxychilus sp.	-	4	-	-	-	-	1	-	8	2	-	-	-	-	-	-	-	-	-	31	-	12	-	-	-	-	-	3	12
Euconolus fulvus (Müller)	-	-	-	-	-	-	-	-	-	-	-	-	-	-	-	-	-	-	-	-	-	-	-	-	-	-	-	-	-
Ceciloides acicula (Müller)	-	1	-	1	-	-	-	-	-	-	-	-	-	-	-	-	-	-	-	-	-	-	-	-	-	-	-	-	-
Clausilidae sp.	-	-	-	-	-	4	-	1	1	-	-	-	-	-	-	-	-	-	-	-	1	-	-	-	-	-	-	-	-
Trichia striolata (Pfeiffer)	-	-	-	10	-	3	1	-	-	1	-	-	-	-	-	-	-	-	-	-	-	2	-	-	-	1	-	-	-
Trichia hispida (L)	-	-	-	1	-	6	4	5	2	4	1	-	-	-	-	-	-	-	-	1	1	-	-	-	-	-	-	-	-
Arianta arbustorum (L)	-	-	-	2	-	-	-	-	-	-	-	-	-	-	-	-	-	-	-	-	-	-	-	-	-	-	-	-	-
Cepaea nemoralis (L)	-	-	-	-	-	-	-	-	-	-	-	-	-	-	-	-	-	-	-	-	-	-	3	-	2	-	-	-	-
Cepaea hortensis (Müller)	-	-	-	-	-	-	-	-	-	-	-	-	-	-	-	-	-	-	-	-	-	-	-	-	-	-	-	1	-
Cepaea sp.	-	-	-	-	3	17	1	-	-	-	-	-	-	-	-	-	-	-	-	-	-	-	-	1	-	-	-	-	-
Helix aspersa (Müller)	-	-	-	-	-	-	1	-	-	3	-	-	-	-	-	-	-	-	-	-	-	3	-	-	-	-	-	-	-
TOTAL INDIVIDUALS	0	19	13	49	6	59	16	28	24	29	7	0	0	0	0	0	0	0	0	143	8	62	10	13	5	3	4	21	39

FRESHWATER MOLLUSCA	SPECIES																												
	1	2	3	4	5	6	7	8	9	10	11	12	13	14	15	16	17	18	19	20	21	22	23	24	25	26	27	28	29
Valvata piscinalis (Müller)	-	-	-	-	-	-	-	-	-	-	-	-	-	-	-	-	-	-	-	1	-	-	-	-	-	-	-	-	-
Potamopyrgus jenkinsi (Smith)	-	7	214	-	5	-	-	-	-	8	-	-	-	-	-	-	-	-	-	1	-	-	-	-	-	-	-	11	20
Lymnaea peregra (Müller)	-	1	36	-	-	-	-	-	-	-	-	-	-	-	-	-	-	-	-	-	-	-	-	-	-	-	-	-	-
Planorbis planorbis (L)	-	-	-	-	-	-	-	-	-	-	-	-	-	-	-	-	-	-	-	-	-	-	-	-	-	-	-	-	1
Armiger crista (L)	-	-	4	-	-	-	-	-	-	-	-	-	-	-	-	-	-	-	-	-	-	-	-	-	-	-	-	-	-
Ancylus fluviatilis (Müller)	-	-	1	-	-	-	-	-	-	-	-	-	-	-	-	-	-	-	-	-	-	-	-	-	-	-	-	-	-
Pisidium amnicum (Müller)	-	-	-	-	-	-	-	-	-	-	-	-	-	-	-	-	-	-	-	-	-	-	-	-	-	-	-	-	-
Pisidium casertanum (Poli)	-	-	-	-	-	-	-	-	-	-	-	-	-	-	-	-	-	-	-	-	-	-	-	-	-	-	-	-	-
Pisidium subtruncatum (Malm)	-	-	-	-	-	-	-	-	-	1	-	-	-	-	-	-	-	-	-	-	-	-	-	-	-	-	-	-	1
Pisidium nitidum (Jenyns)	-	1	-	-	-	-	-	-	-	1	-	-	-	-	-	-	-	-	-	-	-	-	-	-	-	-	-	5	4
Pisidium sp.	-	-	-	-	-	-	-	-	-	1	-	-	-	-	-	-	-	-	-	-	-	-	-	-	-	-	-	-	-
TOTAL INDIVIDUALS	0	9	255	0	5	0	0	0	0	11	0	0	0	0	0	0	0	0	0	2	0	0	0	0	0	0	0	16	26

30	31	32	33	34	35	36	37	38	39	40	41	42	43	44	45	46	47	48	49	50	51	52	53	54	55	56	57	58	59	60	61	62	63	64	65	66	67	68
-	-	-	-	-	-	-	-	-	-	-	-	-	-	-	-	-	-	1	-	-	-	-	-	-	-	-	-	-	-	-	-	-	-	-	-	-	-	-
35	-	2	16	-	-	-	3	-	-	-	-	-	-	1	-	3	1	-	-	-	-	-	-	-	-	-	-	-	-	1	-	-	-	-	-	-	-	-
-	-	-	-	-	-	-	-	-	-	-	-	-	-	-	-	-	-	-	-	-	-	-	-	-	-	-	-	-	-	-	-	-	-	-	-	-	-	-
-	-	-	-	-	-	-	-	-	-	-	-	-	-	-	-	-	-	-	-	-	-	-	-	-	-	-	-	-	-	-	-	-	-	-	-	-	-	-
-	4	10	2	-	-	-	1	-	6	1	-	-	-	9	4	4	6	3	1	3	5	-	3	-	-	-	2	4	-	-	1	-	-	-	1	1	-	2
-	-	-	-	-	-	-	1	-	-	-	-	-	-	-	-	-	-	-	-	-	-	-	-	-	-	-	-	-	-	-	-	-	-	-	-	-	-	-
-	-	-	-	-	-	-	-	-	-	-	-	-	-	-	-	-	-	-	-	-	9	1	-	-	-	-	-	-	-	-	-	-	-	-	-	-	-	-
-	-	-	-	-	-	-	-	-	-	-	-	-	-	-	-	-	-	-	-	-	1	-	-	-	-	1	-	1	1	-	1	-	-	-	-	-	-	-
2	-	-	-	-	-	-	3	-	-	-	-	-	-	-	-	-	-	-	-	-	-	-	-	-	-	-	-	-	-	-	-	-	-	-	-	-	-	-
-	-	-	-	-	-	-	-	-	-	-	-	-	-	-	-	-	-	-	-	-	-	-	-	-	-	-	-	-	-	-	-	-	-	-	-	-	-	-
-	-	-	-	-	-	-	-	-	-	-	-	-	-	-	-	-	-	-	17	-	2	2	1	-	-	1	3	1	3	-	-	-	-	-	2	-	-	1
16	4	8	-	2	-	1	-	-	3	-	-	-	-	6	5	6	1	-	1	4	8	-	6	-	-	-	6	8	1	-	-	-	-	2	5	-	-	2
-	-	5	-	-	-	-	-	-	-	-	-	-	-	-	-	-	-	-	-	-	-	-	-	-	-	-	-	-	-	-	-	-	-	-	3	-	-	-
-	-	-	-	-	-	-	-	-	-	-	-	-	-	-	-	-	-	-	1	1	8	1	2	-	-	-	-	1	-	-	-	-	-	-	-	-	-	5
26	1	29	13	1	-	-	3	-	4	1	-	-	-	6	5	17	1	2	2	4	-	1	-	-	-	3	1	-	4	-	-	1	-	1	7	-	-	8
-	-	-	-	-	-	-	-	-	-	-	-	-	-	2	-	-	1	-	-	1	6	1	-	-	-	-	1	3	-	-	-	-	-	-	2	-	-	3
3	-	10	-	-	-	2	-	-	-	-	-	-	-	-	-	-	-	-	1	-	1	-	-	-	-	1	-	-	-	-	-	-	-	-	-	-	-	-
7	2	-	2	-	-	-	-	-	5	1	-	-	-	-	-	10	1	1	-	-	-	-	-	-	-	-	-	-	-	-	-	-	-	-	1	-	-	2
7	-	-	-	2	-	-	1	-	-	-	-	-	-	-	-	-	-	-	2	-	1	1	2	-	-	-	3	1	-	-	-	-	-	-	-	-	-	-
-	-	-	-	-	-	-	-	-	-	-	-	-	-	-	-	-	-	-	-	-	-	-	-	-	-	-	-	-	-	-	-	-	-	-	-	-	-	-
-	1	-	-	-	-	-	-	-	-	-	-	-	-	-	-	-	-	-	-	-	-	-	-	-	-	-	-	-	-	-	-	-	-	-	-	-	-	-
-	-	-	-	-	-	-	-	-	-	-	-	-	-	-	3?	-	-	-	-	-	-	-	-	-	-	-	-	-	-	-	-	-	-	-	-	-	-	-
-	-	-	-	-	-	-	-	-	-	-	-	-	-	-	-	-	-	-	-	-	-	-	-	-	-	-	-	-	-	-	-	-	-	-	-	-	-	-
-	-	-	18	1	-	-	-	-	-	-	-	-	-	-	1	-	-	1	1	1	1	1	-	-	-	-	2	5	1	-	-	-	-	-	2	-	-	-
-	-	1	-	-	-	-	-	-	-	-	-	-	-	-	-	-	-	-	-	1	36	-	2	-	-	-	-	-	-	-	-	-	-	-	-	-	-	-
-	-	-	-	-	-	-	-	-	-	-	-	-	-	-	-	-	1	-	-	-	-	-	-	-	-	-	-	-	-	-	-	-	-	-	-	-	-	-
-	-	-	-	-	-	-	-	-	-	-	-	-	-	-	-	-	-	-	-	-	-	-	-	-	-	-	-	-	-	-	-	-	-	1	-	-	-	-
-	-	-	-	-	-	-	-	-	-	-	-	-	-	-	-	1	-	-	-	-	-	-	-	-	-	-	-	-	-	-	-	-	-	-	-	-	-	-
-	-	1	-	-	-	-	-	-	-	-	-	-	-	-	-	-	1	-	-	-	-	-	-	-	-	-	-	-	-	-	-	-	-	-	-	-	-	-
-	-	-	-	-	-	-	-	-	-	-	-	-	-	-	-	-	-	-	-	-	-	-	-	-	-	-	-	-	-	-	-	-	-	-	-	-	-	-
-	-	-	-	-	-	-	-	-	-	-	-	-	-	-	-	-	-	-	-	-	-	-	-	-	-	-	-	-	-	-	-	-	-	-	-	-	-	-
-	-	-	-	-	-	-	-	-	-	-	-	-	-	-	-	-	-	-	-	-	-	-	-	-	-	-	-	-	-	-	-	-	-	-	-	-	-	-
-	-	-	-	-	-	-	-	-	-	-	-	-	-	-	-	-	-	-	-	-	-	-	-	-	-	-	-	-	-	-	-	-	-	-	-	-	-	-
-	-	-	-	-	-	-	-	-	-	-	-	-	-	-	-	-	-	-	-	-	-	-	-	-	-	-	-	-	-	-	-	-	-	-	-	-	-	-
96	12	66	51	6	0	3	12	0	18	3	0	0	0	24	18	41	13	8	26	15	78	9	16	0	0	6	18	24	10	1	2	1	0	4	23	1	0	23

30	31	32	33	34	35	36	37	38	39	40	41	42	43	44	45	46	47	48	49	50	51	52	53	54	55	56	57	58	59	60	61	62	63	64	65	66	67	68
1	-	-	-	-	-	-	-	-	-	-	-	-	-	-	-	-	-	-	-	-	-	-	-	-	-	-	-	-	-	-	-	-	-	1	-	-	-	-
36	1	27	90	80	52	231	299	1	29	-	-	-	-	-	-	-	1	-	-	-	1	280	-	-	-	-	-	-	6	1	-	-	-	4	4	-	-	25
1	1	2	1	-	2	3	2	-	1	-	-	-	-	2	-	-	1	-	-	-	-	-	-	-	-	-	-	-	1	-	-	-	-	-	-	-	-	-
-	-	-	1	-	-	-	-	-	-	-	-	-	-	-	-	-	-	-	-	-	-	-	-	-	-	-	-	-	-	-	-	-	-	-	-	-	-	-
-	-	-	-	-	-	-	-	-	-	-	-	-	-	-	-	-	-	-	-	-	-	-	-	-	-	-	-	-	-	-	-	-	-	-	-	-	-	-
1	-	-	3	-	-	2	43	-	-	-	-	-	-	-	-	-	-	-	-	-	-	1	-	-	-	-	-	-	1	-	-	-	-	-	-	-	-	-
1	-	-	-	-	-	-	-	-	-	-	-	-	-	-	-	-	-	-	-	-	-	-	-	-	-	-	-	-	-	-	-	-	-	-	-	-	-	-
-	-	-	-	-	-	-	1	-	-	-	-	-	-	-	-	-	-	-	-	-	-	-	-	-	-	-	-	-	-	-	-	-	-	-	-	-	-	-
3	-	-	4	1	1	5	45	-	-	-	-	-	-	-	-	-	-	-	-	-	-	29	-	-	-	-	-	-	-	-	-	-	-	3	-	-	-	-
6	-	2	6	1	1	6	60	2	-	-	-	-	-	-	-	-	-	-	-	-	-	28	-	-	-	-	-	-	-	-	-	-	-	1	-	-	-	-
-	-	-	10	-	-	-	-	-	-	-	-	-	-	-	-	-	-	-	-	-	-	-	-	-	-	-	-	-	-	-	-	-	-	-	-	-	-	-
49	2	31	115	82	56	247	450	3	30	0	0	0	0	2	0	0	2	0	0	0	1	338	0	0	0	0	0	0	8	1	0	0	0	9	4	0	0	25

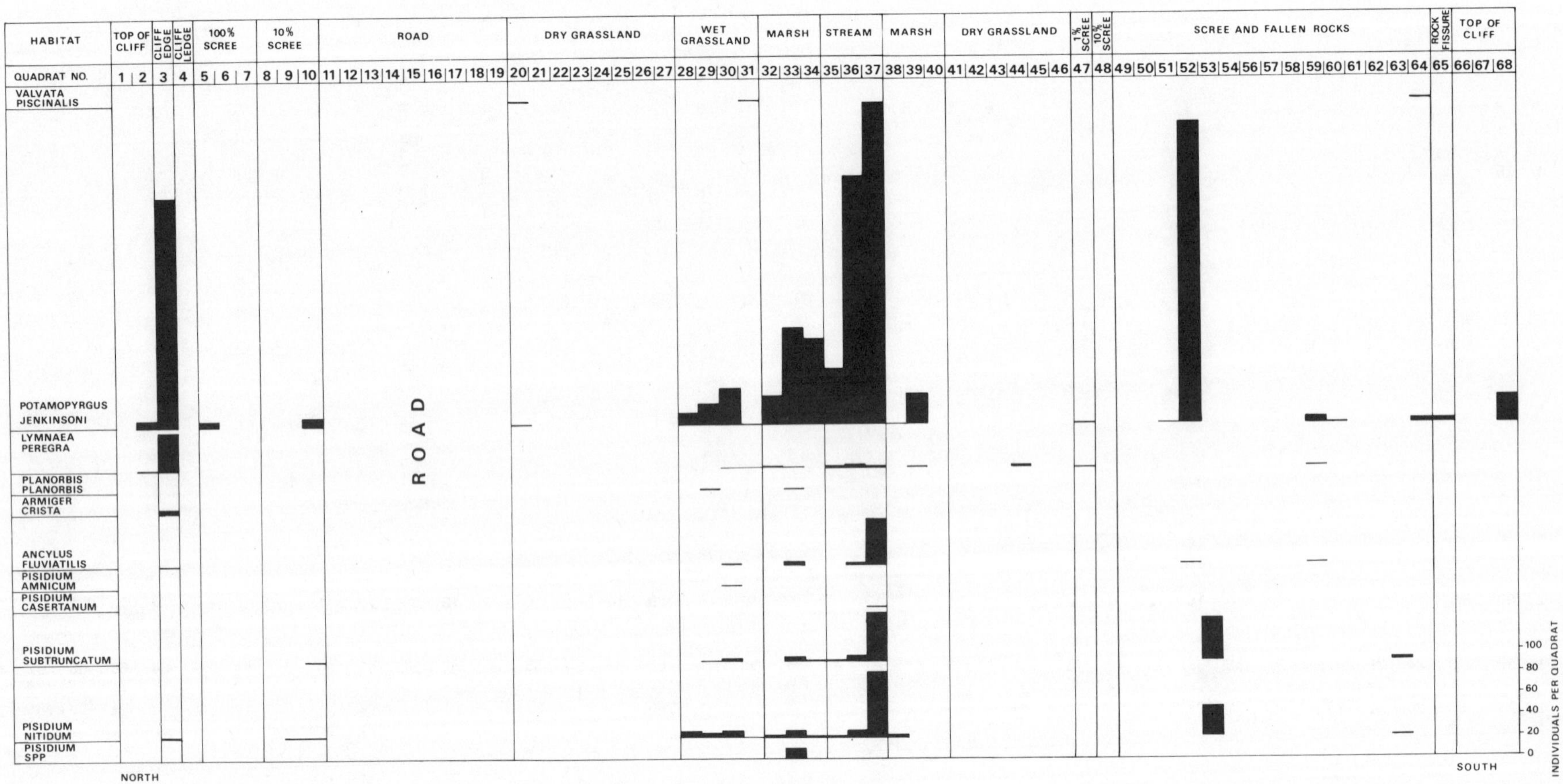

Figure 9. Distribution of freshwater molluscs along Transect Q across Creswell Crags Gorge. Note the extent of transportation of the aquatic fauna by birds to perching places on the gorge walls.

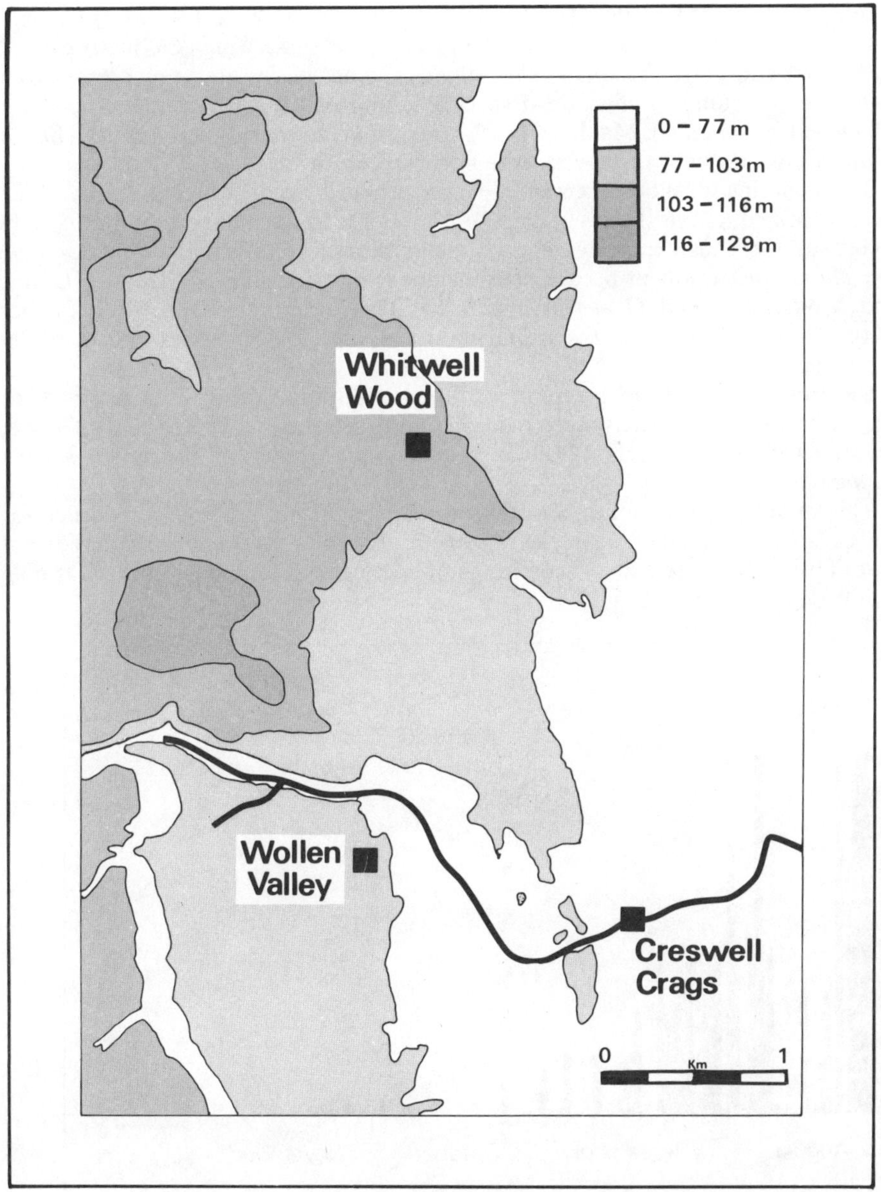

Figure 10. Map showing the location of trapping sites established during the moth survey.

Invertebrates—Moths

Moths are dry land creatures which are able to colonise most of the world's surface. They are absent only from the most inhospitable regions of extreme cold and drought. Directly or indirectly their life depends upon temperature and vegetation. Temperature thresholds vary greatly from species to species, most prefer to develop in a temperature range between 5°C–10°C but cold-hardy species can survive and breed at temperatures approaching freezing point. Moths depend on plants and their distribution in any one locality often reflects the diversity of the area's vegetation.

Some moth species permanently reside in Britain. They cope with seasonal fluctuations in temperature and the availability of food by breeding and developing during the summer months and spending the colder winter months in dormancy or hibernation. This life cycle is often interrupted by periods of quiescence, that is, periods when either temperature or food resources are temporarily unfavourable and where the moth may, as a result, arrest its development.

In addition to resident moths, there are a number of migratory species. Migration can be deliberate, where a southern species flies to Britain, a good example being the Silver Y (*Autographa gamma*) which actually migrate from Central Europe to Britain. Other immigrants can arrive accidentally, perhaps being blown over by winds.

In these circumstances, it is to be expected that the moth fauna in any one locality will include residents, living and breeding locally, migrants arriving each summer from more southerly latitudes and accidentals, unusual species, caught up by air currents and carried to areas outside their normal distribution.

Although moth remains are extremely rare from archaeological sites, the study of modern moth populations at Creswell provides an insight to a rich and diverse element of the fauna present in the current Flandrian warm stage.

Moths of the Creswell Crags Area The larger Lepidoptera or moths have been studied in detail at Creswell Crags since 1981. This study sets out to describe the diversity and frequency of moths at three localities within the Creswell Crags area, and to establish the range of species in each different habitat.

Methods The survey was carried out using standard Mercury Vapour Moth Traps. These were used at the three locations described below:

1. **Creswell Crags**—Three trapping sites were established (*Figure 10*) during the last week of each month between March to September for three years. This provided a total of 27 trapping observations. Two traps were located adjacent to the Creswell Crags Visitor Centre which is set in predominantly Austrian Pine (*Pinus nigra*) and Sycamore (*Acer pseudoplatanus*) woodland. A third trap was located on a north facing grassland slope to the south of the Visitor Centre (*Figures 4 and 10*).

2. **Wollen Valley**—a single trap was established on 276 occasions during the three years of study. This location is a northeastern facing slope of the River Wollen Valley (*Figures 5 and 10*) and is adjacent to a wide range of habitats. Nearby open gardens provide a flora of apple (*Malus sylvestris*), pear (*Pyrus communis*) and other fruit trees with adjacent zones of Poplar (*Populus canescens*). To the east of the trapping site are grass fields bisected by a railway embankment and rough marshy land in the valley floor. The site is two kilometres from Creswell Crags and three kilometres from Markland Grips, an extensive limestone gorge with a rich flora.

3. **Whitwell Wood**—the third location is an old woodland which was clear felled during 1914–18 and subsequently acquired by the Forestry Commission. The present flora is a mixture of deciduous trees and recently planted conifers interspersed by broad open rides. Trapping surveys were undertaken here at monthly intervals between March and September during 1983.

Results The survey recorded 201 species of moths for which the identification and nomenclature follows that given by South (1961). The results for each locality are given in *Tables 3, 4 and 5*, where the total numbers recorded for each species are shown for each month during 1981–83. It can be seen from these tables that there are significant differences between the three localities.

The most diverse fauna was recorded from the Wollen Valley site, where a total of 4526 individuals were identified to 177 species. Of the species, the most commonly recorded (*Table 4*) were Large yellow underwing (*Noctua pronuba*), Garden carpet (*Xanthorhoë fluctuata*), Lesser yellow underwing (*Euschesis cornes*) and Heart and Dart (*Agrotis exclamationis*). Some species are known only from single or low numbers of trapped specimens and of these the Chamomile shark (*Cucullia chamomillae*), Maiden's blush (*Cosymbia punctaria*), Oak beauty (*Biston strataria*) are thought to be very rare occurrences locally.

The sampling localities at Creswell Crags provided records of 244 moths which were identified to 146 species (*Table 3*). At this site lower numbers of moths were recorded, the most common species being Large yellow underwing (*Noctua pronuba*). Other frequent occurrences include Common quaker (*Orthosia stabilis*) and Mother of Pearl (*Pleuroptya paralis*). This locality also provided further records of Oak beauty (*Biston stratavia*) already noted as a species that is locally very rare.

Records from the third trapping locality at Whitwell Wood were obtained for 1983 when 107 individuals were recorded and identified to 35 species. Of these, Lesser swallow prominent (*Pheosia gnoma*) and Mother of Pearl (*Pleuroptya paralis*) are frequent.

This survey provides a number of interesting results not previously recorded for the Creswell Crags area. It is clear from the results given here that the current moth fauna is diverse with a wide range of species represented from the trapping localities.

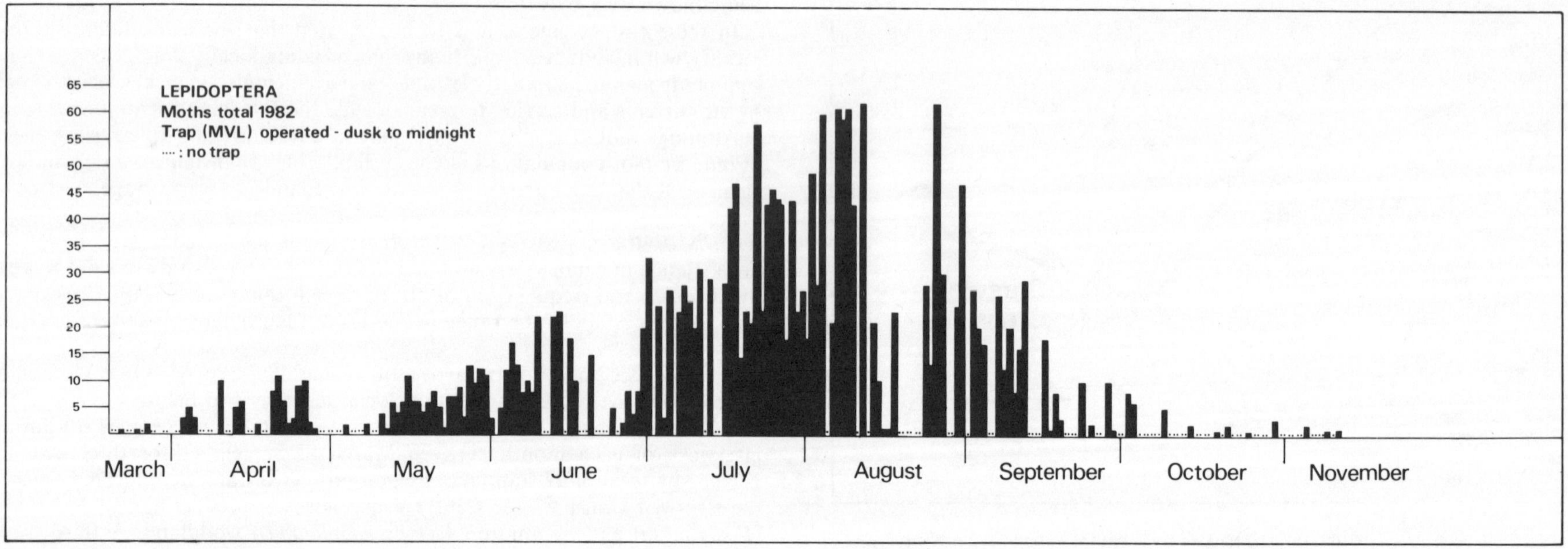

Figure 11. Frequency of moth populations recorded during the 1982 survey.

Figure 12. Moth species from the Creswell Crags area.

Table 3. Moth species trapped at Creswell Crags during 1981–3

		1981									1982									1983									
SPECIES	**MONTH**	**M**	**A**	**M**	**J**	**J**	**A**	**S**	**O**	**N**	**M**	**A**	**M**	**J**	**J**	**A**	**S**	**O**	**N**	**M**	**A**	**M**	**J**	**J**	**A**	**S**	**O**	**N**	**TOTAL**
Drepana falcataria	(Pebble Hook-tip)					1																		1					2
Drepana binaria	(Oak Hook-tip)														1														1
Dasychira pudibunda	(Pale Tussock)												1																1
Euxoa nigricans	(Garden Dart)															1													1
Diarisa rubi	(Small Square Spot)						4																						4
Axylia putris	(Flame)																							1					1
Euschesis comes	(Lesser Yellow Underwing)					2	11	4							1														18
Noctua pronuba	(Large Yellow Underwing)					3	34									14													51
Orthosia stabilis	(Common Quaker)		3									16									3								22
Tholera popularis	(Feathered Gothic)						2																						2
Leucania pallens	(Common Wainscot)					1																		2					3
Leucania impura	(Smoky Wainscot)						1																						1
Leucania comma	(Shoulder-striped Wainscot)																								1				1
Cucullia verbasci	(Mullein Shark)				3																								3
Mormo maura	(Old Lady)						1																						1
Apamea lithoxylaea	(Light Arches)														1														1
Apamea monoglypha	(Dark Arches)						1								1														2
Apamea remissa	(Dusky Brocade)																								2				2
Apamea secalis	(Common Rustic)						2																	3					5
Procus literosa	(Rosy Minor)						1																						1
Eremobia ochroleuca	(Dusky Sallow)						1																						1
Luperina testacea	(Flounced Rustic)						1																						1
Phlogophora meticulosa	(Angle Shades)																1								3				4
Phalpophila matura	(Straw Underwing)																							1					1
Plusia chrysitis	(Burnished Brass)					1																							1
Plusia jota	(Plain Golden Y)					1	1								3														5
Unca triplasia	(Spectacle)						1																						1
Scolioptera libatrix	(Herald)	2																									2		4
Hypena proboscidalis	(Snout)					3	1								1														5
TOTAL TRAPPED SPECIMENS		**2**	**3**	**-**	**3**	**12**	**62**	**4**	**-**	**-**	**-**	**16**	**1**	**-**	**8**	**15**	**1**	**-**	**-**	**-**	**3**	**-**	**-**	**8**	**6**	**-**	**2**	**-**	**146**

SPECIES	MONTH	1981									1982									1983									TOTAL
		M	A	M	J	J	A	S	O	N	M	A	M	J	J	A	S	O	N	M	A	M	J	J	A	S	O	N	
Poecilocampa populi	(December Moth)																											1	1
Philudoria potatoria	(Drinker)																							1					1
Lithosia lurideola	(Common Footman)																							3					3
Spilosoma lutea	(Buff Ermine)				2									1	1								2						6
Phragmatobia fuliginosa	(Ruby Tiger)																								1				1
Arctia caja	(Garden Tiger)																							1	1				2
Sterrha aversata	(Riband Wave)						2																	1					3
Sterrha biselata	(Small Fan-footed Wave)						2																						2
Xanthorhoë montanata	(Silver Ground Carpet)				1																								1
Xanthorhoë fluctuata	(Garden Carpet)						4																						4
Xanthorhoë ferrugata	(Dark-barred Twin-spot Carpet)						5																						5
Perizoma alchemillata	(Small Rivulet)						1																						1
Ecliptopera silaceata	(Small Pheonix)						4																	1					5
Cidaria fulvata	(Barred Yellow)						1																						1
Hydriomena furcata	(July Highflier)						1																						1
Epirrhoe alternata	(Common Carpet)					2	4																						6
Eupithecia absinthiata	(Wormwood Pug)						2																						2
Eupithecia virgaureata	(Golden Rod Pug)						3																						3
Abraxas grossulariata	(Magpie)														2	1								1					4
Deuteronomos fascantaria	(Dusky Thorn)						1																						1
Selenia bilunaria	(Early Thorn)																				4								4
Gonodontis bidentata	(Scalloped Hazel)																						2						2
Colotois pennaria	(Feathered Thorn)								1																			4	5
Poisthographis luteolata	(Brimstone)				1	1	1	1																					4
Biston strataria	(Oak Beauty)												1																1
Cleora rhomboideria	(Willow Beauty)						3																						3
Alcis repandata	(Mottled Beauty)																							1					1
Ectropis crepuscularia	(Small Engrailed)																							1					1
Zygaena trifolii	(Five-spot Burnet)														3														3
Hepialus sylvina	(Orange Swift)																							1					1
Pleuroptya paralis	(Mother of Pearl)													2	3								4	11					20
TOTAL TRAPPED SPECIMENS		-	-	-	**4**	**3**	**34**	**1**	**1**	-	-	-	**1**	**3**	**9**	**1**	-	-	-	-	**4**	-	**8**	**22**	**2**	-	-	**5**	**98**

Table 4. Moth species trapped at Wollen Valley during 1981–3

		1981									1982									1983									
SPECIES	**MONTH**	**M**	**A**	**M**	**J**	**J**	**A**	**S**	**O**	**N**	**M**	**A**	**M**	**J**	**J**	**A**	**S**	**O**	**N**	**M**	**A**	**M**	**J**	**J**	**A**	**S**	**O**	**N**	**TOTAL**
Operinia dilutata	(November Moth)																		1								1		2
Eupithecia icterata	(Tawny Speckled Pug)														1														1
Eupithecia virgaureata	(Golden Rod Pug)						5																						5
Operophtera bramata	(Winter Moth)										2								1										3
Abraxas grossulariata	(Magpie)					5	6							4	7	2								10	2				36
Lomaspilis marginata	(Clouded Border)																							2					2
Ligdia adustata	(Scorched Carpet)																						1						1
Deilinia pusaria	(Common White Wave)						2																						2
Ellopia fasciria	(Barred Red)																							1					1
Campaea margaritata	(Light Emerald)																							2					2
Ennomos quercinaria	(August Thorn)															1													1
Deuteronomos alniaria	(Canary Shouldered Thorn)						2										2									4	1		9
Deuteronomos fascantaria	(Dusky Thorn)							3								2									1				6
Deuteronomos erosaria	(September Thorn)																3												3
Selenia bilunaria	(Early Thorn)		4									2	2								5	3							16
Gonodontis bidentata	(Scalloped Hazel)											1	10									2	22						35
Colotois pennaria	(Feathered Thorn)																	3									2	1	6
Crocallis elinguaria	(Scalloped Oak)					1																		2	18				21
Ourapteryx sambucaria	(Swallow-tailed Moth)					16								1	60									39					116
Plagodis dolabraria	(Scorched Wing)													1															1
Poisthographis luteolata	(Brimstone)					5	1						7	5	1								9	27					55
Epione repandaria	(Bordered Beauty)					1																							1
Theria rupicapraria	(Early Moth)																			1									1
Eramis marginaria	(Spotted Border)																				1								1
Phigalia pilosaria	(Pale Brindled Beauty)																			1									1
Lycia hirtaria	(Brindled Beauty)											2									1	3							6
Biston betularia	(Peppered Moth)												1										1	10					12
Cleora rhomboideria	(Willow Beauty)						4	6							16	32	2												60
Alcis repandata	(Mottled Beauty)																							16	1				17
Ectropis biundulata	(Engrailed)																							41	32				73
Ematurga atomaria	(Common Heath)																								1				1
Bupalus piniaria	(Bordered White; Pine Looper)														1									109					110
Itame wauaria	(V Moth)															1													1
Lithina chlorosata	(Brown Silver-line)												1										3						4
Chiasmia clathrata	(Latticed Heath)																							1					1
Hepialus humuli	(Ghost Moth)					3																		1					4
Hepialus lupulina	(Common Swift)													4									2	1	4				11
Hepialus hecta	(Gold Swift)													1															1
Pleuroptya paralis	(Mother of Pearl)													2										10	81	3			96
Evergostis forficalis	(Garden Pebble)													1									1		4				6
Eurrhypara hortulata	(Small Magpie)													1	6	2							7	15	1				32
Hypsopygia costalis	(Gold Fringe)																						1	2	1				4
Pterophorus pentadactyla	(White Plume)					1	1																	3	4				9
Yponomeuta padella	(Small Ermine)													1										2					3
TOTAL TRAPPED SPECIMENS		-	4	-	-	32	21	9	-	-	2	5	21	21	92	40	7	3	2	2	7	8	47	294	150	7	4	1	779

SPECIES	MONTH	1981 M	1981 A	1981 M	1981 J	1981 J	1981 A	1981 S	1981 O	1981 N	1982 M	1982 A	1982 M	1982 J	1982 J	1982 A	1982 S	1982 O	1982 N	1983 M	1983 A	1983 M	1983 J	1983 J	1983 A	1983 S	1983 O	1983 N	TOTAL
Pyrrhia umbra	(Bordered Sallow)													1									1						2
Cosmia trapezina	(Dun-bar)						6																		4				10
Pseudoips prasinana	(Scarce Silver Lines)														1														1
Colocasia coryli	(Nut-tree Tussock)																						1						1
Plusia chrysitis	(Burnished Brass)					4	1								13	1	1							37	2				59
Plusia festucae	(Gold Spot)																							2		1			3
Plusia jota	(Plain Golden Y)													7	28								1	9					45
Plusia pulchrina	(Beautiful Golden Y)													4										9					13
Plusia gamma	(Silver Y)				2	40										2	4						8	15	10	9	2		92
Unca triplasia	(Spectacle)						1								1														2
Episema caeruleocephala	(Figure of Eight)																	2									1		3
Hypena proboscidalis	(Snout)						6							2	17	2									5	1			33
Trichiura crataegi	(Pale Oak Eggar)																								1				1
Celama confusalis	(Least Black Arches)					2																							2
Lithosia lurideola	(Common Footman)			1	1										2									16	1				21
Spilosoma lubricipeda	(White Ermine)												3	4									16	11					34
Spilosoma lutea	(Buff Ermine)				1	2							7										12	12					34
Cycnia mendica	(Muslin Moth)																								2				2
Phragmatobia fuliginosa	(Ruby Tiger)													1	1	1									1				4
Arctia caja	(Garden Tiger)						2								1									44	2				49
Alsophila aescularia	(March Moth)											2								5	2								9
Cosymbia punctaria	(Maiden's Blush)															1													1
Sterrha dimidiata	(Single-dotted Wave)																							1					1
Sterrha subsericeata	(Satin Wave)																							1					1
Sterrha straminata	(Plain Wave)																							1					1
Sterrha aversata	(Riband Wave)						2																	7					9
Xanthorhoë montanata	(Silver Ground Carpet)				1																		2	1					4
Xanthorhoë fluctuata	(Garden Carpet)			1	1		11	15				1	30	27	10	9	22				1	1	1	58	34	3			225
Xanthorhoë ferrugata	(Dark-barred Twin-spot Carpet)						5										1					1	12						19
Ortholitha chenorodiata	(Shaded Broad-bar)													1									1	1	1				4
Europhila badiata	(Shoulder Stripe)																				1	2							3
Perizoma alchemillata	(Small Rivulet)					2	1																	1	1				5
Euphyia bilineata	(Yellow Shell)					2	3								1	1									3				10
Ecliptopera silaceata	(Small Pheonix)						4						4		1								5		1				15
Lygris pyraliata	(Barred Straw)																							1					1
Lygris mellinata	(Spinach)					1								1	1														3
Dysstroma truncata	(Common Marbled Carpet)																11	4							2	2	1		20
Hydriomena furcata	(July Highflier)					1	1																						2
Hydriomena coerulata	(May Highflier)														6								21	4					31
Anaitis efformata	(Lesser Treble Bar)												1												5	1			7
Anaitis plagiata	(Treble Bar)																						3		11				14
Epirrhoë alternata	(Common Carpet)				1	6	10	4					15	11	8	11	7						8	6	21				108
Epirrhoë tristata	(Small Argent and Sable)														1														1
Eupithecia pulchellata	(Foxglove Pug)												1																1
Eupithecia vulgata	(Common Pug)																1												1
TOTAL TRAPPED SPECIMENS		**-**	**-**	**2**	**7**	**60**	**53**	**19**	**-**	**-**	**-**	**3**	**61**	**59**	**92**	**28**	**47**	**6**	**-**	**5**	**4**	**4**	**92**	**237**	**107**	**17**	**4**	**-**	**907**

SPECIES	MONTH	1981 M	A	M	J	J	A	S	O	N	1982 M	A	M	J	J	A	S	O	N	1983 M	A	M	J	J	A	S	O	N	TOTAL
Deilephila elpenor	(Elephant Hawk-moth)				2	2																	4	16					24
Laothoe populi	(Poplar Hawk-moth)														3								6	7					16
Pheosia tremula	(Swallow Prominent)					1							1		1	1								2	5				11
Pheosia gnoma	(Lesser Swallow Prominent)														1														1
Notodonta dromedarius	(Iron Prominent)			1																									1
Lophopteryx capucina	(Coxcombe Prominent)					2	1								1								1	9					14
Pterostomax palpina	(Pale Prominent)						1																						1
Phalera bucephala bucephala	(Buff Tip)																							2					2
Habrosyne pyritoides	(Buff Arches)					6									16									26					48
Thyatira batis	(Peach Blossom)																							2					2
Tethea ocularis	(Figure of Eight)																							1					1
Drepana acertinaria	(Scalloped Hook-tip)						4																		1				5
Cilix glaucata	(Chinese Character)						1						1		1	4							5	13	9				34
Dasychira pudibunda	(Pale Tussock)												2																2
Euproctis similis	(Yellow Tail)														1	1													2
Leucoma salicis	(White Satin)																							1					1
Euxoa nigricans	(Garden Dart)					1		4							4	103									24	22			158
Euxoa tritici	(White-line Dart)																							1	1				2
Agrotis segetum	(Turnip Moth)													1									2	1					4
Agrotis exclamationis	(Heart and Dart)													13	11								39	140	24				227
Graphiphora augur	(Double Dart)																						1	1					2
Diarisa mendica	(Ingrailed Clay)													8	2								11						21
Diarisa rubi	(Small Square Spot)																						73	2					75
Ochropleura plecta	(Flame Shoulder)													1									1	7					9
Amathes baja	(Dotted Clay)																							1					1
Amathes c-nigram	(Setaceous Hebrew Character)																	1						5		3			9
Amathes sextrigata	(Six Striped Rustic)																								1				1
Amathes xanthographa	(Square Spot Rustic)						10										20	1							69	1			101
Axylia putris	(Flame)													1	1								1	17	13				33
Euschesis comes	(Lesser Yellow Underwing)					3	43	44						1	1	10								37	84	4			257
Euschesis interjecta	(Least Yellow Underwing)																								1				1
Noctua Pronuba	(Large Yellow Underwing)					10	115	72						3	37	112	17							18	27	2			413
Naenia typica	(Gothic)													2	5	1								12	1				21
Maestra brassicae	(Cabbage Moth)					3	5						1	1	6								9	23	64				112
Melanchra persicariae	(Dot)																							1	1				2
Diataraxia oleracea	(Bright-line Brown-eye)													4	6	2							7	78					97
Discestra trifolii	(Nutmeg)																						1						1
Hadena thalassina	(Pale-shouldered Brocade)														1									1	1				3
Hadena bicolorata	(Broad-barred White)					1																	1	2					4
Hadena conspersa	(Marbled Coronet)														1														1
Hadena lepida	(Tawny Shears)													1															1
Orthosia gothica	(Hebrew Character)										2	28	12	7							60	43	4						156
Orthosia cruda	(Small Quaker)																			2									2
Orthosia stabilis	(Common Quaker)											56									3	4							63
TOTAL TRAPPED SPECIMENS		**-**	**-**	**1**	**2**	**29**	**210**	**120**	**-**	**-**	**2**	**84**	**17**	**43**	**99**	**234**	**37**	**2**	**-**	**2**	**63**	**47**	**166**	**426**	**326**	**32**	**-**	**-**	**1942**

SPECIES		1981									1982									1983									
	MONTH	M	A	M	J	J	A	S	O	N	M	A	M	J	J	A	S	O	N	M	A	M	J	J	A	S	O	N	TOTAL
Orthosia incerta	(Clouded Drab)											6	4								30	13	1						54
Orthosia gracilis	(Powdered Quaker)												1																1
Leucania pallens	(Common Wainscot)						10							3	41	14								41	14				123
Leucania impura	(Smoky Wainscot)					3	7							2	57	20	3							45	2				139
Leucania comma	(Shoulder-striped Wainscot)													1	2									10	1				14
Leucania lythargria	(Clay)					1									6	1													8
Lucania conigera	(Brown-line Bright-eye)													8									5	4	2				19
Cucullia chamomillae	(Chamomile Shark)																					1							1
Brachionycha sphinx	(Sprawler)																		1										1
Aporophyla nigra	(Black rustic)																1										3		4
Xylocampa areom	(Early Grey)											9									10	14							33
Allophyes oxyacanthae	(Green-brindled Crescent)																1									4	6		11
Antitype chi	(Grey Chi)															2													2
Omphalescelis lunosa	(Lunar Underwing)																									1			1
Agrochola lychnidis	(Beaded Chestnut)																4									12	25		41
Anchoscelis helvola	(Flounced Chestnut)																1						1						2
Anchoscelis litura	(Brown-spot Pinion)																1									2			3
Atethmia xerampelina	(Centre-barred Sallow)															1													1
Tiliacea aurago	(Barred Sallow)							2																					2
Conistra vaccinii	(Chestnut)																					1				8			9
Cryphia perla	(Marbled Beauty)														2	1								4					7
Apatele leporina	(Miller)													1	1									1					3
Apatele psi	(Grey Dagger)					4	3							3	7								1	10	1				29
Apatele rumicis	(Knot Grass)														3								6	11					20
Amphipyra berbera	(New Copper Underwing)																1										2		3
Amphipyra tragopaginis	(Mouse)																	6								9			15
Apamea lithoxylaea	(Light Arches)														21									39	4				64
Apamea monoglypha	(Dark Arches)														3	3								49	1				56
Apamea crenata	(Clouded-bordered Brindle)																						6						6
Apamea sordens	(Rustic Shoulder-knot)													1									11						12
Apamea remissa	(Dusky Brocade)													1									6		1				8
Apamea unanimis	(Small Clouded Brindle)																						1						1
Apamea secalis	(Common Rustic)														2									3	1				6
Procus strigilis	(Marbled Minor)													1									1	66					68
Procus latruncula	(Tawny Marbled Minor)																						7	58					65
Procus fasciuncula	(Middle-barred Minor)																							1					1
Eremobia ochroleuca	(Dusky Sallow)						1	1									1								1	2			6
Euplexia lucipara	(Small Angle Shades)													1	2								1	1	1				6
Phlogophora meticulosa	(Angle Shades)							2							1	1	1	3					2	2	1	8	7		28
Thalpophila matura	(Straw Underwing)															3	1								3				7
Meristis trigrammica	(Treble Lines)					1																							1
Caradrina morpheus	(Mottled Rustic)						1																						1
Gortyna micacea	(Rosy Rustic)																1								1	7	2		11
Gortyna flavago	(Frosted Orange)							1									1									2	1		5
TOTAL TRAPPED SPECIMENS		**-**	**-**	**-**	**-**	**9**	**22**	**6**	**-**	**-**	**-**	**15**	**5**	**22**	**148**	**46**	**17**	**9**	**1**	**-**	**40**	**29**	**49**	**345**	**34**	**55**	**46**	**-**	**898**

Table 5. Moth species trapped at Whitwell Wood during 1983.

SPECIES		1983 Months M	A	M	J	J	A	S	O	N	TOTAL
Pheosia tremula	(Swallow Prominent)						5				5
Pheosia gnoma	(Lesser Swallow Prominent)					10					10
Lophopteryx capucina	(Coxcombe Prominent)				1						1
Phalera bucephala bucephala	(Buff Tip)					8					8
Amathes xanthographa	(Square Spot Rustic)						3				3
Axylia putris	(Flame)						3				3
Leucania lythargria	(Clay)					1					1
Omphaloscelis lunosa	(Lunar Underwing)								1		1
Conistra vaccinii	(Chestnut)			1							1
Cryphia perla	(Marbled Beauty)							1			1
Euplexia lucipara	(Small Angle Shades)					3					3
Cosmia trapezina	(Dun-bar)						4				4
Colocasia coryli	(Nut-tree Tussock)				1						1
Philudoria potatoria	(Drinker)					1					1
Lithosia lurideola	(Common Footman)						1				1
Geometra papilionaria	(Large Emerald)						2				2
Calothysanis amata	(Blood Vein)						1				1
Xanthorhoë montanata	(Silver Ground Carpet)						1				1
Ortholitha chenopodiata	(Shaded Broad-bar)					1	1				2
Colostygia pectinataria	(Green Carpet)					2					2
Anticlea derivata	(Streamer)			1							1
Chloroclystis rectangulata	(Green Pug)					1					1
Campaea margaritata	(Light Emerald)					1	1				2
Deuteronomos fascantaria	(Dusky Thorn)						2				2
Selenia bilunaria	(Early Thorn)						8				8
Selenia tetralunaria	(Purple Thorn)						1				1
Gonodontis bidentata	(Scalloped Hazel)				2						2
Crocallis elinguaria	(Scalloped Oak)						2				2
Lycia hirtaria	(Brindled Beauty)			9							9
Alcis repandata	(Mottled Beauty)						6				6
Ectropis biundulata	(Engrailed)			1							1
Ectropis crepuscularia	(Small Engrailed)				2						2
Hepialus sylvina	(Orange Swift)						1				1
Hepialus lupulina	(Common Swift)					1	4				5
Pleuroptya paralis	(Mother of Pearl)				7	5					12
TOTAL TRAPPED SPECIMENS		**0**	**0**	**12**	**13**	**34**	**46**	**1**	**1**	**0**	**107**

Interestingly, the greatest diversity of species is present from the Wollen Valley locality. The frequency of moths from this locality, which is essentially open ground, contrasts strongly with those recorded from the remaining two localities which are both woodland with diverse floras. This point is illustrated by the results for 1983, where the numbers of moths recorded from Whitwell Wood was 107, from Creswell Crags 60, whilst the Wollen Valley locality provided 2648 individual moths. This observation suggests that locally, open ground provides a preferred habitat for large numbers of species and that local woodland faunas are impoverished by comparison. The woodland faunas also appear to be dominated by resident species, particularly Large yellow underwing, Lesser yellow underwing and Common quaker. In comparison, the open ground at Wollen Valley has additional species occurring in low numbers. Many of the locally uncommon species occur in this context and in particular Silver Y which has migrated into the area from Central Europe in considerable numbers especially during 1983.

Discussion This study highlights the need for care in interpreting environmental conditions from invertebrate faunas. The three chosen sampling sites illustrate the diversity and differences that are present within an overall small area. Many species, thought to prefer woodland habitats are shown in this study to be more numerous in open ground habitats. This observation has a number of implications for conservation of moth faunas. The flora and fauna of Creswell Crags and Whitwell Wood are protected by legislation. Conversely, the richest moth fauna in this area at the Wollen Valley site occurs in an open area intensely used agriculturally and industrially, for which there is little protection.

The diversity of modern moth faunas in the Creswell area demonstrates the degree to which our knowledge of past environments is limited. Moth remains are unknown from the archaeological deposits of the Creswell area which provide outstanding evidence for past warm stage vertebrate and molluscan faunas.

There is no reason to believe that moth faunas have not been at least as diverse in past warm stages as they are today, but the systematic study of this tantalising area of life is hampered by their poor preservation in the archaeological record, and inadequate recovery techniques.

MAP, PICTORIAL AND DOCUMENTARY EVIDENCE OF PAST ENVIRONMENTS

The origins of human settlements in the Creswell gorge are well known from extensive archaeological finds dating to the prehistoric period. The nature of human settlement in the early historic periods at Creswell is, however, shrouded in mystery. Few historic records survive and the first clear reference to settlement in the Creswell area is around AD 1175 when Thomas de Cuckney endowed the

Abbey of Welbeck (Thompson 1938, Turberville 1938). At this time it is likely that a small settlement centred around a water mill was established nearby in a woodland clearing on the River Wollen near the eastern end of the Creswell Gorge. Later in the period between 1539–1767, there is 'fragmentary' documentary evidence for this small settlement which had remained part of Welbeck Abbey.

An unusually detailed picture of a small settlement at the western end of Creswell Crags has been left by the artist George Stubbs, who, with his colleague Barret, was employed by the Duke of Portland between 1767–70 to paint views of Welbeck (Egerton 1978). During these years Stubbs produced *Two Gentlemen Going Shooting, with a view of Creswell Crags, taken on the spot*, which is shown in the complimentary postcard. Behind the sportsmen in this illustration can be seen a timber framed, thatched water mill complete with undershot wheel. It is seen beside a small mill pond, presumably formed by damming the River Wollen. The cliff faces are barely visible under a dense foliage of elderberry, elm and oak.

Stubbs was clearly impressed by the scene which he may have also used as background in a number of other works, particularly *Horse devoured by a lion* produced in 1763 (Egerton pers. comm.). The small settlement appears to have remained relatively unchanged for the following hundred years. The gorge was visited by Laing in 1821, who describes it as a "wild place" impassable for travellers and carriages.

This idyllic scene changed dramatically in 1854 when a new limestone quarry was opened just behind the southern outcrop of the Creswell gorge and quarry staff were accommodated in newly built cottages at the western end of the gorge in proximity to the mill (*Figure 4*). The area was changed beyond recognition in 1865 when extensive landscaping of Welbeck Abbey Lands was undertaken. At Creswell, the small hamlet, water mill and the now disused quarry cottages were demolished. The mill pond was drained and the present, much larger, lake created at the eastern end of the gorge (*Figure 4*). It was during this work that Richard Tebbet the quarry supervisor discovered the first fossil bones from the Creswell Crags which led in 1875 to a major scientific exploration.

DEPOSITS IN THE FLOOR OF THE CRESWELL CRAGS GORGE

Study of the sediments preserved in the floor of the gorge has provided a great deal of very tantalising information about the recent ecological and geological history of the lake and gorge. *Figures 13 and 14* show in schematic form the general character and stratigraphic relationships of sediments found in shallow excavations and boreholes into the floor of the gorge. These deposits are:

Oldest

Layer H—Magnesian Limestone—the bedrock which also forms the walls of the gorge. This rock occurs 4.2m below the Mill Bridge. At this location the rock is hardened by partial silicification reaching over 28% silicon dioxide at a depth of 9.5m below the present ground surface. Excavations and coring in the centre of the lake have not reached bedrock.

Layer G—Talus and slope deposits—this is a complex layer, at least 3 metres thick, comprising angular to rounded cobbles and boulders of Magnesian Limestone in a matrix of finer limestone debris. In the talus at the foot of the gorge walls, the boulders reach over 1m in diameter. These coarse deposits have accumulated as a result of rockfall and past freeze-thaw activity shattering the cliffs and talus. Layers of much finer silt size deposits are also present. The materials may derive from weathering of the limestone, and/or by being blown in as dust by stronger winds in the past.

No dating evidence has yet been found in the sections studied on the gorge sides. However, the many differences between the size and shape of the materials present, when compared to the sediments collecting on the gorge floor today, suggest the gorge floor cobbles and boulders probably date to the period 10,000 to 80,000 years ago, (possibly 10–25,000 years ago) when the climate of the Creswell area was often extremely cold and arctic. In much of the latter period a major ice sheet extending from Scandinavia as far as Norfolk, pressed up against the Lincolnshire hills to the east. The climatic changes associated with this glacial event probably had the effect of shattering the exposed limestone cliffs and detaching boulders from the rock faces.

In the area of Pin Hole, Church Hole, Robin Hood's and Mother Grundy's Parlour, deposits of this general age have yielded important palaeolithic archaeological remains. These are described in Campbell (1977) and Jenkinson (1984).

Layer F—Coarse sands and gravels with angular limestone debris and Bunter pebbles—these sediments probably owe their origin to reworking by stronger streams, lake waves and currents of finer debris from the underlying talus and slope deposits as they were produced by the frost shattering described above. Further study will probably reveal a much more complex picture of their age and origin.

Elsewhere in the Creswell area they may be much older in age. Within the gorge these deposits form an important aquifer supplying water to the lake.

Layer D—Black humose silts and sands—this layer is up to 1.2m thick, very soft, frequently laminated, sometimes sulphurous. There is an abundant content of coal debris, and occasionally cobbles are present. Molluscan fossils and plant debris are common. In the upper levels, laminations occur which are up to 5mm thick. These comprise light grey and brown/black couplets, and represent deposition in shallow water marshes, streams, and lakes. The abundance of partially decomposed, organic remains and the presence of hydrogen sulphide, suggest that the lake floor was sometimes poorly oxygenated. The marsh soils also lacked adequate aeration, which otherwise would have helped break down the only partially decayed biological remains accumulating on them. The much paler laminations suggest better aquatic conditions. The origins of the laminations are not known with certainty. The coarse elements may correspond to higher discharges and floods, the finer layers to more quiescent periods.

The angular coal debris known from this layer may derive by natural erosion from the small surface outcrops of the Clowne coal seam which are known upstream to the north-west (Eden, Stevenson and Edwards 1957). These outcrops are also known to have been quarried from Roman times; mined coal being found in a Romano-British farmstead at nearby Scratta Wood (White pers. comm.).

Layer E—Black humose silts and peats—this layer is at least 3 metres in thickness. These fossiliferous deposits have been found at the western entrance to the gorge, where they collected in a biologically rich marsh and lake margin. The presence of angular coal debris in their upper levels (e.g. Unit MB1/8) suggests that at least these upper levels might have been contemporary with coal mining upstream. Unfortunately the stratigraphic relationships between layers D and E are not fully clear. It is probable that much of layer E predates layer D.

Three large wooden timbers, square in section with mortice and tenon joints were found at the top of this layer and are described later. The extent to which they may have sunk or been pushed into layer E is not clear.

Layer C—A complex of man-made and alluvial deposits—these sediments occur at the western end of the gorge. They are at least 1.5m thick and comprise red clay/silts, coal rich lenses, and yellow made ground. The red/clay silt layers may be a 'puddling' of water-proof materials laid in or near the former millpond floor at this site.

Table 6. Table describing the augering and sediments from Borehole 1.

STRATIGRAPHY AND SEDIMENT DESCRIPTION BY CONTRACTOR BOREHOLE 1		SAMPLES TAKEN	
Ground level	= Nettles and firm brown clay with fragments of limestone	0.1m–0.6m 0.7m	Bulk sample
0.7m–1.2m	= Very soft dark brown silty clay	0.7m–1.2m 1.3m	U/4 sample
1.6m	= Very soft brown silty clay	1.3m–1.8m 1.9m 2.0m	Bulk sample sample
2.0m	= Sand, gravel and stones	2.0m–2.5m 2.5m–3.0m	Bulk Bulk
3.0m	= Limestone? Had to use chisel	3.0m–3.4m	Bulk

Layer B—brown sand, silt loams with limestone pebbles—these deposits indicate former marsh and lacustrine environments.

Layer A—Dark brown silty clay—up to 0.5m in thickness, these deposits are rather humose, extremely soft, marsh soils.

SEDIMENTOLOGY

Sedimentology of Borehole 2

The stratigraphy and sediments found here (*Figures 13 and 14*) are probably fairly typical of those of the north and south lake margins. The samples were obtained by Exploration Associates Limited, using a shell and auger drilling rig mounted on a pontoon.

The field sediment description logs of boreholes 1 and 2 are given in *Tables 6 and 7*. A detailed sedimentological description and the results of analysis of deposits from borehole 2 are given in *Figure 15*.

Undisturbed samples in U4 tubes to a depth of 2m were provided. These were extruded in the Department of Civil Engineering at the University of Sheffield. The sedimentological properties of the samples were determined using standard techniques, to quantify their physical and chemical properties.

Results and Discussions

Borehole 2—the basal layer of borehole 2 was comprised of coarse sands and gravels of layer F. These were very brecciated and angular fragments, dominantly

Table 7. Table describing the augering and sediments from Borehole 2.

BOREHOLE 2		SAMPLES TAKEN	
Ground level	= Nettles and top soil		
0.1m–0.6m	= Very soft dark brown silty clay	0.1m–0.6m 0.7m	U/4 sample
1.3m	= Grey brown silty sand	0.7m–1.2m 1.3m 1.3m–1.8m 1.9m 2.0m	U/4 sample U/4 sample sample*
2.0m	= Sand, gravel, stone and pieces of pottery	2.0m–2.5m 2.5m–3.0m	Bulk Bulk
3.0m	= Limestone? had to use chisel	3.0m–3.3m	Bulk

* Seepage of water 1.9–0.8m

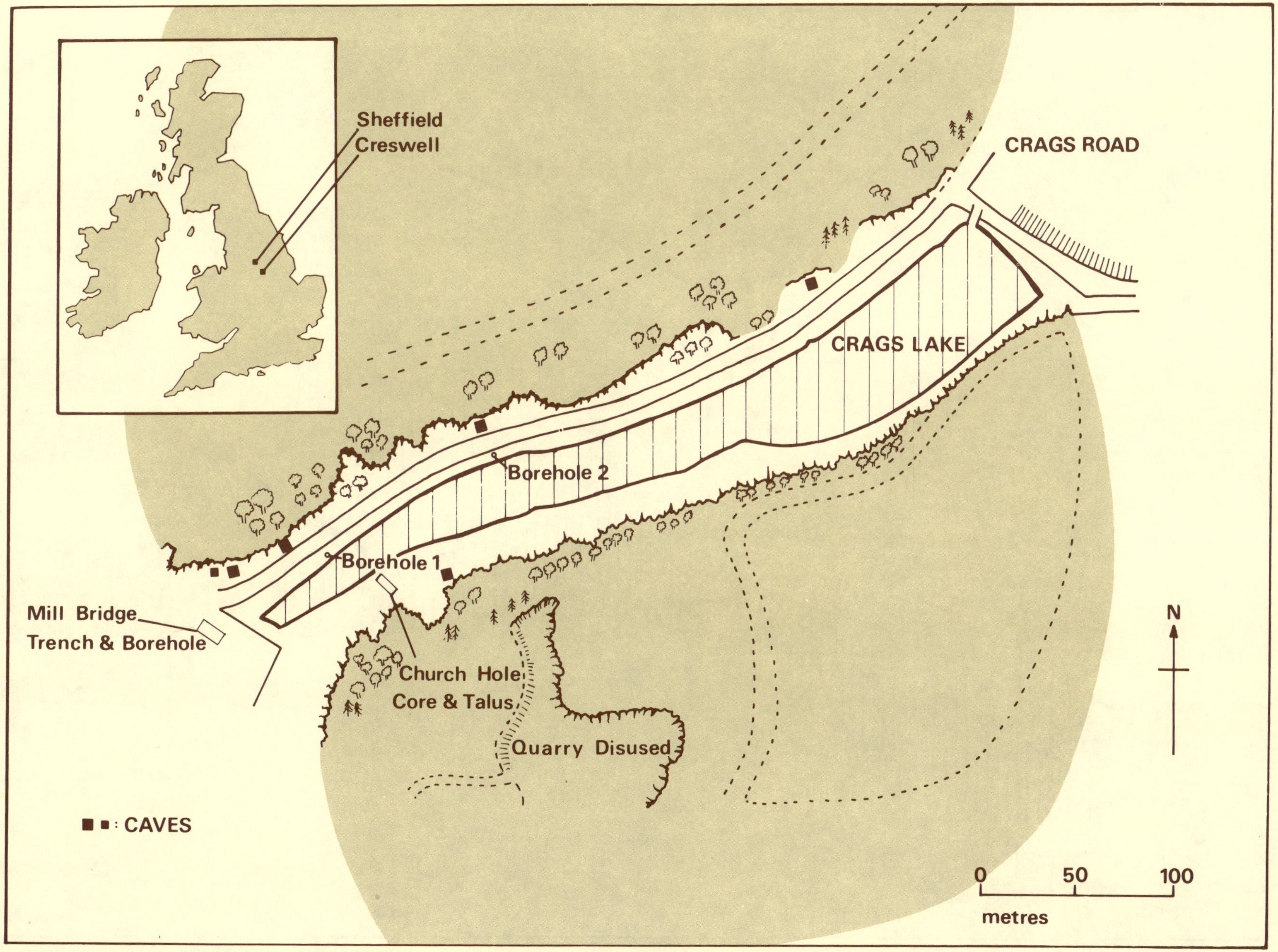

Figure 13. Map of Creswell Crags Gorge showing the location of boreholes and temporary exposures.

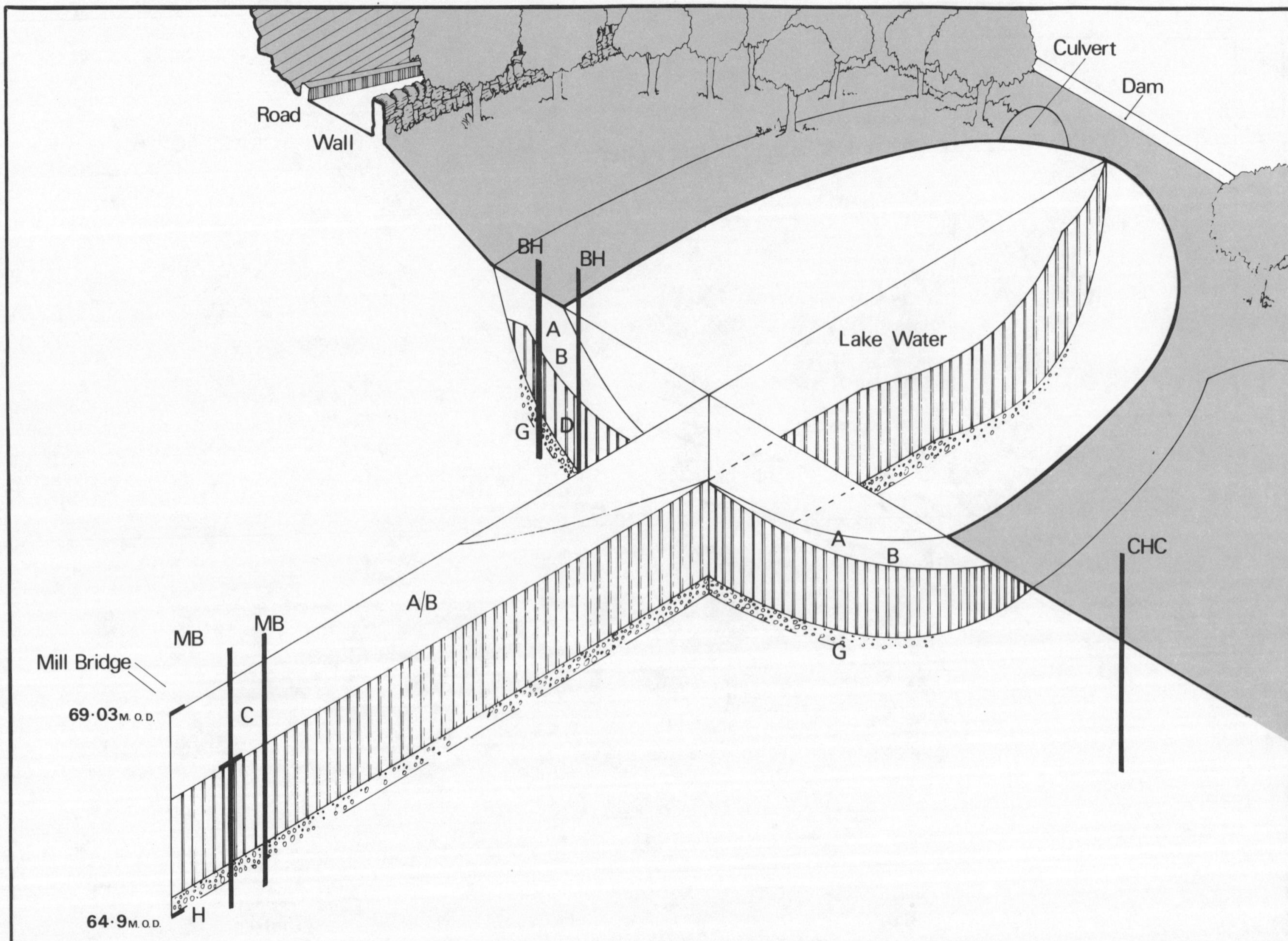

Figure 14. Schematic diagram showing the stratigraphic relationships of the deposits within the Creswell Crags Gorge.

limestone but pebbles from the Sherwood sandstone group (previously known as the Bunter formation) were also present. Coal was recovered from between 2 and 3m depth, as was pottery.

The carbonate 'equivalent' is a measure of the total carbonate in the sample that can be estimated from dissolution in 3N HCl. For layer F in Borehole 2 the carbonate values increase from 45% to 80% with depth possibly due to the fact that the majority of the fine earth fraction is comprised of limestone debris and sand.

The angularity of many of the limestone pebbles suggest that this layer is probably the finer material which has been derived from freeze-thaw action on the limestone cliffs, and then accumulated as a result of slope wash, strong stream and lake currents. In terms of dating, the presence of coal fragments in the upper 1m is ambiguous. Some of the material may be of ancient origin, however in-washing might have occurred as recently as the Roman period when the extraction of coal began nearby.

Overlying the sands and gravels in Borehole 2 are black humose silts and sands of layer D, approximately 1m in thickness. Most of the material extruded by U4 cores was of the fine earth fraction, the stones present making up less than 2% by weight and being rounded. The sediments are markedly laminated, especially in the upper .75m of the deposit where there are well developed alternate layers of brown/black sands or clays, and light brown/grey sands or silts.

Between 1.5m and 2m depth, there is a greater proportion of silt and clay in the sediments with mean size generally smaller than 4.5∅. These lower sediments show fewer laminations but coal fragments and molluscan remains are still present.

This contrasts with the overlying 0.3m where the average particle size is in the fine sand fraction greater than 4∅ diameter. Here the laminations are more pronounced and up to 5mm thick, comprising couplets of dark brown sands and light grey sands.

Loss-on-ignition measurements for organic carbon are between 23% and 29%, while carbonate range from 14% to 20%. The high organic carbon is the abundance of vegetable matter, coal fragments, and molluscs present within the limestone debris.

The laminations are probably due to varying flow conditions in the stream, marsh and lake environments. The supply of material to this depositional environment will depend on the rate of erosion of the catchment. This in turn is related to climatic, geological and vegetational factors. In addition, the amount and type of material settling in the lake or stream bed is determined by the exact nature of the bed, particle retention time, and stratification within the lake water. These conditions are related to temperatures, exposure to wind, and rate of outflow and inflow.

Therefore as external conditions vary, the nature of sedimentation on the lake or stream bed will also vary, so giving rise to the laminations. The dark brown, finer bands are probably due to more quiescent periods with anaerobic conditions causing partial decay of vegetation debris. The coarser, paler laminations suggest more rapid flow or a greater volume of water, thereby increasing the competence of the system to remove finer material. The presence of coal fragments in the whole depth of laminated sediments suggests that the alternating conditions of greater or lesser flow might have occurred since the onset of mining in the area.

The uppermost layers of Borehole 2 correspond to layers B and A which comprise a brown sandy, silt loam with limestone pebbles, and a dark brown, sandy loam in turn overlain by a very soft, silty clay deposit respectively.

The sandy silt loam of layer B lies between 0.8m and 1.1m depth and has a mean particle diameter of less than 4.5∅ in the fine earth fraction. Organic carbon contents are between 10% and 13% and appear to be concentrated in the upper layers which have a carbonate value of 17%. In contrast, the lower levels of layer B have a slightly lower organic carbon content. The greater carbonate content of 30% is due to the presence of limestone pebbles, up to 5cm in diameter, plus the many molluscan remains. As with layer D, this heterogeneous sediment type probably results from fluctuations in character of the lacustrine depositional environment.

Layer A comprises soft marsh deposits and marsh soils overlying a paler sandy material. These represent the most recent sediments accumulating at the present time. They have a mean particle diameter of greater than 4∅. A small quantity of coal is present. This probably accounts for the lower organic carbon levels between 14% and 16% compared with the underlying sediments between 1.2 and 2.0m where there is more decaying vegetation. Carbonate levels average 16.5%, which is lower than underlying layers and probably results from the relative absence of limestone pebbles and detritus.

Mill Bridge—Detailed Description of its Stratigraphy

The sediments of the Mill Bridge samples (MB1 and MB3) were obtained from temporary trenches dug in the western end of the gorge (*Figures 13 and 16*). Trench MB1 exposed and facilitated the sampling of the upper 2m of sediments, pollen samples being taken only from the lower 1m. Trench MB3 was at right angles and almost adjacent to MB1, exposing 3m of sediments. Samples were collected from the lowest metre, together with the interface between the peaty deposit and overlying complex.

The deepest unit, which was exposed in MB3 and partially exposed in MB1, was Unit MB1/9 and is the equivalent of layer E; it is made up of black humose silts and peats. Molluscs were abundant and the organic debris suggest that it is possibly the remnant of a marsh or lake on which the mill was situated.

Layer C is a series of complex man-made and alluvial deposits. Its interface with layer E was highly irregular due to compaction from above. The material

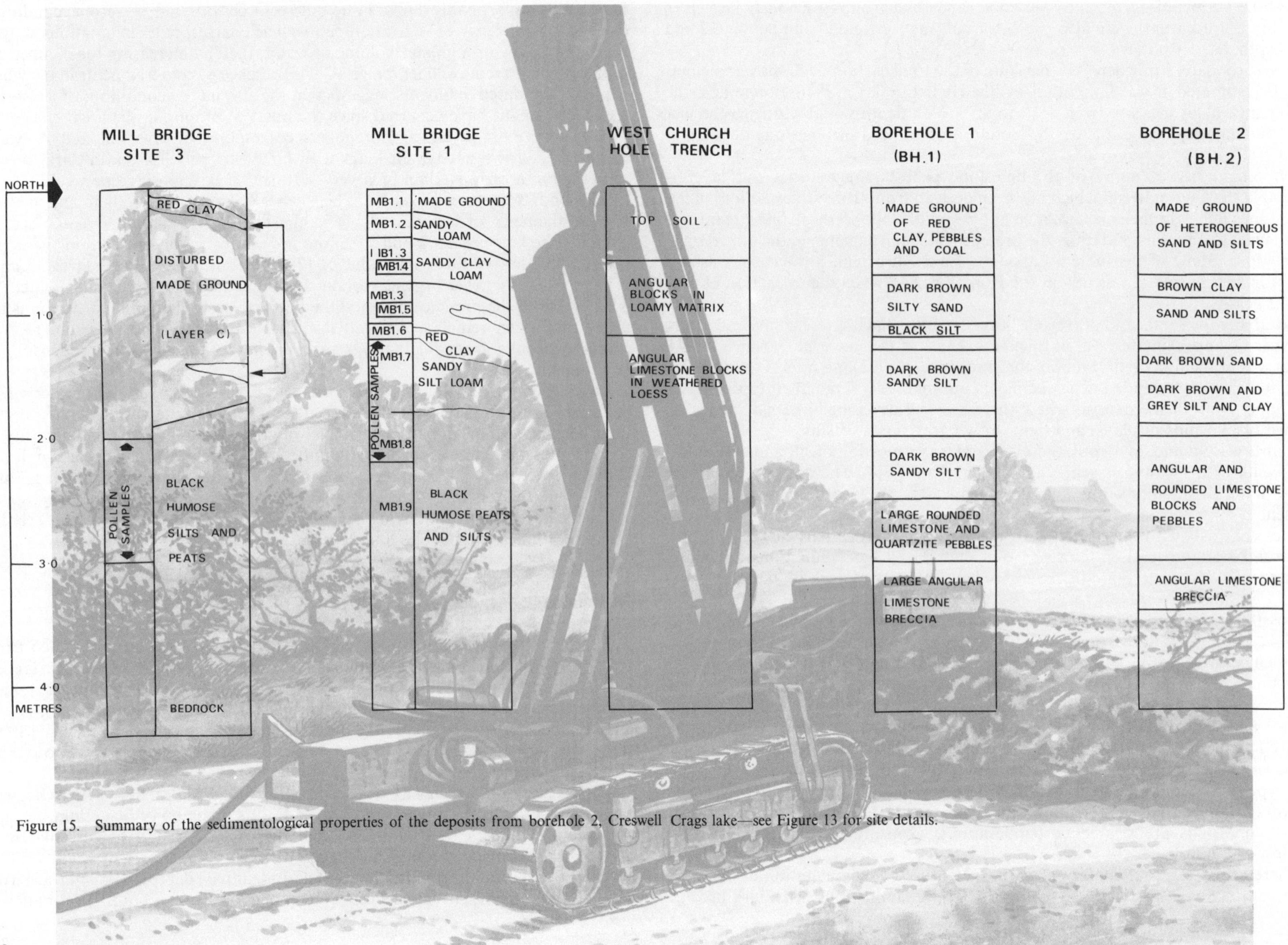

Figure 15. Summary of the sedimentological properties of the deposits from borehole 2, Creswell Crags lake—see Figure 13 for site details.

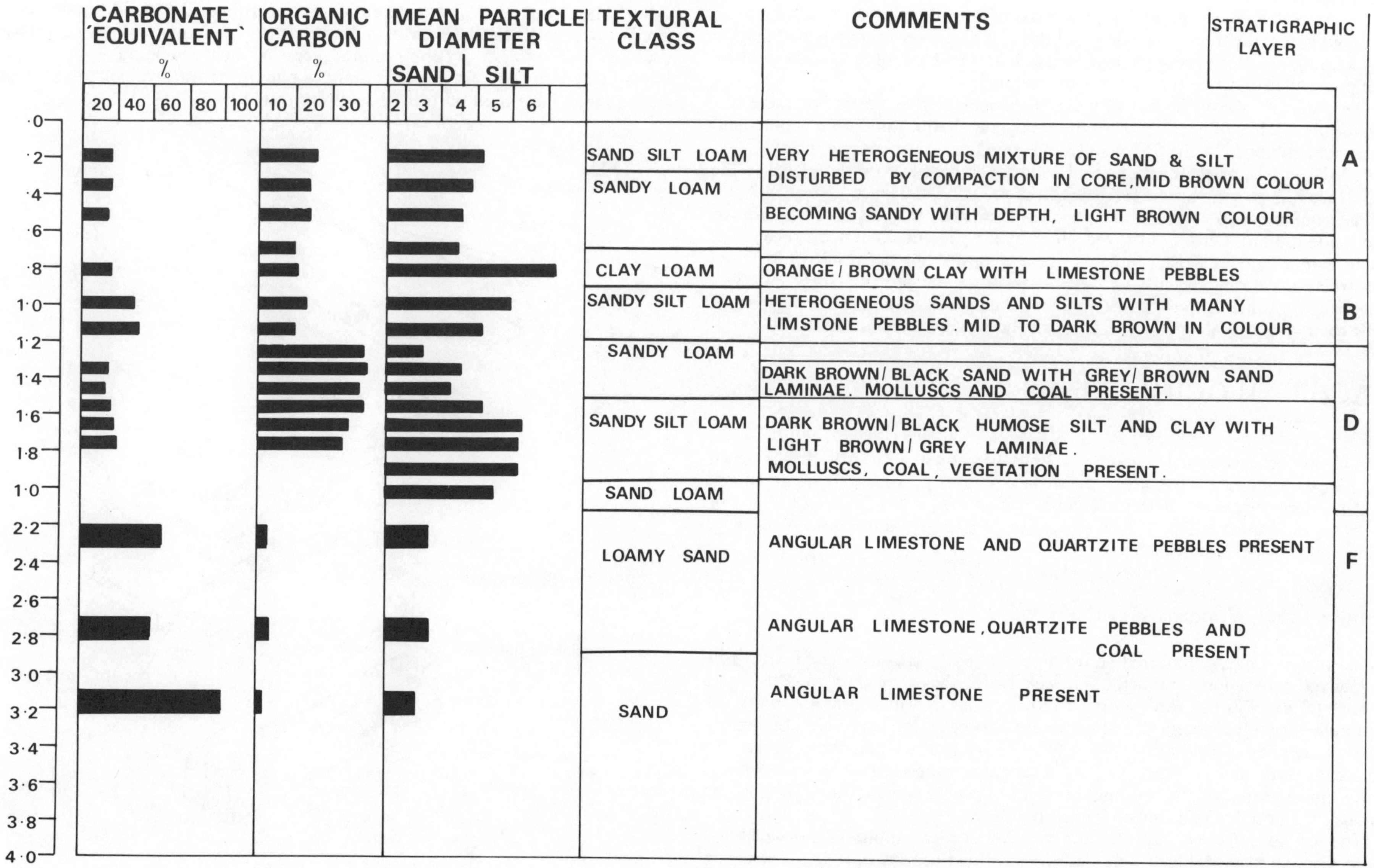

Figure 16. Stratigraphy and sediments at Mill Bridge.

immediately overlying layer E is a dark grey/brown, sandy silt loam containing molluscan remains and coal fragments, plus large limestone blocks. In MB1, one metre above the layer E/C interface, a band of red silty clay up to 20cms thick thins out across the trench. The origin of this clay rich layer is unknown; it may be a 'puddling'—water-proofing—layer placed at the base of a stream or lake occupying the site when the mill was operational.

The sediment above the red silty clay is similar to that below but there is a greater abundance of coal debris in the sandy clay loam. Limestone pebbles and quartzite pebbles from the Sherwood sandstone formation are present.

In MB3, a lens of charcoal material is present which is possibly related to the Mill since it is at comparable levels with the red silty clay layer.

The uppermost 20–40cms in the trenches comprises very disturbed sediments, and made-ground. Lenses of the red silty clay are present. Coal debris occurs, as do limestone and quartzite pebbles. These deposits are the result of building constructions during the last two centuries, since the present Crags lake was established. In this period landscaping has taken place, as well as the very recent construction of a drainage system through the western entrance to the gorge.

ARCHAEOLOGICAL FINDS

Important post-medieval archaeological finds were found in the Mill Bridge trench (*Figure 13*). Here, 1 to 1.5m below the surface in layer E, three well preserved oak timbers were uncovered. These are illustrated in *Figure 17*. Detailed analysis of these wood fragments shows them to be part of a large, timber-framed building, which once stood near Mill Bridge.

Timbers and Woodworking

None of the timbers recovered shows signs of tool marks associated with their felling and conversion to timber, but it is likely that they were all sawn. The largest timber (*Figure 17*) has three stopped mortices, all of which bear the marks of spoon auger on their base. The mortices are unpegged, indicating that the timber joints were not expected to be subject to any parting strain and were merely used to locate three upright timbers. This observation suggests that this timber is a fragment of groundsill, the spacings of the mortices are comparable with those for 'studs', the uprights in a timber-framed building.

The second timber (*Figure 17*) has a massive mortice cut into its end which has been through pegged, illustrating that it was a load bearing part of the structure and must therefore have been from a different area of the structure from piece 1. The last timber (*Figure 17*) has three unpegged mortices cut by spoon augers and designed as the first piece, to locate tenons where no parting strain is present. This timber has two unexplained drilled holes in its surface. The function of this timber is unknown but as it was associated with the other two pieces, it probably belongs to the same structure. With the exception of the groundsill none of the timbers is specific to a particular section of a timber-framed building. All three timbers would be compatible with the structural pieces of such a building.

It is likely that these fragments belong to one of the watermills known on the site, and may have been part of the mill illustrated by Stubbs (1767).

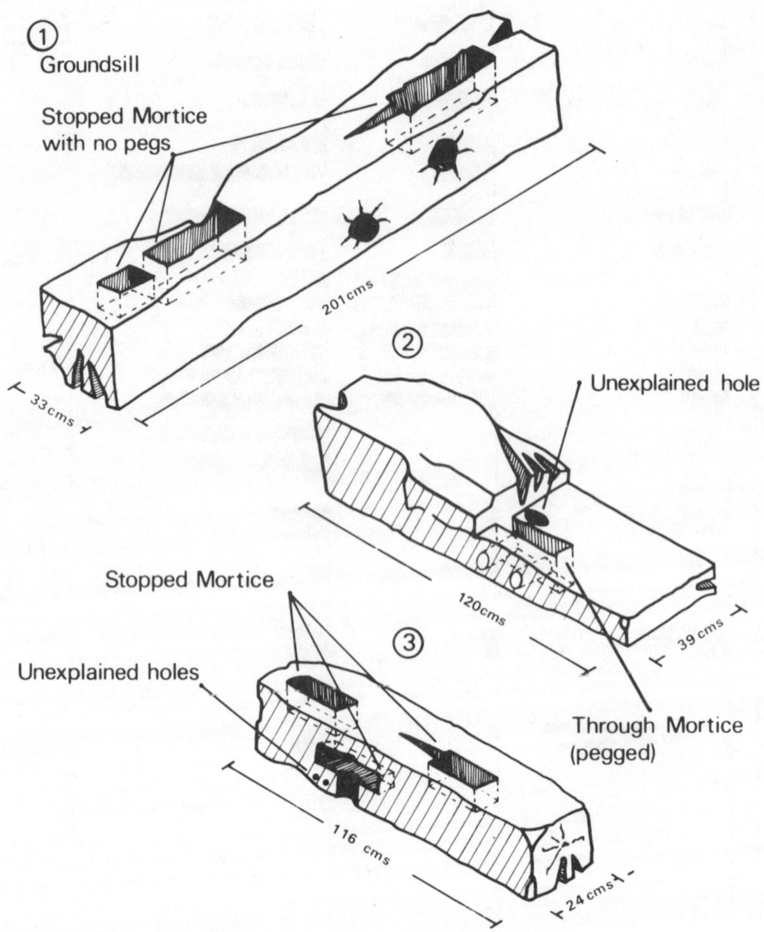

Figure 17. Tudor timbers and woodworking recovered from Mill Bridge marsh deposits.

Dendrochronology

Samples of all three timbers were removed for tree-ring dating. Only one of the samples from the groundsill had enough well preserved rings to allow dating by this method. This piece had 125 complete growth rings preserved. Measurements of these rings were compared with two dating tree ring sequences from the Sherwood Oak and the Yorkshire tree ring chronologies. Sections of these chronologies are shown in *Figure 18*. It can be seen in this figure that the Creswell specimen matches well with the sequence dated between 1405–1529 AD. The outer rings of the Creswell timber are in transition from sapwood to heartwood. Allowing 32 ± 9 years for completion of this process (Baillie 1982), we conclude the tree from which the groundsill was made was felled within a decade either side of 1561 AD.

This activity, probably involving woodland clearance and the establishment of a water mill in the western end of the gorge, is of considerable interest in that it is dated to the late 16th century, a period when documentary evidence of development in the area is especially poor.

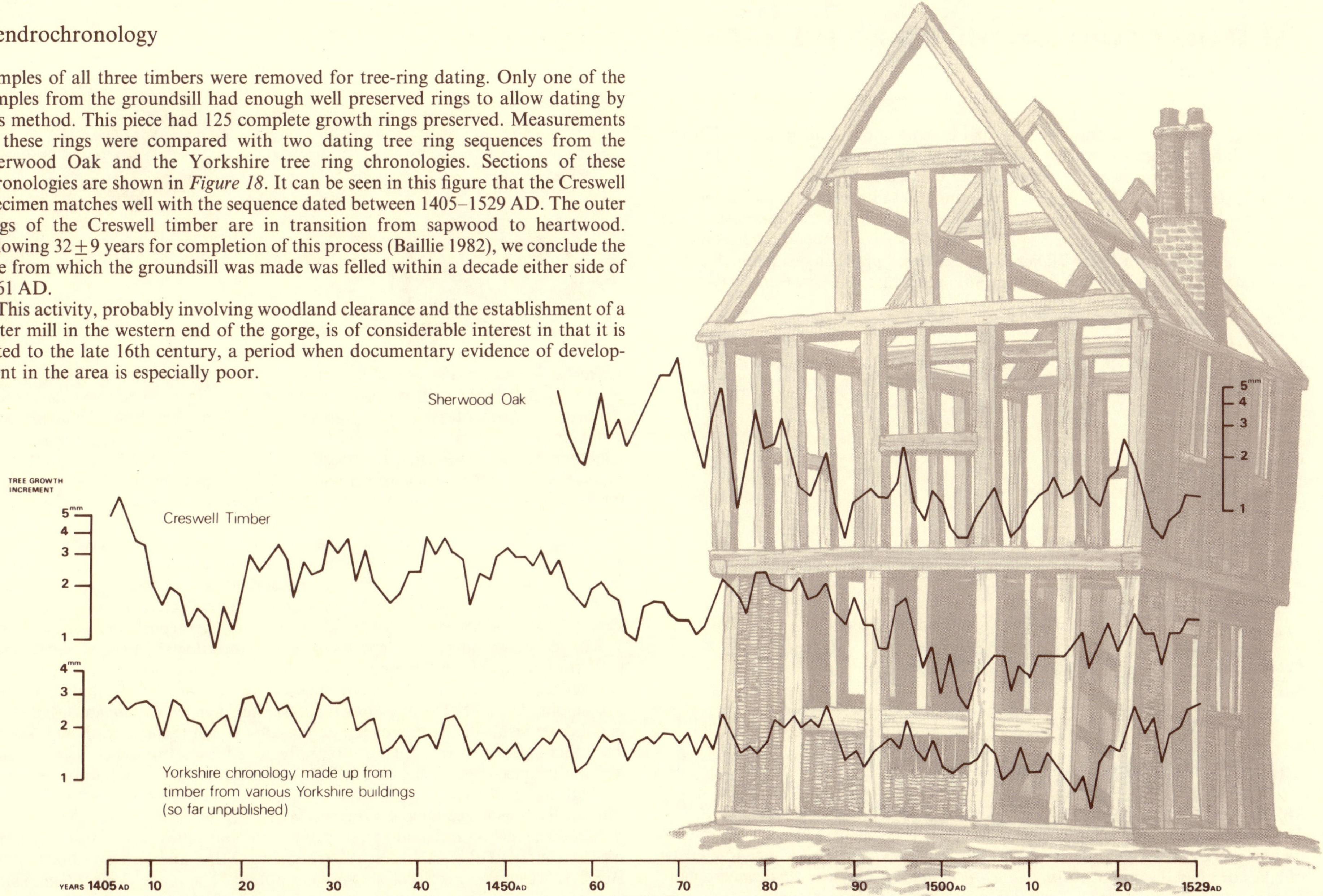

Figure 18. Diagram showing the match and age of the Mill Bridge 3 groundsill and the dendrochronological sequences for the Sherwood Oak and Yorkshire.

PALAEOECOLOGY OF THE LAKE—THE FAUNAL EVIDENCE

Molluscan remains constitute the principal type of faunal evidence found in this study. Many molluscan species are restricted to particular types of habitat. Consequently their presence in deposits may be used as an aid to reconstruct the nature of past environments. In this study, some 53 samples of at least 1 kilogram, from sites MB1, MB3, Boreholes 1 and 2 were sieved through a 0.5mm sieve and the molluscan remains extracted and identified using a binocular stereo-microscope. The counts recorded in *Tables 8—11* are based upon single identifiable shell parts such as apices or lip parts. Important species are illustrated in *Figure 8*.

Table 8. Molluscan species recovered from the Mill Bridge 1 sequence.

SPECIES	Top MB1/1	MB1/2	upper MB1/3	lower MB1/3	MB1/4	MB1/5	MB1/6	Bottom MB1/7
Potamopyrgus jenkinsi			2					
Valvata piscinalis				1				
Bithynia (operculum)						1		
Lymnaea peregra				3		1		1
Gyraulus laevis				1				1
Ancylus fluviatilis				1				
Carychium minimum								1
Discus rotundatus				1		1		
Zonitidae sp.				2				
Vallonia costata								2
Vallonia pulchella						1		3
Vallonia(?) excentrica						1		
Punctum pygmaeum						1		
Ceciliodes acicula							1	
Clausiliidae sp.	1							
Pisidium subtruncatum			1	1		1		
Pisidium sp.			2	2		1		
TOTAL	1	0	5	12	0	8	1	8

Environmental Reconstruction

Mill Bridge 1
The results of mollusc counts of this trench are given in *Table 8*. The species present represent several different environments. *Valvata piscinalis* is characteristic of lakes or quiet deep pools. *Bithynia tentaculata* and *Pisidium amnicum* are more common in streams. *Ancylus fluviatilis* occurs on cobbles in flowing water, or on the wave-washed lake-beach margins. Species which tolerate a wide variety of aquatic habitats are *Potamopyrgus jenkinsi, Lymnaea peregra, Planorbis planorbis,*

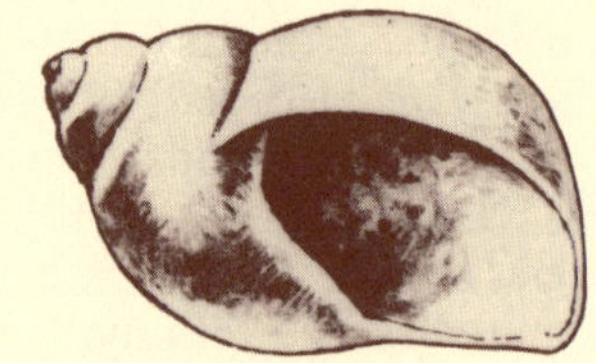

Planorbis vortex, Pisidium milium and *Pisidium subtruncatum.* The following species prefer weed-rich water: *Armiger crista, Segmentina complanata* and *Acroloxus lacustis.* Marsh or wet grassland habitats are represented by *Carychium minimum, Vallonia pulchella* and *Trichia hispida.* The specimens of *Vallonia costata* might have been occupying drier grassland or scrub covered soils nearby. *Punctum pygmaeum* suggests the soils were litter covered. The presence of *Discus rotundatus,* the Zonitidae, and the Clausiliidae suggest the nearby presence of woodland scrub, and possibly scree.

Section MB1 is characterised by very low numbers of shells deriving from the whole range of environments mentioned above. Units MB1/2 and MB1 are completely sterile. Given the general widespread and abundant distribution of molluscs at Creswell, and the relatively lime rich characteristics of the enclosing sediments, the absence of molluscan remains in these particular layers is best explained by assuming these deposits have been introduced after quarrying nearby red Permian silts/clays; these naturally lack shells. Units MB1/1 and MB1/6 may also reflect this process. The single shell of the tree snail Clausiliidae is clearly anomalous. Unit MB1/6 possesses a single specimen of *Ceciloides acicula.* This may be the result of the burrowing activity for which this species is well known. The other layers may owe their ecologically mixed faunas to the occasional floods which introduced specimens from all the aquatic and terrestrial habitats swept by the high flood waters.

Mill Bridge 3 sequence Unlike sequence MB1, this series of samples lies below the presumed disturbed and made ground of the red and yellow clays. The majority of species found (*Table 9*), were also found in MB1 and are described above. However, several other species have been found. These are *Segmentina complanata, Acroloxus lacustris* and *Pisidium milium*, all of which favour weed-rich pools and streams: *Pisidium subtruncatum* which might also occur in these habitats or together with *Pisidium amnicum* in faster flow in streams or lakes.

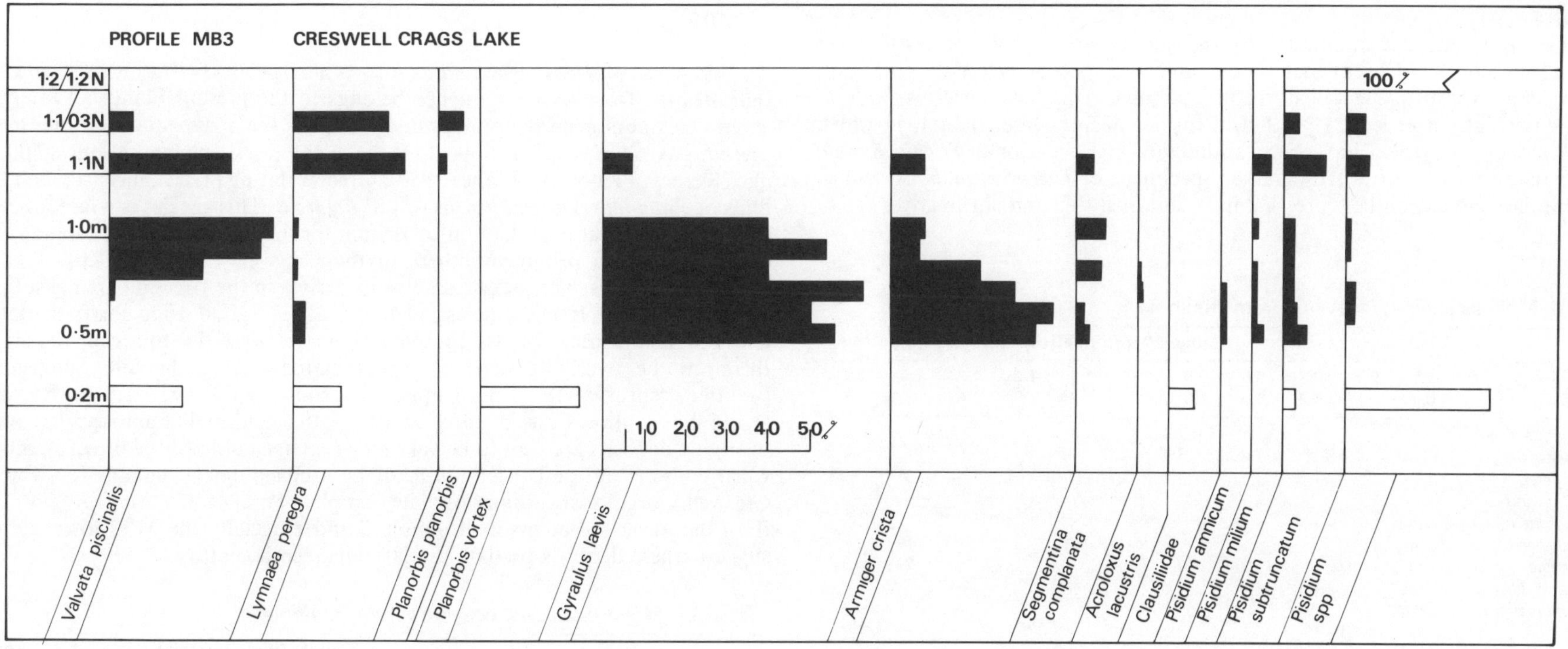

Figure 19. Frequency and stratigraphic distribution of molluscs from the Mill Bridge 3.

The number of specimens found in each sample are given in *Table 9*. These data have been re-calculated as percentage frequencies in *Figure 19* to indicate how the relative abundance of each species changes through the sedimentary sequence.

Several interesting points emerge: First, the richness of the upper layers, which culminates in peak numbers at 0.8m; and second, the general dominance of species favouring marsh, shallow-water, weed-rich, pool or stream environments. The nearby swamp environment apparently lacked a tree or shrub cover. There is no indication of drier land adjacent to the site. The changes in relative abundance of the principal deeper, quiet water species—*Valvata piscinalis*—point to either the increasing importance through time of either (a) deeper pools in the swamp and/or (b) closer proximity to the main lake, perhaps prone to more frequent flooding and hence introduction of 'lake' species as dead shells. The abundance of *Gyraulus laevis* is especially interesting. This species appears to dislike polluted waters, nowadays being most common in large open water bodies such as the lakes in the western Lake District.

Table 9. Molluscan species recovered from the Mill Bridge 3 sequence.

	Top			Sample Depth (Metres) MB3							Bottom	
SPECIES	**0.2**	**0.3**	**0.4**	**0.5**	**0.6**	**0.7**	**0.8**	**0.9**	**1.0**	**1.1**	**1.1**	**1.2**
Valvata piscinalis	3					4	181	95	131	17	43	
Lymnaea peregra	2			1	7	1	6		4	15	16	
Planorbis planorbis										1	5	
Planorbis vortex	4											
Gyraulus laevis				29	105	227	271	141	129	4		
Armiger crista				18	81	107	152	18	27	5		
Segmentina complanata				1	5	1	43		24	2		
Acroloxus lacustris						4	4					
Clausiliidae sp.	1											
Pisidium amnicum				1		1						
Pisidium milium					1	2	2		3	2		
Pisidium subtruncatum	2			2	6	8	20	6	5	6	2	2
Pisidium sp.	5				4	7	6		2	3	3	
TOTAL	**17**	**0**	**0**	**52**	**209**	**362**	**685**	**260**	**325**	**55**	**69**	**2**

Borehole 1

This lakeside borehole is dominated by the aquatic and marsh species listed in *Table 10* found in the MB sequence. The numbers of specimens found in the cores are too small to justify detailed reconstructions. The 'lake' species *Valvata piscinalis* is common at level 1.3–1.8m, a former deeper water habitat in which *Lymnea peregra* may also have been abundant. The occasional *Trichia hispida* suggests damp pasture or nearby marsh. Specimens of *Discus rotundatus*, and of the Zonitidae, indicate either scree habitats and/or a tree and shrub cover.

Table 10. Mollusc species recovered from Borehole 1.

	Top				Sample Depth (metres)						Bottom
SPECIES	0.1 0.6	0.7	0.7 0.8	0.8 0.9	0.9 1.0	1.0 1.1	1.1 1.2	1.3	1.3 1.8	1.9	2.0
Potamopyrgus jenkinsi			1	2				1	3		
Valvata piscinalis									12		
Lymnaea peregra			1	1	2	1			11	13	
Planorbis planorbis								1	2		
Planorbis vortex								1	1		
Gyraulus laevis						1					
Armiger crista										2	
Ancylus fluviatilis			1								
Discus rotundatus				1							
Zonitidae sp.			1					2			
Vallonia(?) excentrica	1										
Trichia hispida			1	1							
Pisidium casertanum			1	1							
Pisidium milium			1								
Pisidium subtruncatum			2	3	1	2			4		
Pisidium sp.				5	2	2		1			
TOTAL	1	0	9	14	5	6	0	6	33	15	0

Borehole 2

The specimens found are listed in *Table 11*. The palaeoenvironments indicated are the same as those described in Borehole 1. Interesting new finds are the specimens of *Carychium minimum* and *Cochlicopa lubrica*. These also suggest the presence of marsh/damp pastures. A single specimen of *Pupilla muscorum* was noted. This latter species usually favours drier, exposed habitats. It may have been transported into the lake by erosional processes, or on a bird's feet. There are rare instances where this species has been observed to be part of a marsh community.

Dating

The presence of *Discus rotundatus* and other species favouring tree and shade indicates the fossiliferous sequence belongs to the present Flandrian interglacial stage. This commenced approximately 10,000 years ago and continues to the present day. *D. rotundatus* appears to have colonised England about 8,500 years ago (Kerney, Preece and Turner 1980). Greater dating precision is provided by the finds of *Potamopyrgus jenkinsi* shown in *Figure 8*. This species is a late nineteenth century, accidental introduction to Britain, probably from New Zealand. Nowadays it occurs in prolific numbers in the Creswell Crags lake and associated streams and pools. The precise date of its arrival in the Creswell area is subject to current research. It nevertheless provides a very good zone fossil to date the Creswell lake sequences. Its presence indicates that the following layers, and therefore the overlying deposits, accumulated during the late nineteenth or twentieth century: MB3/Unit 3 upper; Borehole 1 (1.3–1.8m depth); Borehole 2 (1.1–1.2m depth). Consequently much of the coal rich humose silts and the overlying deposits are seen to be very recent in age, and of little direct significance when considering the conservation of the archaeological remains for which the Creswell Gorge is world famous. The complete absence of *Potamopyrgus jenkinsi* from the lower sediments in Borehole 2 and especially the MB3 lower deposits, suggests these deposits predate the late nineteenth century.

Table 11. Mollusc species recovered from Borehole 2.

	Top						Sample Depth (metres)								Bottom
SPECIES	0.1 0.2	0.2 0.3	0.3 0.4	0.6 0.7	0.7 0.8	0.8 0.9	0.9 1.0	1.1 1.2	1.3 1.4	1.4 1.5	1.5 1.6	1.7 1.8	1.8 1.9	2.0	2.1
Potamopyrgus jenkinsi	7		10	4			5								
Valvata piscinalis		1	2												
Lymnaea peregra		2			1	1		3		1		4		2	2
Planorbis vortex		1													
Armiger crista								1							
Ancylus fluviatilis								3						4	4
Carychium minimum	1														
Cochlicopa lubrica	1														
Discus rotundatus			1				1	1							
Zonitidae sp.							1	1							
Vallonia pulchella						1									
Vallonia sp.								1							
Pupilla muscorum								1							
Trichia hispida			1												
Pisidium casertanum			2	1											
Pisidium milium			2	1				1		1	1				
Pisidium subtruncatum	1	2	2	6			1	14	1	5	4	5		2	4
Pisidium sp.				1			1	6	8	13	7	2			4
TOTAL	10	6	20	13	1	2	9	32	9	20	12	11	0	8	14

PALAEOECOLOGY OF THE LAKE, CRAGS AND SURROUNDING DISTRICT: THE BOTANICAL EVIDENCE

Pollen and Spores

Palynology is the study of pollen and spores. Typical examples of pollen and spores are shown in *Figures 21a and b*. These microscopic grains are liberated from plants as part of their reproductive process.

Some species emit enormous quantities of pollen into the air. In other species, the pollen is transported by insects or birds. In many aquatics, the pollen or spores are moved by water currents. There are very large differences in the quantities of pollen or spores produced by species. Spores of the Scots Pine (*Pinus sylvestris*) are liberated in millions. They are also equipped with bladders which enable some to travel thousands of miles in the atmosphere. Others, such as the pollen of the Lime tree (*Tilia*) are relatively heavy and are often transported by insects. Consequently these grains are less likely to travel far from their parent tree. Wet marsh surfaces, like that of Creswell, are therefore in constant receipt of grains by air, water and very occasionally by insects. If the surface is peaty, poorly oxygenated and buried relatively rapidly, the grains have a good chance of being preserved. Laboratory treatments enable these grains to be extracted from the sediments. They are then identified and counted using high powered microscopes. The species and numbers of grains at each level enable a general picture to be reconstructed of the former vegetation on the accumulating surface and in the surrounding countryside. Fortunately, interpretation is aided by the excellent botanical survey of the Creswell Crags area by Daphne Row (1978–82).

The Pollen Diagrams

The pollen from flowering plants and spores from the non-flowering plants at each sample level are recorded and studied using a pollen diagram such as *Figures 20 and 21*. These diagrams illustrate the relative abundance of each species' pollen or spores at each level, respectively, in one sequence. Examination of the diagrams shows that whilst the pollen or spores of our major tree genera can be reliably identified and attributed to the appropriate genus (e.g. *Quercus*—the oaks), we cannot as yet identify which species of our two common oaks is represented (i.e. *Q. robur* or *Q. petraea*). In the case of the Cyperaceae and the Graminae, it is not yet possible to attribute the pollen found beyond the family level—i.e. to the sedges or grasses. One exception is the probable identification of pollen from the Cereals, previously growing in nearby arable fields. Otherwise, members of the grass family may be found in fields, hedges, woods, cliffs, pasture, marshes, as well as underwater.

Pollen Diagram from the Lake Sediments Adjacent to the Victorian Dam

A section was excavated on the southern side of the gorge, 50m to the west of the dam (SK 536733) (*Figure 13*). The sequence of deposits is:
1.65m and below—Coarse sands and gravels with angular and sub angular limestone pebbles (5YR 4/2) (layer G).
1.65–1.45m—Silty sand with many small limestone pebbles (5YR 4/4), gradually fining upwards to clayey silt with some find sand (7.5YR 3/4) (layer F).
1.45–1.2m—Black humose silt (7.5YR 3.2), closely matted with organic matter, with coal fragments and fine laminations of sand (layer D). An abrupt transition to:
1.2–1.1m—Coarse silty sand (5YR 4/4) with woody material. Coal fragments are present throughout (layer B). A gradual transition to:
1.1–0.0m—Black organic silty clays (5YR 2.5/1) with many coal fragments, showing a gradual transition at 0.3m to dark reddish brown silty clays (5YR 2.5/2) (layer A). Thin silty sand lenses occur throughout the sequence.

Pollen samples were taken at intervals of *c.* 0.2m. From each sample a 2ml sub-sample was processed with methods given by Hunt (1984). Each slide was counted to 200 grains. The results of the pollen analysis are presented in *Figure 20*. This shows the pollen concentrations per species per ml of sediment.

Within the diagram the species recognised have been grouped according to preferred habitat. This enables comparison with the ecological zones noted at Creswell Crags by Row (1980). Row notes seven zones; north and south facing cliffs, north and south facing screes, the marsh and lake covered gorge floor, the stream and the surrounding woodlands. Comparison with Row's species lists shows that the preponderence of plant species recorded in the pollen analysis are present today within the gorge. Plants from all the zones noted by Row are present in the diagram.

Two distinct assemblages are present in the sediments: The lower assemblage (between 1.65 and 1.6m) is characterised by relatively low proportions of trees, shrubs and grasses. Herb species account for over half of the total land pollen. *Pinus* and *Quercus* dominate the arboreal pollen, but *Fagus* is also present. Shrubs include rare *Salix*, Coryloid and Ericaceae. The herbs (excluding Gramineae) are dominated by Cyperaceae and Compositae. Rare *Sinapis* (type) and *Cirsium* (type) suggest open ground and low counts of *Bidens* (type) and *Typha augustifolia* indicate marshy ground. Aquatic species are absent from the assemblage. Spores of *Pteridium* and Filicales (undifferentiated) are abundant, *Lycopodium* and *Polypodium* spores are rare.

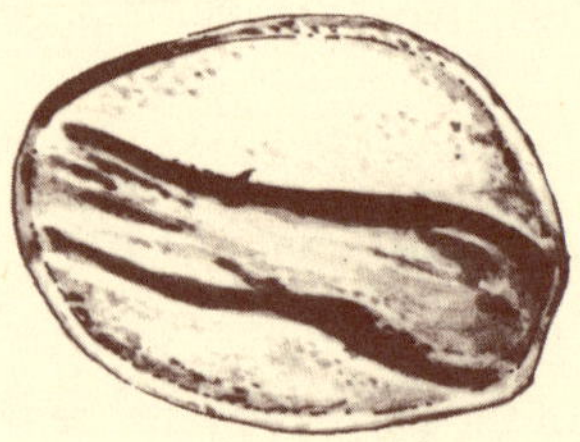

Oak

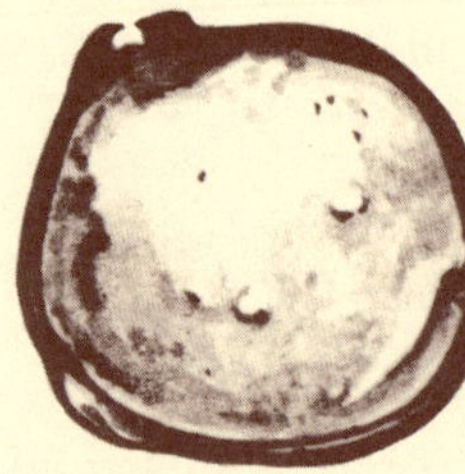

Birch

The assemblages above 1.4m show sufficient similarity to be considered together. The arboreal pollen is dominated by *Pinus*, except at 0.6–0.65m. *Ulmus* and *Quercus* are also important and dominate the AP at 0.6–0.65m. *Fagus* is a constant but minor component, while *Tilia* and *Betula* also occur rarely and sporadically. *Carpinus* is only present between 1.45 and 1.0m.

All the shrubs presently found at Creswell occur sporadically in the diagram; most surprising are the very low and sporadic counts of *Corylus*. Ericaceae pollen occurs regularly but in small amounts and probably represents distant vegetation since no Ericaceae presently grows at Creswell Crags.

Woodland and woodland margin herbs are poorly represented by a single grain of Ciraea at 0.6–0.65m. Open ground herbs are more numerous. They include Compositae (Liguliflora), *Rumex acetosa* and *Cirsium* (type). The Chenopodiceae and Caryophyllaceae make sporadic appearances, while *Anthemis* and *Carduus* are recorded only by single grains. Gramineae are common, rises in Gramineae correspond closely with declining arboreal pollen, in particular with falls in *Pinus*. Very low counts of cereal pollen are occasionally noted.

Many herb pollen types cannot be assigned to species. Because of wide differences in habitat preference within a single family these are grouped as herbs with varied habitat preference. These are represented by *Ranunculus*, *Serratula* (type) *Lamium* (type) and a single grain of *Allium*. Row (1980) records the growth of *Allium oleraceum* (Field Garlic) as a minor component of the gorge flora.

Damp/Marshland species are a noteable component of the pollen spectra. All the species recorded as pollen are present in the modern gorge flora (Row 1980). Cyperaceae dominate the marshland pollen, while *Bidens* (type) and *Typha augustifolia* occur intermittently throughout the assemblages. *Filipendula*, *Caltha* and *Ephilobium* are represented by single grains.

Pollen of aquatic species is relatively rare, only two species being identified; *Callitriche* is present between 1.4–1.45m and 1.2–1.25m, reappearing in the top sample; *Potamogeton* is more abundant but has a similar distribution.

Pteridium is the dominant Cryptogam, while Filicales (undifferentiated) and *Sphagnum* are also present in quantity throughout. Rare *Lycopodium* and *Polypodium* are intermittently recorded. A single grain of *Equisetum* is noted at 1.0–1.05m.

Concentration totals have been presented for 'recycled grains'; these compose a group of pre-Quaternary spores largely of Carboniferous age (Hunt, pers. comm.). They are present throughout and show a gradual rise to very high levels at 0.4–0.45m, followed by a very marked decline.

Dating Evidence

1.65–1.45m—Dating is uncertain, but must predate lake formation.
1.45–1.2m—Immediately predates lake formation; for the start of deposition the increasing presence of *Pinus* suggests a later period (post 1700). Davis and Turner (1979) noted increasing *Pinus* as a characteristic of the recent historical period in several pollen diagrams.
1.2–1.1m—Lake formation is indicated by a rapid change in sedimentation. This would mark the construction of the dam in 1865. 1.0m—Arrival of the freshwater mollusc *Potamopyrgus jenkinsi c.* 1890–1900.
0.0m—Draining of lake, sedimentation ceases: 1982.

The lower assemblage shows preferential preservation of structurally strong, pollen grains, in particular the Compositae and *Pinus*. A high proportion of badly damaged, unrecognisable, grains are present. It is suggested that this assemblage represents stream bed deposition with attendant sorting and weathering of the pollen load; as a result conclusions cannot be drawn as to the flora of the gorge.

The upper pollen assemblage indicates lateral changes in the course of the stream probably gave rise to the gradual upward fining of the sediments, giving way to black humose silts. These contain matted organic matter suggesting grass roots. The presence of pollen from both marshland and aquatic species suggests marsh with small pools of standing water. Periodic flooding of the marshy stream banks is indicated by sand bands.

The overall ecology of the woodlands, gorge cliffs and screes appears to have been substantially similar to that of today, though *Pinus* would seem to have been a less important component of the woodlands than it is nowadays.

The band of sands and gravels above the black humose silts probably represents further stream bed deposition, however, the pollen assemblage is not significantly abraded.

After 1.5m the sediments rapidly become finer grading, upwards into the black silty clays. These suggest a quiet water, low energy, depositional environment (occasional thin sandy bands recording storm water deposition). The transition almost certainly marks the impounding of the lake in 1865.

Most changes in arboreal pollen are probably related to localised changes in a single tree species, nevertheless there is documentary and photographic evidence of the clearance of the woodlands surrounding Creswell Crags in the 1914–18 period. The large reduction in *Pinus* and the reduction in *Ulmus* and *Quercus* at 0.6–0.65m may be related to this clearance. The decrease in *Ulmus* and *Quercus* is

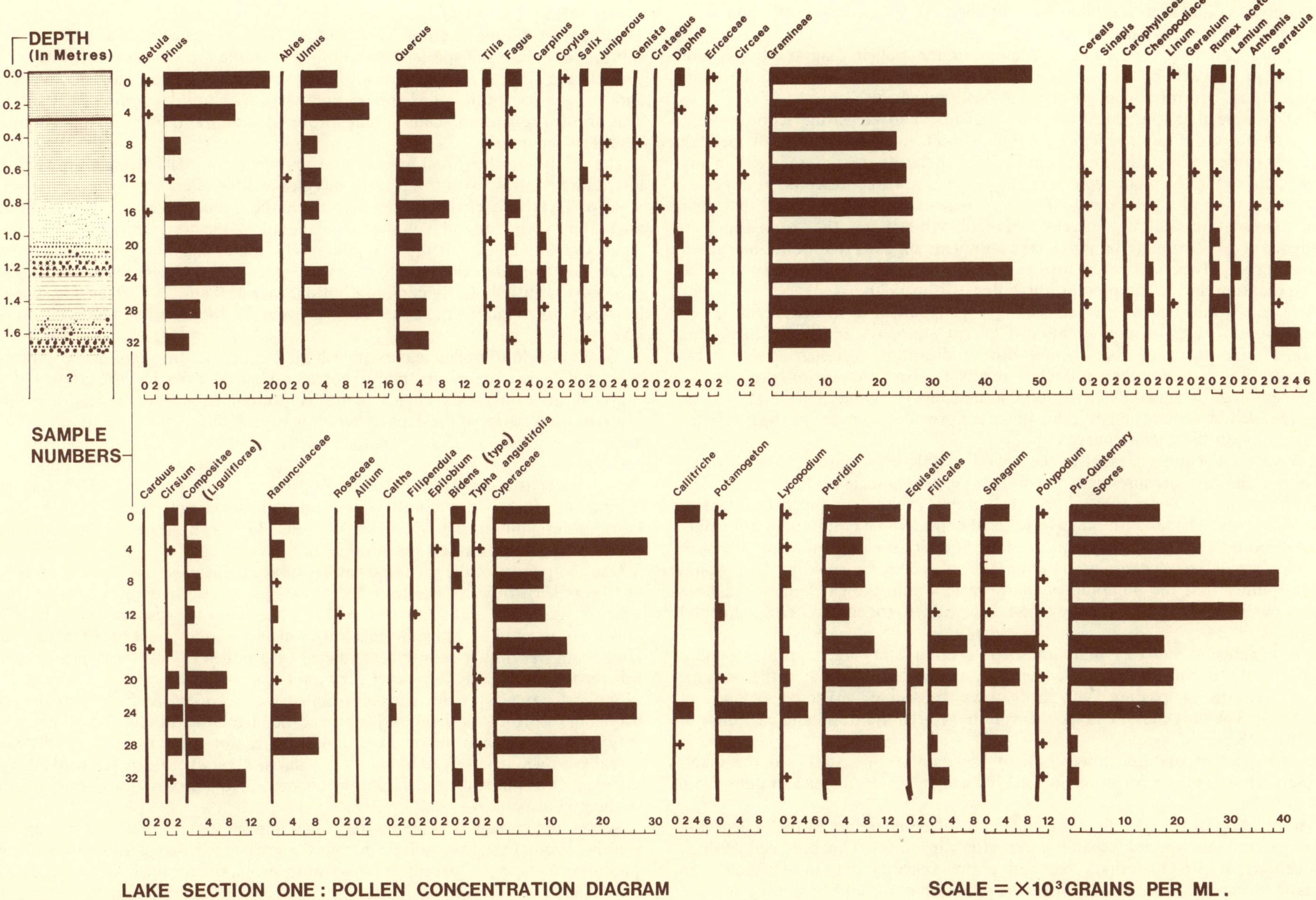

Figure 20. Pollen diagram from recent lake sediments taken from near the Victorian dam.

not as great as that seen for *Pinus*, possibly because isolated and hedgerow oaks and elms were generally not subject to clearance.

Carpinus betulus (Hornbeam) is present in the pollen diagram but is not recorded at Creswell by Row (1980), though it is noted by Howitt and Howitt (1962:174) as "not infrequent throughout Nottinghamshire".

It is notable that the transition from marshland to lacustrine sedimentation produced no recognisable shift in the pollen spectrum. The creation of the lake evidently caused only a slight relocation of plant habitats and did not result in any marked change in the plant ecology of the gorge as a whole. It would be expected that the creation of a permanent lake would benefit aquatic plants and that their total representation should increase markedly; this is not the case. The high incidence of recycled material in the lake sediments suggests that pollution caused by mining activity is responsible for the paucity of aquatic flora noted both in the pollen diagram and in the present gorge flora (Row 1980).

Recycled grains show marked changes in abundance which seem to be independent of rates of sedimentation. Concentrations rise markedly during the period of lake silt deposition when all other indications suggest relatively stable sedimentation rates (and by inference relatively constant erosion rates in the catchment area of the lake). It is probable that this pre-Quaternary material has been recycled by mining activity, this therefore provides an index of the impact of coal mining on the Creswell area.

The very low counts present in the lowest sample may represent the 'natural' erosion of the coal measures near Creswell or very small scale coal extraction. The high point in the deposition of recycled grains probably represents intensive mining activity. The lake would have suffered considerable pollution and possibly proved too hostile an environment for many aquatic species. Following this peak the number of recycled grains entering the lake declines rapidly. This would suggest either that the dumping of mine waste within the catchment had been vastly curtailed or that measures had been taken to control environmental pollution.

The conclusion suggests that landscape around the gorge appears to have changed little during the period covered by the pollen diagram; with the same overall pattern of pasture with hedgerows and small scattered patches of woodland. The only major change seems to have been the woodland clearance of the 1914–18 period.

It is suggested that the lower half of the dam section (prior to the lake's formation), dates from sometime in the 1700's to 1865. The upper half dates from 1865 to 1982.

The creation of the lake did not significantly alter the nature of the pollen rain, however, aquatic species became rarer after this time. The presence of high frequencies of pre-Quaternary recycled grains suggests that this reduction in aquatic species probably resulted from the pollution of the lake by mining activity.

Profile MB3—Unit MB3

These pollen diagrams from Mill Bridge (*Figures 21a and 21b*) also record a substantial number of species known to occur in the area at the present day. The study found six tree species, five shrub species, 21 herbaceous species, four ferns and six aquatics; a total of 42 species, compared with today's figure of 151 species. This profile predates the Dam profile; probably also pre-dating the Tudor timbers described previously.

The study of the fossil pollen and spores from Mill Bridge provides an interesting contrast with the present day flora of the site.

All of the arboreal (tree) species detected in the former pollen rain at Mill Bridge are present at the site today in the woodland above the gorge. Birch (*Betula*) has a distinctive trend through the pollen diagram, increasing as a component of the pollen rain from the core base to core top. Alder (*Alnus*) has a similar trend. Oak (*Quercus*) is initially fairly common but declines at 0.4m. Pine (*Pinus*) is sparsely distributed throughout the core, today it occurs in the woodland adjacent to the lake.

Hazel (Coryloid) pollen is present in large frequencies throughout the diagram, occurring more frequently than arboreal pollen. Willow (*Salix*), as would be expected in a lake-side environment, is present in approximately the same proportions to hazel in the deposit, and it was probably a stable component of the lake-side vegetation. Crack Willow (*Salix fragilis*) is currently on the site occupying the gorge floor and stream habitats. Hawthorn (*Crataegus*) and Gorse (*Ulex*) are sparsely distributed in the top 0.5m of the core, probably suffering competition from Hazel (both Hawthorn and Gorse are presently at the site). Gorse occurs only in the woodland, whereas Hawthorn occurs in the woodland, on the gorge floor, and on the south cliff.

One component of the shrub pollen, Hornbeam (*Carpinus*), is not present today at Creswell. Hornbeam was recorded at two places in the core, 0.2m and 0.4m, where it was 1.3% and 0.6% of the total pollen rain for respective depths. This pollen was most likely blown in as a longer distance component of the pollen rain. Hornbeam was only a minute percentage of the pollen rain at the depths where it was recorded and probably never grew on the site.

Similarly, Heath species (Ericoid) pollen was recorded at five intervals from 0.8–0.3m (being lost at 0.4m); it is not recorded from the present flora. This taxon may have been blown in from surrounding areas or it might just possibly have actually grown at Creswell in the peaty-marsh area where the MB1–MB3 were sampled. It did not form a significant element of the ecology of Creswell in the studied time span.

Sedges and Grasses dominated the pollen rain throughout the core, presumably growing around the lake margin forming a grass, reed, sedge and willow fringe. The arboreal species (except Willow) were probably confined to the cliffs and woodland.

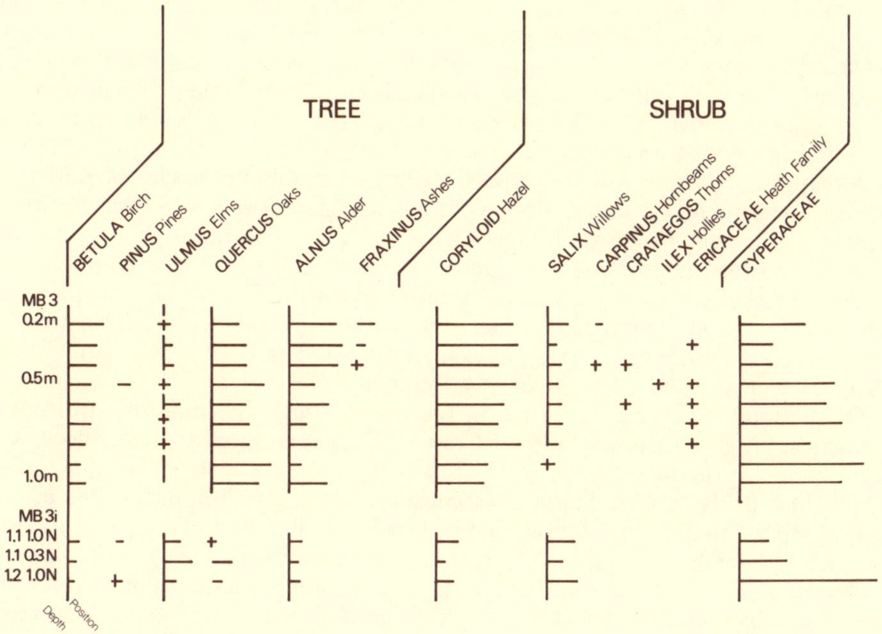

Figure 21a. Pollen diagram showing the frequency of tree, shrub and herb pollen recovered from Mill Bridge 3.

Oak

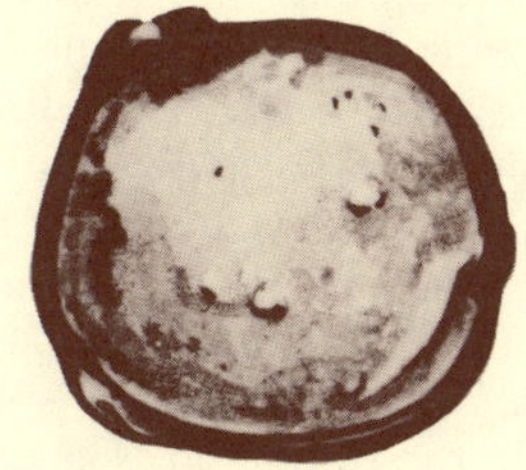

Birch

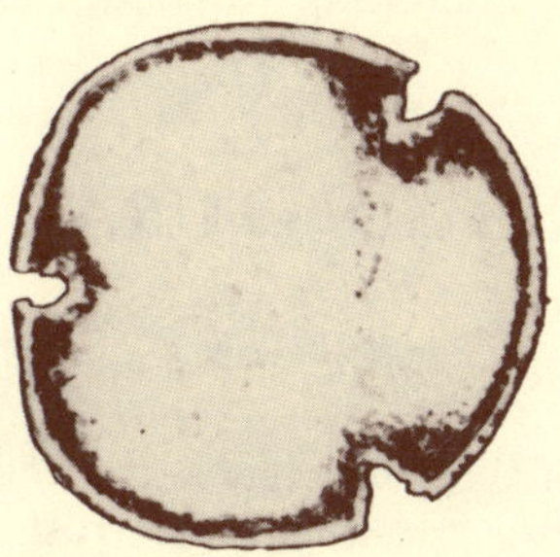

Lime

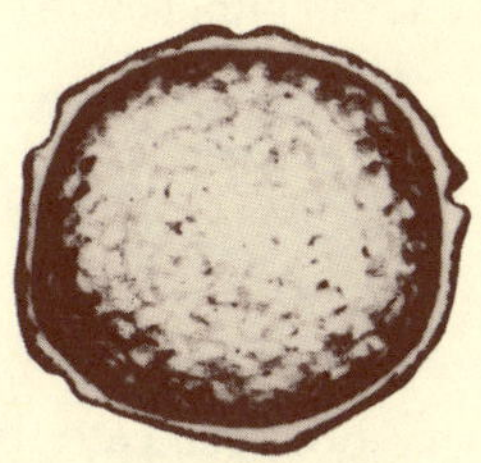

Elm

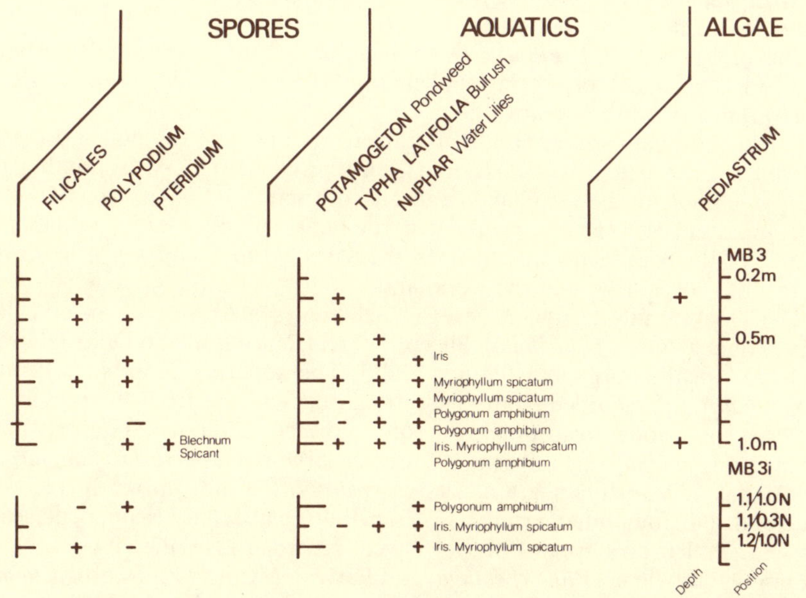

Figure 21b. Pollen diagram showing the frequency of spores, aquatics and algae recovered from Mill Bridge 3.

Cereal pollen is represented at all levels sampled, this pollen would have been blown in from surrounding arable farmland.

There are a number of flowering plant families represented by the pollen rain. The Beet family (Chenopodiaceae) are sparsely, though continuously, represented from the core base to top. Today members of this family are absent on the gorge floor. The Pink family (Caryophyllaceae) is also sporadically represented, with its main appearance between 0.4–0.2m. Nowadays members of this family include Red campion (*Silene diocia*) and White campion (*Silene alba*), both in the gorge and woodland, with a hybrid Campion (*S. diocia* x *alba*) occurring only in the gorge. Common mouse-ear (*Cerastium fontanum*) occurs on both scree slopes, in the gorge and woodland. Common chickweed (*Stellari media*), Greater stitchwort (*Stellari holostea*), and Lesser stitchwort (*Stellari minea*) all occur on the gorge floor and in the woodland. The carrot family (Umbellifereae) are recorded in low quantities. Members of the Umbelliferae at Creswell today are: Rough chervil (*Chaerophyllum temulentum*) on the Gorge floor; Cow parsley (*Anthriscus sylvestris*) and Upright hedge parsley (*Torilis japonica*) are also in this habitat; Hogweed (*Heracleum sphondylium*) on both scree slopes and on the gorge floor. Members of the Mallow family (*Malvaceae*) also occur at intervals on the pollen diagram; Common mallow (*Malva sylvestris*) is presently located on the gorge floor and the north scree.

Pollen of the Dandelion family (*Taraxacum* sp.) occurs in significant proportions throughout the core. At present, Dandelion (*T. officinale*) grows on both screes, gorge floor and woodland.

The moisture loving *Filipendula*, a member of the Rose family, is another frequent component of the last pollen rain. Today, Meadowsweet (*Filipendula ulmaria*) grows on the stream side.

Thistles (*Cirsium* sp.) are another stable component of the pollen diagram; at present Spear thistle (*C. vulgaris*) and Creeping thistle (*C. arvense*) both grow on the gorge floor, in the woodlands and on both screes.

Common nettle (*Urtica diocia*) is recorded in small, but steady, amounts in the middle of the core, being absent from the base and top. Today it grows on both screes, the gorge floor and the woodland.

The Dock family (Polygonaceae) is well represented by four species. Broad-leaved dock (*Rumex obtusifolia*), Sheep's sorrel (*R. acetòsa*) and Dock (*Polygonum* sp.) grow in the gorge and the north cliff. The aquatic Amphibious bistort (*P. amphibium*) was recorded from the section, but is absent from the present flora.

Other occasional recordings are of bindweed (*Calystegia*) (absent today); Primrose (*Primula*) (also absent); Lesser spearwort (*Ranunculus flamma*) and a single flax (*Linum* type) grain. Lesser spearwort is not currently recorded at Creswell, but four other members of the Buttercup family (Ranunculaceae) are present. Pollen of a species of violet were recorded at MB3i/(1.1–0.3m); today Common dog-violet (*Viola riviniana*) and Early dog-violet (*V. reichenbachiana*) are present; the former on the gorge floor and the woodland, the latter in the woodlands only.

Four types of the Pteridiophyta were found. Members of the Filicales were the dominant, and these genera occurred throughout the pollen diagram, peaking at 0.6m. Bracken (*Pteridium*) was absent from 0.3m and 0.2m only. It is presently recorded from the north cliff. *Polypodium* (Polypody) is sporadically recorded and today can be found only on the south scree. There was an isolated occurrence of Hard fern (*Blechnum spicant*) from 1.0m. It occurred nowhere else in the sampled area and is absent from the site today.

Aquatics were reasonably well represented by six species in the sample, only two of which can be found today. Pondwood (*Potamogeton*) was a frequent component of the former pollen rain, especially at 0.7m and below. At present Broad-leaved pondweed (*P. natans*) grows in the streams. Bulrush (*Typha latifolia*) was also recorded at several depths, but in small frequencies. Today it too inhabits the stream. Present on the pollen diagram, but absent from the modern flora, are *Iris* and Spiked water-milfoil (*Myriophyllum spicatum*). The only alga recorded was *Pediastrum* at 0.3 and 1.0m; it was not frequent.

Of the total 42 species recorded in the pollen study, the majority are today present in the seven habitat types at Creswell Crags and most probably occupied these niches in the recent past.

The Mill Bridge pollen diagram indicates that the vegetation in the area in the period represented by the section studied was not unlike that of today. Wetlands comprising marsh pools and possibly a lake were probably fringed with willows and alders. Scree, cliff sides and the gorge sides supported a deciduous woodland dominated by Oak, Birch and occasional Elms, and in the later stages Ash trees. Species favouring more open or cleared ground—Birch, Ash—become increasingly important with time at the expense of Oak. This may suggest some selective felling for timber. Alder and Willow also increase slightly in importance. There are several possible explanations for this, but colonisation of marsh seems the most likely. Arable fields with their associated crop of weed species appear to have existed in the area throughout the period, represented by the section. Unfortunately in the absence of radiocarbon dates this interesting sequence can only be referred to the Tudor or pre-Tudor period.

CRESWELL CRAGS: TOWARDS A NATURAL HISTORY

These initial observations indicate the floor of the gorge has had an interesting ecological history. The oldest deposits currently known are the frost shattered screes and breccias probably dating from an extremely cold, sub-arctic phase 10–26,000 years ago. Subsequently, lake-waves and streams reworked these deposits, open water probably being present during the period 10–15,000 years before present.

The next phase currently identified was marked by the deposition of peats and peaty silts in a marsh and pool at the western entrance to the gorge at Mill Bridge. A lake may have been present further east in the gorge. The presence of angular coal debris in the upper parts of these deposits may indicate natural erosion or that they collected fairly recently, during the period in which coal has been mined upstream. The oldest date for coal mining known so far is the 3rd century AD. Consequently the deposits may date at any time—from this period up to the early Tudor period.

During this episode, the character of the vegetation of the area was generally the same as today. Cereals were being grown on the arable land. Alder and Willow scrub was probably encroaching on the swamp. However, in the Oak dominated woodland, Oaks might have been felled and the cleared area re-colonised by Birch and Ash. A mill and small hamlet were constructed in a lakeside clearing at approximately 1175 AD.

During and possibly after this phase, the lake has been in existence. Its molluscan fauna was dominated by lake and marsh species. The former became increasingly important through time. Coal debris, possibly acid run-off, and poor aeration all led to the lake sediments incorporating much partially decayed organic sediments, now identifiable by their black, sulphurous character. The water snail *Gyraulus laevis*, possibly sensitive to this pollution, declined in numbers.

The duck-shooting lake was created during 1865, thus deepening and extending the area of standing water. The general depth and water quality conditions prevailed until well after the late nineteenth century, when the water snail *Potamopyrgus jenkinsi* invaded the region to become the most abundant water snail of today. The land at Mill Bridge continued to be reinforced by the introduction of clay-rich soils, burying the old mill. In more recent times, the amount of introduced coal debris entering the lake declined and the water quality appears to have improved as grey-brown silts were deposited over the black, sulphurous silts previously forming the floor of the lake and marsh.

The next major stage in the ecological history of the lake was the mandatory recent removal of much of the grey-brown marsh silts and former black, sulphurous lake silts. Armed with the evidence of these studies, this work caused no damage to the important plants, animals and prehistoric archaeological remains of Creswell Crags. Archaeological and palaeoecological resources were preserved for future generations to study.

Blackham, A., Briggs, D.J., Cartledge, K.M., Coles, G.M., Gilbertson, D.D., Griffin, C.M., Hillam, J.A., Hunt, C.O., Jenkinson, R.D.S., Norris, M., Pyatt, R.B., Row, D. and Row, R. 1984. Creswell Crags: Towards a Natural History. Chapter 2 in Jenkinson, R.D.S. and Gilbertson, D.D. *In the Shadow of Extinction: a Quaternary Archaeology and Palaeoecology of the Lake, Fissures and Smaller Caves at Creswell Crags S.S.S.I.* Sheffield: Department of Prehistory and Archaeology, University of Sheffield. Pp. 13 to 53.

CHAPTER 3: DEATH, DISARTICULATION AND DECAY IN AN EIGHT THOUSAND YEAR OLD ROCK FALL

with D.J. Briggs, C.M. Griffin, R.E. Stebbings and C.M. Watts

CONTENTS

This report discusses an investigation of the geomorphology, sedimentology, vertebrate and molluscan remains of a small fissure—the Dog Hole Fissure. A complex history has been found.

After initial opening of the fissure by rockfall and partial infilling with coarse clastic debris, the already partially disarticulated remains of a wolf and pig fell into the fissure, whereupon their corpses were colonised by carnivorous molluscs. Further rock movement occurred fracturing the wolf skull and inducing loss of teeth and their infiltration through the lower coarse breccias. Subsequently the fissure developed its own fauna comprised of bats, frogs, a substantial and diverse troglophile molluscan fauna, and eventually became the site of predation and denning by a red fox. Transport and introduction to the site of aquatic molluscs, probably by birds, has been shown to be common in the area today and to have occurred at several points in the development of the fissure. In its latter stage the fissure became waterlogged and the deposition of travertine commenced.

Biostratigraphic evidence indicates the fauna and travertine are of Flandrian age. A radiocarbon date of 9960 ± 140 BP (HAR 4309) is thought to be at least 1000 years too old as a result of the 'hard water' effect caused during the period of water-logging.

Flandrian occurrences of beaver (*Castor fiber*) and wolf (*Canis lupus*) are noted. These species are now extinct in the British Isles. The present study has also shown that this type of location midway between true caves and open ground traps, may offer a new perspective on palaeoenvironment, palaeoecology and emphasise the complexity of geomorphic and taphonomic processes that can influence the character and composition of the fossil assemblage.

The site has an important role in establishing the palaeoecology and archaeology of Creswell Crags. First it represents largely unknown and obviously interesting Flandrian environments and processes. Second it suggests that previous dating and correlations made between caves on the basis of travertine layers need to be treated with caution.

INTRODUCTION

This report deals with recent work at Dog Hole Fissure in the north western area of the Creswell Crags gorge (*see Figure 5*) and emphasises the complex process of reworking, derivation and decay that can determine the character of the fossil assemblage in cave and fissure sites which are otherwise much better known for their archaeological remains.

The importance of the results presented here are:

1) Information from Dog Hole Fissure has an important bearing upon the now totally excavated and poorly understood Dog Hole Cave. The latter can be grouped with other well known caves at Creswell Crags as important sites of Devensian/Flandrian human and animal occupation.

2) Results of work upon the faunal material represents a fully comprehensive publication of bats, birds, fish and Mollusca from the Creswell Caves. Some elements of the larger vertebrate fauna (i.e. beaver) are of regional significance in that they are the first regional evidence for particular species from a well stratified, radiocarbon dated Flandrian site. This species is now extinct in the British Isles.

3) Within the overall spectrum of cave environments, the study of the Dog Hole Fissure site is one of the first examinations of a specific type of environment—the small fissure—which has not previously been examined in detail.

4) The Flandrian deposits of the site include travertine which was previously commonly used as a stratigraphic marker horizon in the Creswell Caves and is indicative of uniform environmental factors characteristic of the Late Devensian. The nature of the Dog Hole Fissure deposits tests the validity of this view and assesses the principle of correlation between cave sites on the basis of specific type deposits.

5) The relative absence of large carnivore activity and human occupation from the site is in marked contrast to the majority of the Creswell Crags Caves and provides important detail of a faunal accumulation associated with middle range carnivores.

Dog Hole Cave and Fissure: Excavation History

Dog Hole Cave (73m O.D.), in the north western outcrop of Creswell Crags Gorge (*Figure 5*), consists of a fairly extensive series of phreatic solution cavities formed along a NE-SW axis in the Magnesian Limestone bedrock. Three separate phreatic cavities form prominent entrances to the modern cave.

The existence of the cave has been known for some years; until recently it was used as a pig sty associated with a dwelling that occupied the talus area immediately in front of the largest cave entrance. The archaeological significance of the cave was realised (Jenkinson 1978) when superficial examination revealed evidence of large scale archaeological excavation in many areas of the cave with localised survival of infilling deposits adhering to the cave walls. Research with the available manuscript accounts shows conclusively that there have been three separate excavations within the main cave, each unaware of previous work. All artefactual material from these excavations has been lost since discovery.

Initial excavations were undertaken by Laing, the work being published in a short account (Laing 1889). Comment in the latter confines itself to comparisons with the evidence from the adjacent Pin Hole Cave and fails to discuss anything specifically from Dog Hole Cave. In fact, although the existence of the report has been known for a number of years, the site of the excavation has not, chiefly due to

Laing's failure to state its location. The precise location of the excavation in relation to Dog Hole Cave, however, is clear from a later excursion account given by a contemporary of Laing's (Burr 1910). Laing's excavation appears to have extended throughout the main passage and its adjoining chambers. Remnants of the upper stratigraphic levels, particularly the travertine formation, adhering to that inside the cave and its phreatic fissures.

During March 1978, another substantial rockfall took place in the exact area of the previous collapse (*Figures 22 and 23*). As a result of the latter rockfall, enormous disturbance of the older rockfall debris took place. In particular a large limestone block associated with the older fall was completely detached from the rockface, a process which exposed an area of infilling deposit previously between the rock debris and the limestone cliff and adjacent to one of the subsidiary solution cavities of Dog Hole Cave (*Figure 23*).

The area of exposed sediment (the Dog Hole Fissure site) weathered rapidly. Total destruction of the newly exposed sediments seemed highly likely, particularly by another seemingly imminent rockfall, but also by rapid weathering of the less resilient areas of sediment. As a result, and despite the danger, a rescue excavation was mounted. The potential importance of the relatively small volume of sediment was beyond question, in that they were the most complete sequence of deposits still remaining in the general area of Dog Hole Cave which had an association with the now completely excavated and entirely unknown internal deposits of the main area of the cave. In such circumstances the site offered a last chance to establish an environmental history of the site.

Dog Hole Fissure: Recent Excavations

Detailed examination and mapping of Dog Hole Cave and its environs during 1977 revealed areas of *in situ* sediments. This was particularly the case in the western entrance area of the cave where a substantial rockfall, contemporary with the cave infill, was lodged against the rock face. Subsequently, infilling of the cavities within and around the rockfall had taken place, the resultant sediments being capped by a travertine formation similar to and probably continuous with the cave wall indicate that the total depth of infilling deposit was in the order of three metres.

Unaware of previous work upon the site, further excavation was undertaken by A.L. Armstrong during the 1940's. No detailed record of the work survives to the present day, in fact the sole evidence for the excavation is a photograph taken during the work (Armstrong 1940), which shows a small trench cut across the main entrance of the cave.

Subsequent work was undertaken by Collcutt (1975), who unaware of the previous excavations, referred to the site as West Pin Hole. The small trench excavated by Collcutt in the western area of the cave, showed the existence of greatly disturbed deposits with little *in situ* material (Collcutt 1975:127).

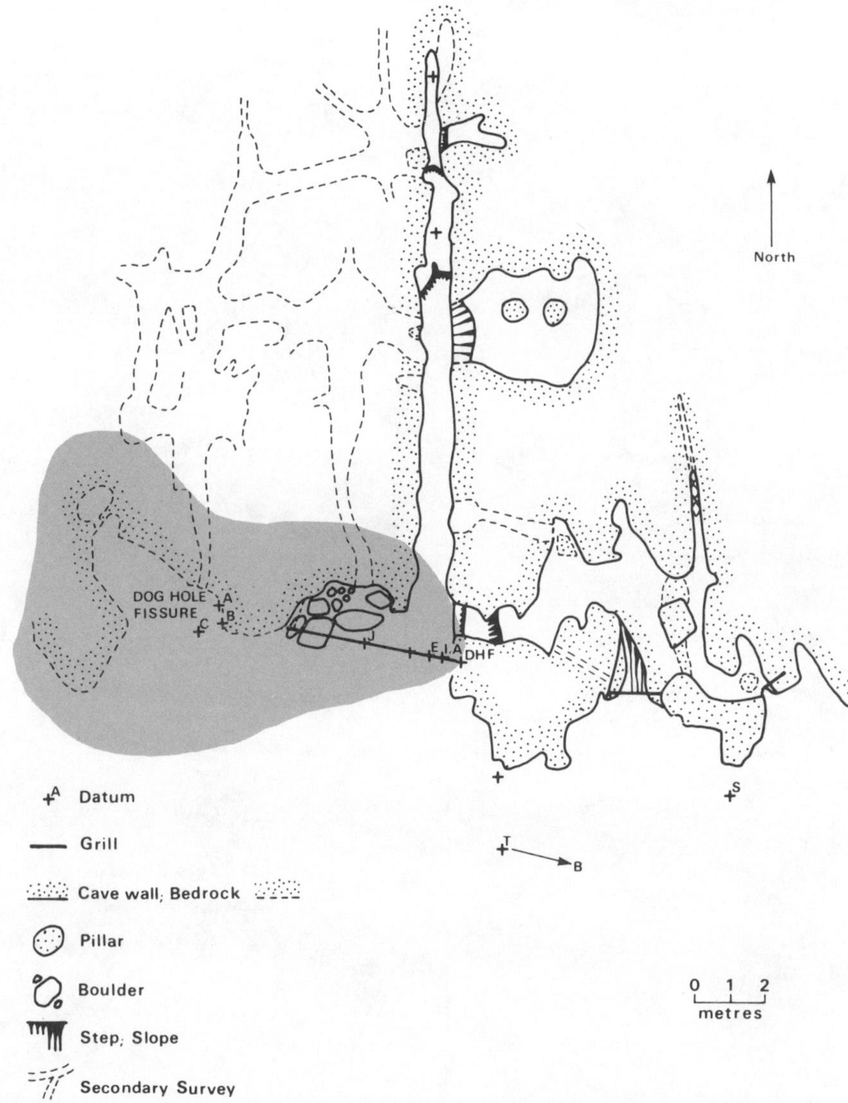

Figure 22. Ground plan of Dog Hole Cave and Fissure, Creswell Crags.

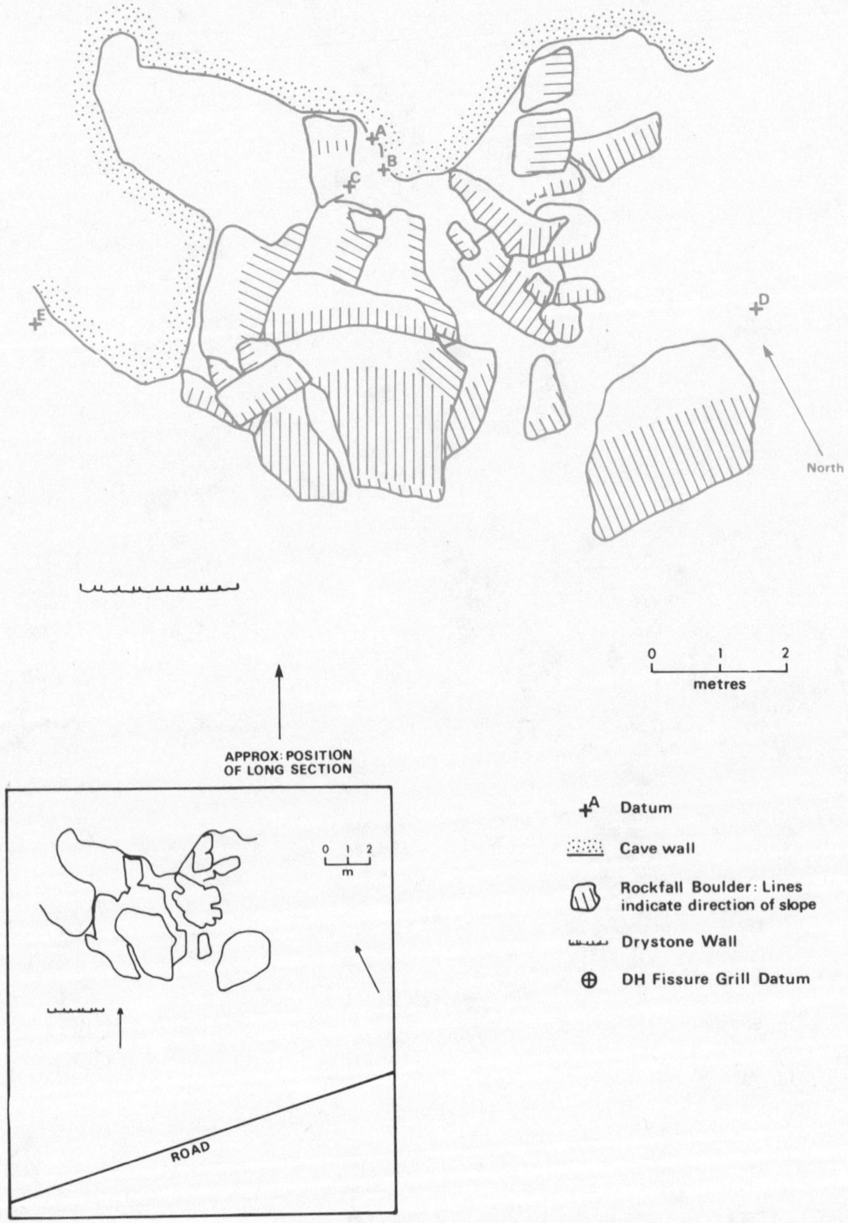

Figure 23. Detailed plan and section of the rock fall at Dog Hole Fissure.

Stratigraphy

The deposits were removed in a series of sixteen spits of variable depth, dependent upon localised concentrations of rock debris shown in *Figures 23 and 24*. The travertine formation, capping the deposits, was removed as one spit. Artefactual and faunal remains were recorded three-dimensionally as found. The total sediment from each excavated spit was sieved (using a minimum sieve size of 2 phi), and hand sorted to recover microfossil remains. During excavation the distribution of rock debris within each spit was recorded, the remaining total sediment from each spit was subjected to sedimentological analysis.

The section is shown in Figure 24 and described below:

Stratigraphic Description			
Layer	Spits	Thickness of Stratum	Description
6	1	0.08m	clay loam—10 YR 7/3
5	2	0.58m	travertine—10 YR 7/3
4	3	0.14m	sandy loam with limestone fragments—10 YR 6/4
3b	4–7	0.20m	sandy loam debris—10 YR 6/3
3a	8–10	0.15m	sandy loam debris—7.5 YR 6/4
2	11–16	0.39m	limestone debris—10 YR 7/4–7/3

SEDIMENTOLOGY

The sediments which filled the fissure showed no marked bedding or stratigraphic variation. The sediments are almost wholly composed of debris derived from the local Magnesian Limestone and there is no evidence of any far-travelled material. The coarser fractions consist of angular limestone blocks, and the finer fraction of irregular concretions of calcium and magnesium carbonate. The basal materials in the fissure were compact and showed evidence of travertine cementation, and contained small pockets of more friable sand. These passed vertically into finer, strongly cemented sandy loam, including large, angular blocks of unweathered limestone. The travertine comprised a compact, cemented deposit enclosing large limestone blocks, and included small pockets of relatively loose sediment. It capped the lower fissure deposits and seemed to pass along the rockwall into the adjacent Dog Hole Cave. Above it occurred a thin veneer of orange sand.

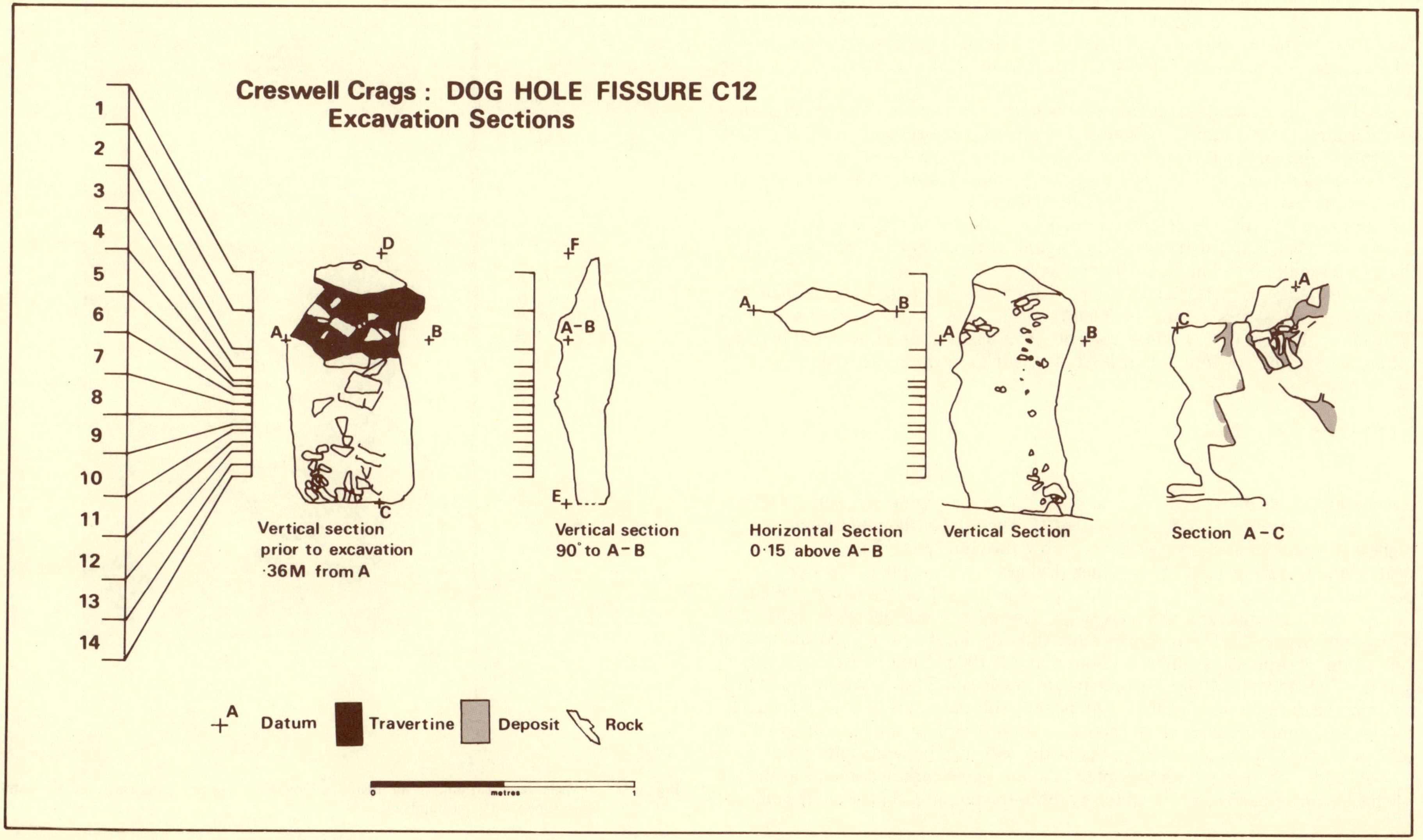

Figure 24. Stratification and excavation details of the Dog Hole Fissure sediments.

Samples from spits 1 to 14 were analysed by standard sedimentological methods, the results are summarised in *Figures 25 and 26*. Standard particle size analyses were carried out on bulk samples (less than 32mm diameter). Silt and clay contents were measured using the hydrometer method (Kaddah 1974). Sand and stone contents were analysed by dry sieving of the material in the 63μ to 32μ range, using standard $\frac{1}{2}$ phi-interval sieves. The results for each sample were plotted as cumulative frequency curves on arithmetic—probability paper from which graphical measures for mean ($\bar{x}$), skewness (Sk), sorting (So) and kurtosis (Kg) were calculated.

Further analyses were carried out on the fine earth fraction (<2000/μ diameter) to determine the calcium carbonate, inorganic phosphorus and organic carbon contents. Total carbonate (carbonate 'equivalent') was measured using 3N HCl in the calcimeter method described by Avery and Bascomb (1974). Inorganic phosphorus extraction was by 2N H_2SO_4 with two hours shaking. This was followed by a colorimetric determination of phosphorus in solution (Murphy and Riley 1962, Dick and Tabatabai 1977). Organic carbon content was calculated by the loss-on-ignition technique of Ball (1964).

Assessments of particle shape were made for two size ranges—coarse sand (500 to 2000μ) and stones (8mm to 32mm)—using the visual comparison chart designed by Powers (1953). Measurements were based upon at least 200 particles in the coarse sand fraction and at least 50 particles in the stone fraction.

Results—Description

Results of the chemical and physical analyses of the sediments indicate several consistent trends, shown in *Figures 25 and 26*. The total carbonate content is at its highest in spit 13 but decreases considerably through spits 12 to 3. It reaches a peak in the travertine (spit 2) layer then declines again in spit 1. The trend of the phosphorus content curve is generally opposite to that of the carbonate curve. Phosphorus contents are relatively high throughout the deposits, apparently indicating enrichment from sources other than the local bedrock. At the base of spit 13 the phosphorus content is about 60mg P $100g^{-1}$ but it rises markedly in spit 3 to 300–450mg P $100g^{-1}$. Contents are low in spit 2 (the travertine) and high again in the sandy residue (spit 1). Significantly this pattern is broadly reflected by the organic content curve which increased from 2.48% at the base of spit 14 to 5.71% in spit 1, with subsidiary peaks in the sequence between spits 3 and 7.

The sudden change in both phosphorus and organic carbon contents at the top of spit 11 can be partly accounted for by the corresponding changes in the amount

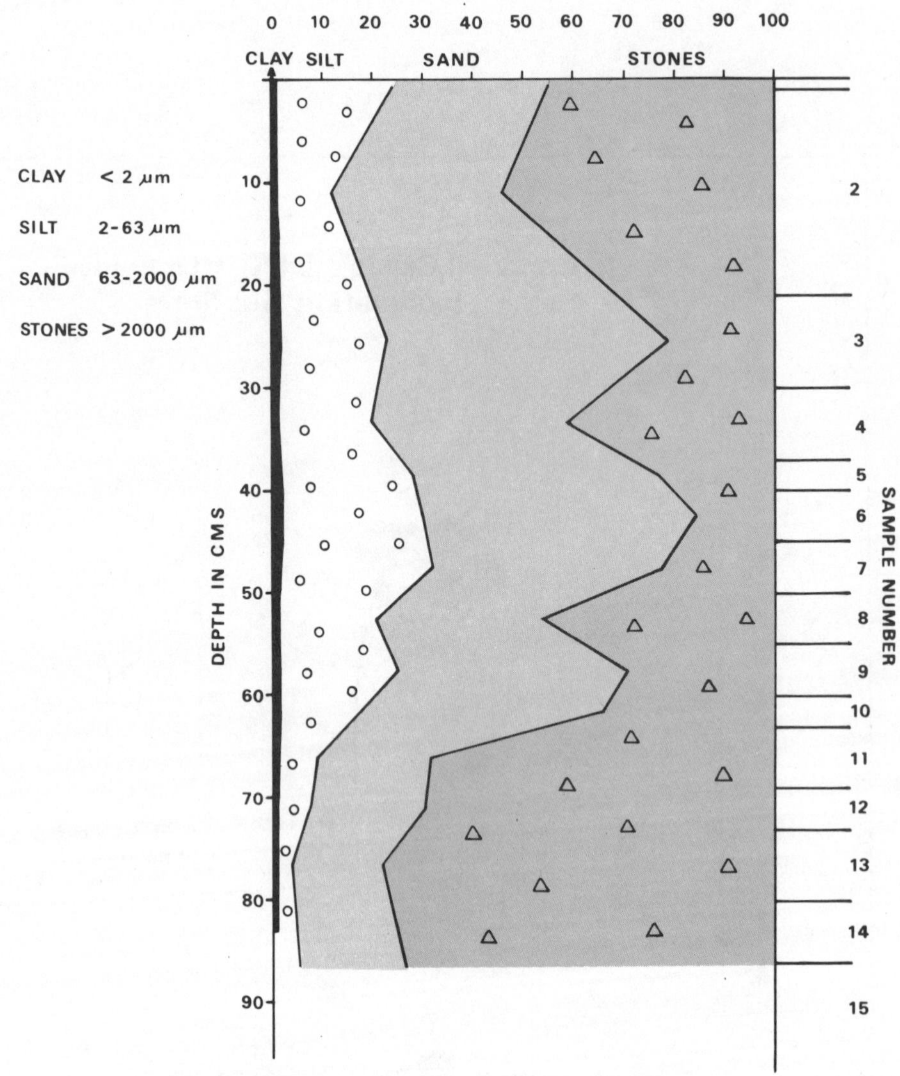

Figure 25. Particle size distribution through the Dog Hole Fissure sediments: sample numbers correspond with spit numbers.

of fine material with which phosphorus and organic carbon are usually associated. The mean particle size of the fine earth fraction follows the general trends shown by organic carbon and phosphorus. Low phi-values (that is, coarse material) occur in spits 11 to 14 and spit 2, but the material is much finer in spits 3 to 10 and in spit 1.

Sorting is very poor throughout the whole fissure and no trend is apparent. Both skewness and kurtosis, however, show a trend related to the change in mean size. Values are high in spits 11–14, fall between spits 3 to 9, rise again in the travertine, then fall once more in spit 1. With the exception of the material in spit 1, all the sediments show a positive skewness, possibly indicating some enrichment by fine grained materials. Kurtosis values show a mesokurtic particle size distribution throughout the deposits. Particle shape varies little up the profile, although the stone fraction is consistently more angular than the coarse sand fraction (with the exception of spit 1). The average particle shape of almost all the samples falls in the angular class on the Powers scale.

To supplement the field classification of the sediments into stratigraphic layers, and indicate the general structure of relationships between the samples, a statistical cluster analysis was performed on the data shown in *Figures 25 and 26*. Analysis was carried out using the clustering algorithm developed by Ward and the CLUSTAN 1C package designed for the ICL 1906S computer (Wishart 1978). Results are presented as a dendrogram in *Figure 27*.

It is apparent from this diagram that the broad morphological classification of the fissure deposits is confirmed by the statistical analysis of the sediments which has grouped the fourteen spit samples into five sedimentary groupings or units.

Unit 1: sandy residue, spit samples–1
Unit 2: sandy pockets within travertine, spit samples–2 and 10
Unit 3: sandy loam infill, spit samples–3, 5, 6 and 7
Unit 4: sandy loam infill, spit samples–4, 8 and 9
Unit 5: rockfall debris, spit samples–11 to 14

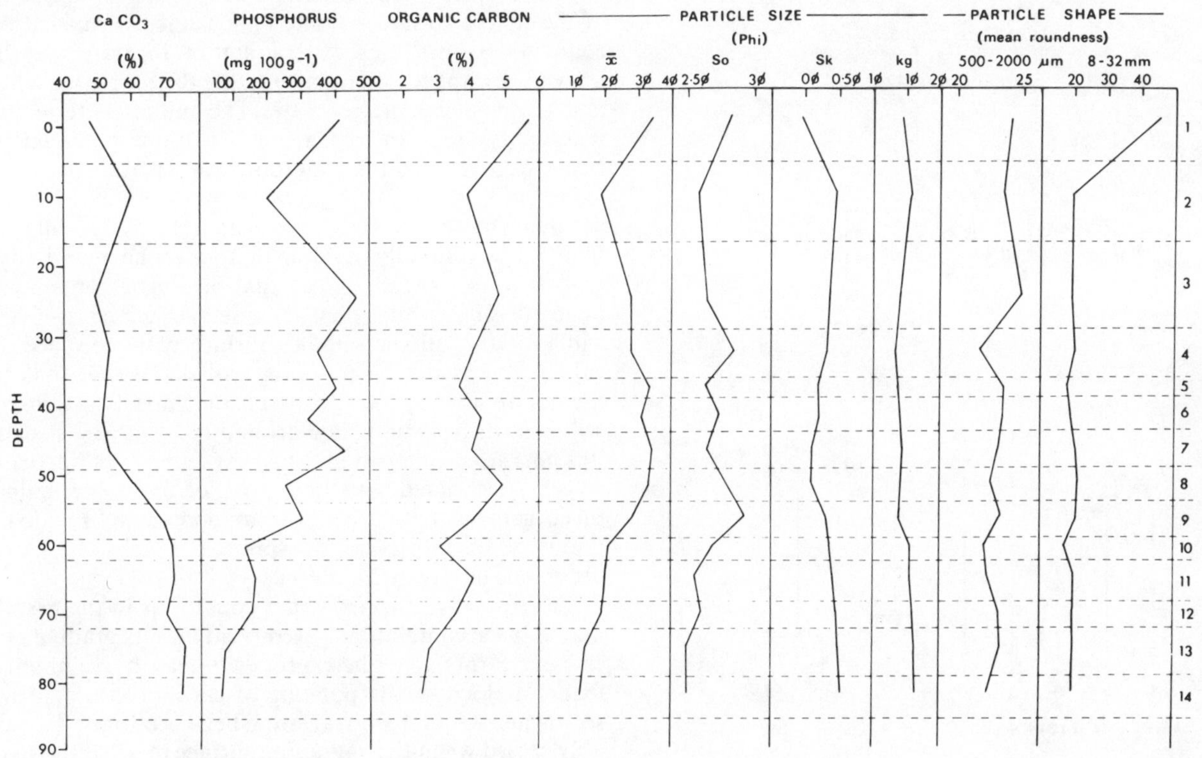

Figure 26. Summary of the textural and chemical properties of the sediments in Dog Hole Fissure: sample numbers correspond with spit numbers.

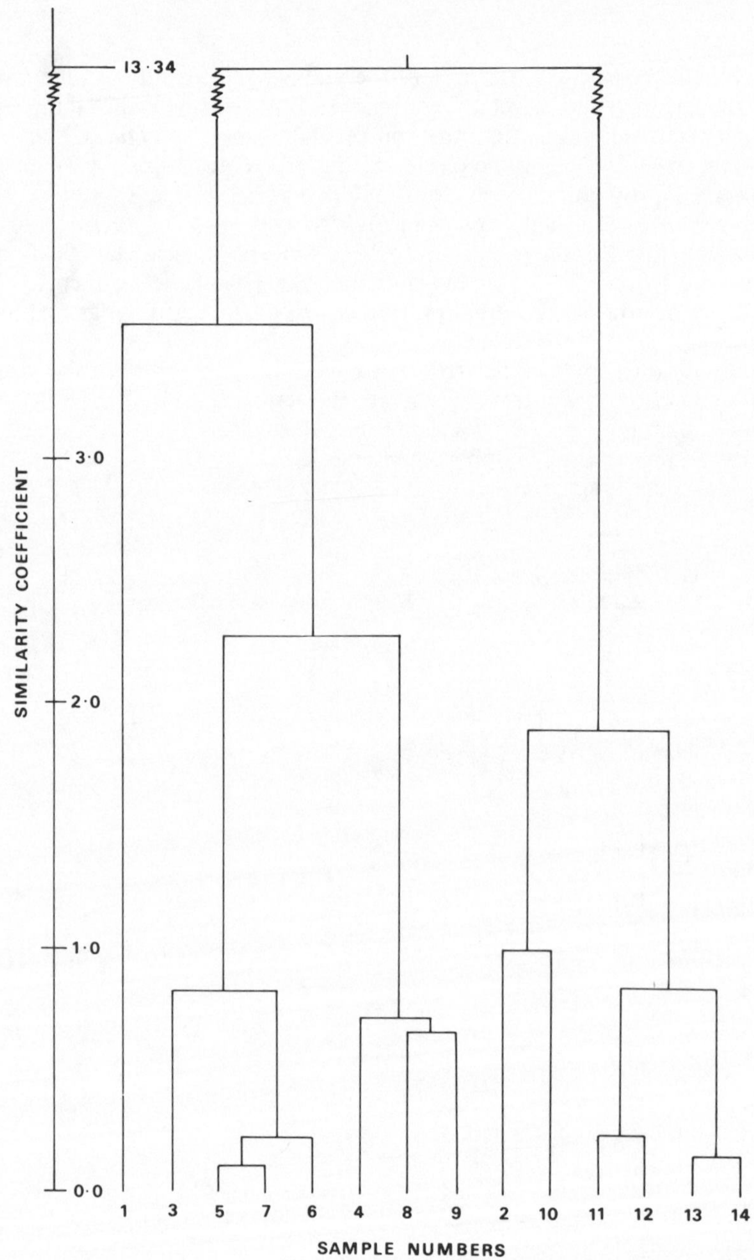

Figure 27. Dendrogram grouping spits of similar textural properties into five sedimentary units recognised at the 1.5 level of similarity coefficient, for details of calculation see text.

The one anomaly in the results is the association of the sample from spit 2 (Unit 2) with samples from spits 10 to 14 from Unit 5 on *Figure 27*. This seems to arise because the material analysed from the travertine layer was derived from the pockets of sediment trapped within the travertine; as such, this material is not wholly representative of the cemented travertine. Nevertheless, results from the cluster analysis indicate that the five units recognised in the sediments provide a satisfactory basis for classification of the fissure deposits.

Interpretation

These characteristics suggest the sequence of formation of the fissure sediments. The basal material (Unit 5, spits 11–14) is regarded as a rockfall deposit, as evidenced by the abundance of stones, the high total carbonate content and relatively open fabric. Exactly when this rockfall occurred relative to opening up of the fissure cannot be determined but by implication it is likely to have been contemporary with, or very soon after, formation of the fissure; clearly there was no ready escape for material entering the fissure and thus these must have been the first sediments to accumulate. The initial material in spit 14 must have been reasonably loose and open, for it is clear that after its accumulation teeth and bones were able to infiltrate downwards from the skull of the wolf that became lodged in spit 11.

Following the rockfall, finer material was deposited, some of it infiltrating into Unit 5, but gradually building up to give the main body of the sediments in spits 3 to 9. The finer texture, lower total carbonate content and compact nature of these materials suggest that they aggraded largely by in-wash of sand and silt down the cliff wall and off the boulder surface with only occasional falls of coarser rock debris. It was during this phase of deposition that the wolf skull fell into the fissure, apparently being broken on impact or subsequently, and it seems that sediment then accumulated around the decaying skeleton. As will be shown later, this phase of deposition was marked by an increased molluscan population, possibly associated with scavenging of the wolf remains. Possibly as a response to this organic activity, there was an increase in organic matter content and a rise in the level of inorganic phosphorus, much of it presumably fixed from the decomposing organic materials.

Subsequently it appears that conditions in the fissure became wetter, probably due to the accumulation of sediment and its gradual cementation with in-washing calcium carbonate. These processes may have inhibited water flow through the fissure and led to the ponding of calcium-saturated waters at the surface of the sediments. As a result, travertine began to form. Travertine precipitation presumably ceased when the aggrading surface reached the top of the fissure, allowing the water to escape laterally. On this surface, a thin residue of fine material developed, probably by further in-wash of sediment from the cliff face. Accumulation here has been limited, however, for the water flowing across the travertine surface has been able to erode the sediment as it formed.

The time scale of this sequence is not known for certain but there is no evidence to suggest that it represents any lengthy period of time. Moreover, there is circumstantial evidence in the distribution of the contained fossil materials to indicate that accumulation was relatively rapid, and that sediment aggraded more-or-less in pace with the decay of the wolf skeleton.

Consequently we note the total time-span up to the start of travertine formation may have been no more than a few years. From current observations of the rate of sediment wash down the cave walls at Creswell this may well have been sufficient to allow the accumulation of sediment to fill the fissure. How long the travertine took to form is a matter of conjecture. Recent observations have indicated that travertine has been forming in environments of this type almost continuously throughout the Flandrian. On the other hand, formation of the depth of travertine found in the Dog Hole fissure would not require a long period of time.

ARTEFACTS

The total artefactual evidence from the site comprised of two flints, recovered from stratigraphic layer 3(b). The first, from spit 6, is a small unretouched, obliquely broken blade, 20mm in length. The second fragment is a cortical waste flake 25mm in length, and lacking any retouch. Both pieces are chronologically undiagnostic. Flint is not found in the vicinity of the fissure and their occurrence on this site must indicate human presence in the vicinity during the accumulation of spits 8–10.

THE VERTEBRATE FAUNA

Numerous fossil bones were recovered by excavation despite the relatively small size of the site. Larger fragments were recorded on site; smaller faunal material was recovered by washing the excavated sediment through a 2 phi sieve and hand sorting the residue with the aid of a low powered stereo-binocular microscope.

Of the 538 bone fragments recovered, 430 (79.92%) were identifiable. The nomenclature used for the vertebrates follows that set out by Kurten (1968). The stratigraphic distribution of vertebrate bone fragments is set out in *Tables 12 and 13*. The variations in frequency of vertebrate remains are illustrated in *Figure 28*. This figure excludes *Canis lupus, Sus scrofa* and *Cervus elaphus* because the remains of a *single* individual of each of these taxa occur throughout a large proportion of the excavated stratigraphic layers.

All recovered fragments were also subjected to fracture pattern analysis (*Table 13*), differentiation being on the basis of their being complete; complete and gnawed; fractured; or fractured and gnawed. It was not possible to reliably distinguish fractures due to carnivore activity and those induced by post-depositional movements. Nevertheless, gnawing patterns were clearly marked. These were probably due directly to small carnivores, especially by *Vulpes vulpes* which was recorded from this site. The results are illustrated in *Figure 28*.

Thirty-three species were recovered from the site. They are all represented by relatively low numbers of individuals. Some single individuals occurring throughout the site suggest a relatively rapid accumulation of the known fauna. Initial accumulation on the site is composed almost wholly of *Rodentia* sp. and *Rana* sp. The number of bone fragments increases dramatically during the formation of stratigraphic layer 3, when 69% of faunal accumulation occurs. The layer marks the appearance of *Canis lupus, Vulpes vulpes, Barbastella barbastellus, Myotis mystacinus, Myotis nattereri, Plecotus auritus, Sus scrofa, Cervus elaphus, Castor fiber, Clethrionomys glareolus, Apodemus sylvaticus, Sorex araneus, Sorex minutus, Turdus iliacus* and *Rana* sp.

Following the faunal climax in spits 4–10, a dramatic reduction occurs in both the quality of fragments and the number of individuals in the upper layers of the fissure infill deposits.

Origin of the Vertebrate Fauna: Post-Mortem Movement

A number of bone fragments can be demonstrated to have been moved 'post-mortem' after their initial inclusion within the Dog Hole Fissure sediment. The origin of the fragments of *Canis lupus* and *Sus scrofa* are a key issue for understanding the nature of accumulation process within the site. The most interesting example concerns the *Canis lupus* remains which all belong to a single adult. Since these are distinct parts of only one individual (the more or less complete skull, mandible and a fibula), but also lack of other parts, we conclude that the wolf bones were already disarticulated before they became incorporated within the fissure. The fracture of the crania (both halves being found in close proximity) and dislodgement of some of the dentition, suggests further disturbance and compression during the accumulation of Unit 3. The post-mortem movement of bones from the wolf infiltrating downwards through coarser sediments has produced a vertical spread through spits 2–16. Similar movement can be demonstrated for *Sus scrofa* remains (particularly those from spits 9 and 15), which belong to the same individual and have been widely separated.

It is likely that the origin of much of the faunal material in spits 11 to 16 owes its origin to post-mortem movement from spits 8 to 10, although this cannot be clearly demonstrated for species other than those already discussed because of the character of the skeletal remains.

Table 12. Stratigraphic distribution of vertebrate bones from Dog Hole Fissure Sediments.

Stratigraphic Layers	Spit		Wolf Canis lupus N	%	Red Fox Vulpes vulpes N	%	Wild Cat Felis sylvestris N	%	Mustelid Mustela sp N	%	Barbastelle Barbastella barbastellus N	%	Whiskered Bat Myotis mystacinus N	%	Natterers Bat Myotis natteri N	%	Long Eared Bat Pleoctus auritus N	%	Bat Plecotus sp N	%
6	1	F																		
		N																		
5	2	F	2	5.55	1	2.77														
		N	1	14.28	1	14.28														
4	3	F	3	2.81	1	0.97	4	3.88			2	1.94	1	0.97	1	0.97				
		N	1	3.44	1	3.44	1	3.44			1	3.44	1	3.44	1	3.44				
3b	4	F																		
		N																		
	5	F									2	5.40	1		1					
		N									2	8.33	1		1					
	6	F	1	2.12	2	4.25														
		N	1	6.66	1	6.66														
	7	F											2	3.84						
		N											1	11.11						
3a	8	F	1	2.77													3	8.33	15	41.66
		N	1	12.50													2	25.00	1	12.50
	9	F	1	2.08							30	62.50								
		N	1	10.00							1	10.00								
	10	F	1	6.66																
		N	1	25.00																
2	11	F	1	50.00																
		N	1	50.00																
	12	F																		
		N																		
	13	F	1	25.00																
		N	1	25.00																
	14	F	1	25.00	1	25.00			1	25.00										
		N	1	25.00	1	25.00			1	25.00										
	15	F																		
		N																		
	16	F																		
		N																		
Total number of individuals			1		4		1		1		4		2		1		1		1	

Stratigraphic Layers	Spit		Bat Chiroptera sp N	%	Hare Lepus sp N	%	Wild Pig Sus scrofa N	%	Horse Equus N	%	Cow Bos taurus N	%	Red Deer Cervus elaphus N	%	Deer Cervid sp N	%	Beaver Castor fiber N	%	Bank Vole Clethrionomys glareolus N	%
6	1	F					1	14.28												
		N					1	16.66												
5	2	F					3	8.33			2	5.55	7	19.44						
		N					1	14.28			1	14.28	1	14.28						
4	3	F	19.	18.44	2	1.94	19.	18.44	1	0.97	1	0.97	5	4.85			1	0.97	3	2.91
		N	2	6.89	1	3.44	2	6.89	1	3.44	1	3.44	1	3.44			1	3.44	1	3.44
3b	4	F	1	2.56	1	2.56	17	43.58												
		N	1	11.11	1	11.11	2	22.22												
	5	F	13	35.13			14	37.83					2	5.40	1	2.70			1	2.70
		N	3	25.00			1	8.33					1	8.33	1	8.33			1	8.33
	6	F					12	25.53							2	4.25	1	2.12	2	4.25
		N					1	6.66							1	6.66	1	6.66	1	6.66
	7	F	38	73.00																
		N	4	44.44																
3a	8	F																		
		N																		
	9	F	1	2.08			5	10.41											2	4.16
		N	1	10.00			1	10.00											2	20.00
	10	F													1	6.66				
		N													1	25.00				
2	11	F																		
		N																		
	12	F																		
		N																		
	13	F	1	25.00											1	25.00				
		N	1	25.00											1	25.00				
	14	F																		
		N																		
	15	F					1	100.00												
		N					1	100.00												
	16	F																		
		N																		
Total number of individuals			12		2		6		1		1		1		1		1		5	

N = number of individuals
F = number of fragments

Common Field Mouse *Apodemus sylvaticus* N %	Rodent *Rodentia sp* N %	Common Shrew *Sorex Araneus* N %	Pygmy Shrew *Sorex minutus* N %	Great Tit *Parus major* N %	Long Tailed Tit *Aegithalos caudatus* N %	Warblers *Muscicapidae sp* N %	Blackcap *Sylvia atricapilla* N %	Redstart *Phoenicurus phoenicurus* N %	Redpoll *Acanthis flammea* N %	Redwing *Turdus iliacus* N %	Fieldfare *Turdis pilaris* N %	Blackbird *Turdus merula* N %	Jackdaw *Corvus monedula* N %	Perching Birds *Passerine sp* N %	Frog/Toad *Rana sp* N %	Salmon *Salmo sp* N %	INDETERMINATE FRAGMENTS N %	% INDENTIFIED FRAGMENTS T %	Total Fragments	
	2 28.57	2 28.57										1 14.28	1 14.28				2	7	9	
	1 16.66	2 33.33										1 16.66	1 16.66				22.22	77.78	100	
	20 55.55														1 2.77		3	36	39	
	1 14.28														1 14.28		7.69	92.31	100	
	11 10.67	3 2.91	1 0.97	1 0.97	1 0.97		1 0.97	1 0.97			1 0.97				18 17.47	2 1.94	32	102	134	
	1 3.44	2 6.89	1 3.44	1 3.44	1 3.44		1 3.44	1 3.44			1 3.44				3 10.34	1 3.44	23.88	76.12	100	
2 5.12	15 38.46	1 2.56							1 2.56						1 2.56		8	39	47	
1 11.11	1 11.11	1 11.11							1 11.11						1 11.11		17.03	82.97	100	
		1 2.70												1 2.70	2 5.40		6	37	43	
		1 8.33												1 8.33	2 16.66		13.95	86.05	100	
	11 23.40	3 6.38												1 2.12	12 25.53		12	47	59	
	3 20.00	2 13.33												1 6.66	3 20.00		20.33	79.67	100	
	3 5.76		1 1.92											2 3.84	6 11.53		10	52	62	
	1 11.11		1 11.11											1 11.11	1 11.11		16.12	83.88	100	
	6 16.66		1 2.77			1 2.77									9 25.00		10	36	46	
	1 12.50		1 12.50			1 12.50									1 12.50		21.74	78.26	100	
	6 12.50									1 2.08					2 4.16		0	48	48	
	2 20.00									1 10.00					1 10.00			100.00	100	
	13 86.66																0	15	15	
	2 50.00																	100.00	100	
	1 50.00																2	2	4	
	1 50.00																50.00	50.00	1	
																	1	0	1	
																	100.00		100	
															1 25.00		2	4	6	
															1 25.[illegible]		33.33	66.66	88.88	
															1 25.00		0	4	4	
															1 25.00			100.00	100	
																	20	1	21	
																	95.23	4.77	100	
1	15	7	2	1	1	1	1	1	1	1	1	1	1	3	15	1	106	430	538	Total
																	20.07	79.93	100%	fragments

Table 13. Distribution of fractured and gnawed vertebrate bones illustrating predator and prey species.

			Predators									Prey								
			Wolf (*C. lupus*)			Red fox (*V. vulpes*)			Wild cat (*F. sylvestris*)			Hare (*Lepus* sp.)			Stoat/Weasel (*Mustela* sp.)			Wild pig (*S. scrofa*)		
Stratigraphic layers	Spit		N	TB%	GF%	N	TB%	GF%	N	TB%	GF%	N	TB%	GF%	N	TB%	GF%	N	TB%	GF%
6	1	TB																1	100	
		GF																1	100	100
5	2	TB	2	100		1	100											3	100	
		GF	0			0												3	100	25
4	3	TB	3	100		1	100		4	100								19	100	
		GF	0			0			2	50	6.25							7	89.47	53.12
3b	4	TB													2	100		17	100	
		GF													1	50	5.88	15	88.23	
	5	TB													1	100		14	100	
		GF													0			13	92.85	76.47
	6	TB	1	100		2	100											12	100	
		GF	0			0												9	75	56.25
	7	TB																		
		GF																		
3a	8	TB	1	100																
		GF	0																	
	9	TB	1	100														5	100	
		GF	0															5	100	71.42
	10	TB	1	100																
		GF	0																	
2	11	TB	1	100																
		GF	0																	
	12	TB																		
		GF																		
	13	TB	1	100																
		GF	0																	
	14	TB	1	100		1	100					1	100							
		GF	0			0						0								
	15	TB																1	100	
		GF																1	100	100
	16	TB																		
		GF																		

			Horse (*Equus*)			Cow (*Bos* sp.)			Red deer (*C. elaphus*)			Deer (*Cervid* sp.)			Beaver (*C. fiber*)			Frog (*Rana* sp.)			Salmon (*Salmo* sp.)		
Stratigraphic layers	Spit		N	TB%	GF%	N	TB%	GF%	N	TB%	GF%	N	TB%	GF%	N	TB%	GF%	N	TB%	GF%	N	TB%	GF%
6	1	TB																					
		GF																					
5	2	TB				2	100		7	100								1	100				
		GF				1	50	8.33	7	100	58.33							1	100	8.33			
4	3	TB	1	100		1	100		5	100					1	100		18	100		2	100	
		GF	1	100	3.12	0			3	60	9.37				1	100	3.12	6	33.33	18.75	2	100	6.25
3b	4	TB																1	100				
		GF																1	100	6.88			
	5	TB							2	100		1	100					2	100				
		GF							2	100	11.76	1	100	5.88				1	50	5.88			
	6	TB										2	100		1	100		12	100				
		GF										1	50	6.25	0			6	50	37.50			
	7	TB																6	100				
		GF																4	66.66				
3a	8	TB																9	100				
		GF																2	100				
	9	TB																2	100				
		GF																2	100				
	10	TB										1	100										
		GF										1	100	28.57									
2	11	TB																					
		GF																					
	12	TB																					
		GF																					
	13	TB										1	100					1	100				
		GF																1	100	100			
	14	TB																1	100				
		GF																1	100	100			
	15	TB																					
		GF																					
	16	TB																					
		GF																					

TB = Total fragments per species
GF = Gnawed or fractured fragments per species
GF% = Gnawed fragments: percent of total gnawed/fractured bone fragments

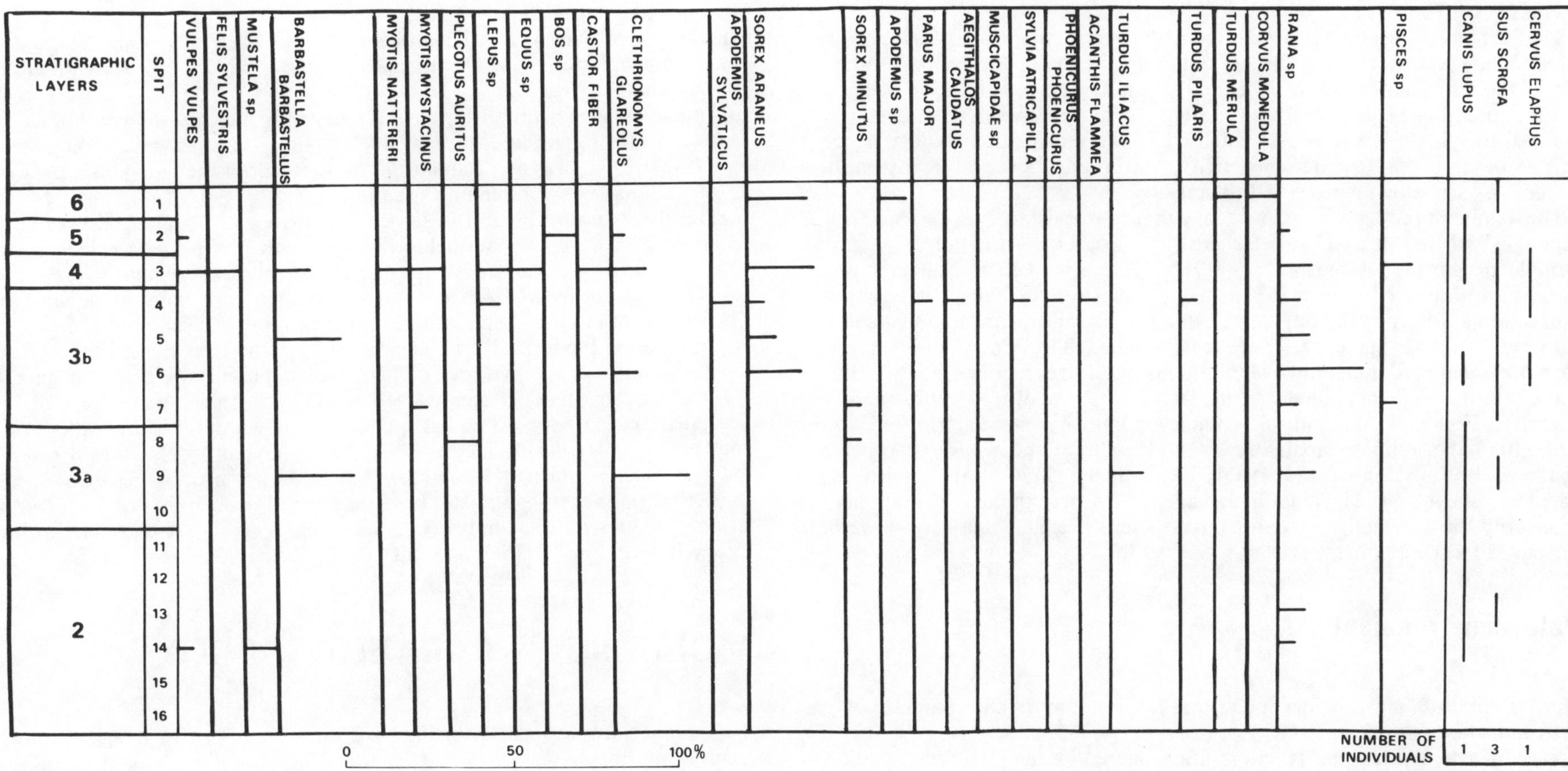

Figure 28. Percentage frequency of vertebrate bones through the Dog Hole Fissure sediments.

Detection of post-mortem movement in faunal material has the potential of overcoming considerable bias imposed upon cave faunal analysis. Its detection in this instance is made easier by low quantities of bone per species and by the character of the Dog Hole Fissure.

Origin of the Vertebrate Fauna: Predatory Behaviour

All faunal remains were examined for evidence of predatory damage, particularly gnawing marks and fracture patterns characteristic of carnivore breakage (*see Figure 28 and Table 13*).

The carnivore assemblage evident from the site is comprised of a single wolf (*Canis lupus*), wildcat (*Felis sylvestris*) and four red foxes (*Vulpes vulpes*), although two of the latter individuals are foetal. The stratigraphic distribution of gnawed and fractured bone shown in *Table 13* suggests that primary carnivore activity is confined to spits 3–7, and is associated with both red fox and wildcat. There is little evidence of wolf predatory activity, the latter, allowing for post-mortem movement (see below) is restricted to spits 4–7.

The dominant prey species associated with predatory activity is pig (*Sus scrofa*), although both red deer (*Cervus elaphus*) and frog (*Rana* sp.) form a high but variable proportion of the prey (*see Table 13*). The skeletal character of the gnawed and fractured bone material strongly suggests scavenging activity rather than hunting. Many of the fragments belong to juvenile or foetal individuals (i.e. *Sus scrofa* = 90.32% juvenile, 9.67% foetal) and adult individuals of other species are represented predominantly by limb fragments. The exceptions are frog and the salmonid fish where individuals, particularly in the case of frog, represent a wide age range. Frog and salmonid fish remains are known from modern studies to be well within the hunting capabilities of both red fox and wildcat (Corbet and Southern 1977, Baranovskaya 1935). Interestingly, 50% of the wildcat bone fragments show signs of predator damage, which may indicate that it was not necessarily the only active predator on the site; its remains may also have been scavenged by the dominant predator, the red fox.

Palaeoenvironment

The vertebrate fauna provides interesting information on the character of past environments at the site:

Macro-environments, that is, information offered by the presence of the larger mammal fauna relevant to habitats and climatic conditions in the area outside the fissure. The predator and prey species found in the fissure indicate a Quaternary warm stage climate, with well developed woodland which prevailed during the period of fissure infilling. The presence of cold-sensitive bat and rodent species argue against the presence of cold, periglacial conditions. Within the vicinity of the site the presence of some habitats is suggested by the finds of *Equus* sp. (horse) and *Cervus elaphus*. The record of *Castor fiber* (beaver), with its well known effects upon trees and streams and *Salmo* sp. (salmon) suggest that a substantial body of water existed within the vicinity of the cave. Both *Vulpes vulpes* and *Felis sylvestris* prefer areas of good ground cover.

Rana sp. is fairly common throughout the sequence (15% of the total individuals present) and clearly indicates the presence of aquatic and well-vegetated habitats.

We conclude that:

(a) the macro-palaeoenvironment represented is that of a warm stage climate with a mature wooded landscape and open glades, and a lake and marsh habitats nearby;

(b) micro-environment: the species present also indicate the conditions found within the fissure and its immediate environs. In particular it is likely that *Vulpes vulpes* was an occupant of the site; half of the individuals present are foetal, indicating a denning situation.

Several species are present in largely complete and undamaged skeletal form and these were probably habitual to the site. Many of these species have small life territories. Typical examples are: *Sorex araneus* and *Sorex minutus, Clethrionomys glareolus* and *Apodemus sylvestris*, and all tolerate a wide range of climates today. Their presence in Dog Hole Fissure must indicate the presence of surface ground cover, either in the form of rock debris, or leaf litter.

All the bat and the majority of bird species present are likely to have been habitual to the site. A prerequisite of such a suggestion must be that it was vegetated, indeed some of the bat species are known in the present day to prefer rock crevices (*Myotis mystacinus, Plecotus auritus*) and well wooded roost sites (*Myotis nattereri, Barbastella barbastellus*). Although no evidence of bat roosting in overhanging vegetation exists above the site today, such environments occupied by bats are present today in ivy covered overhangs and cave entrances within the Creswell gorge and in close proximity to the Dog Hole Fissure site.

MOLLUSCAN PALAEOECOLOGY

The sediments were washed through a 2 phi sieve after disaggregation, and the molluscan remains separated and identified using a low powered stereo-microscope. Normally only apical fragments, or in less abundant taxa, single identifiable parts such as lip fragments have been counted. The lamellibranch data refers to the number of valves counted.

Table 14. Mollusc species recovered from the Dog Hole Fissure sediments.

	SPECIES															
	1	2	3	4	5	6	7	8	9	10	11	12	13	14	15	16
Carychium minimum (Müller)	-	-	-	-	1	-	-	-	-	-	-	-	-	-	-	-
Cochlicopa lubrica (Müller)	-	1	3	2	3	3	6	1	1	-	-	-	-	-	-	-
Lauria cylindracea (Da Costa)	-	-	2	-	1	7	-	1	-	-	-	-	-	1	-	-
Vallonia pulchella (Müller)	-	-	-	-	1	1	-	1	-	-	-	-	-	-	-	-
Ena obscura (Müller)	-	-	-	-	-	-	1	1	-	-	-	-	-	-	-	-
Punctum pygmaeum (Draparnaud)	1	2	2	1	5	2	-	1	-	-	-	-	-	-	-	-
Discus rotundatus (Müller)	10	4	3	3	2	8	10	-	2	-	1	-	-	3	-	-
Arion sp.	-	13	1	1	10	10	-	2	-	-	-	-	-	1	-	-
Vitrina pellucida (Müller)	-	-	-	1	-	1	-	-	-	-	-	-	-	-	-	-
Vitrea crystallina (Müller)	-	-	-	-	2	-	1	3	1	-	-	-	-	-	-	-
Aegopinella pura (Alder)	-	-	-	2	1	-	-	-	-	-	-	-	-	-	-	-
Aegopinella nitidula (Draparnaud)	-	-	-	-	-	-	-	-	-	-	-	-	-	4	-	-
Oxychilus draparnaldi (Beck)	-	-	-	-	-	-	3?	-	-	-	-	-	-	-	-	-
Oxychilus cellarius (Müller)	21	34	21	21	13	64	40	30	10	4	1	-	-	5	-	-
Oxychilus sp.	-	6	-	8	23	88	51	10	-	-	-	-	-	-	-	-
Deroceras reticulatum (Müller)	-	-	-	1	-	-	-	1	-	-	-	-	-	-	-	-
Euconulus fulvus (Müller)	-	2	-	4	-	1	-	-	-	-	-	-	-	1	-	-
Clausilia bidentata (L)	-	-	-	-	-	1	3	3	1	-	-	-	-	-	-	-
Arianta arbustorum (L)	1	-	1	1	-	1	1	1	-	2	-	-	-	-	-	-
Helicigona lapicida (L)	2	-	-	-	-	-	-	-	-	-	3	-	-	-	-	-
Cepaea nemoralis (L)	-	-	-	-	-	-	-	1	-	-	-	-	-	-	-	-
Cepaea sp.	-	-	-	-	-	1	1	-	2	2	-	-	-	-	-	-
Bithynia tentaculata (L)	-	-	1	-	-	-	-	1	-	-	-	-	-	-	-	-
Lymnaea peregra (L)	1	-	-	-	-	-	-	-	-	-	-	-	-	-	-	-
Pisidium subtruncatum (Malm.)	-	2	-	-	-	-	-	-	-	-	-	-	-	-	-	-
TOTAL INDIVIDUALS	**36**	**64**	**34**	**45**	**62**	**188**	**117**	**57**	**17**	**8**	**5**	**0**	**0**	**15**	**0**	**0**

Six hundred and forty-seven (647) molluscs were identified and attributed to 23 taxa (*Table 14 and Figure 29*). Since the spits were necessarily of unequal volume and weight, we have portrayed the results in percentage frequency form with original spit thickness and in recalibrated form (*Figures 28 and 29*), the former expressed as the numbers of molluscs or species per kg dry weight of sediment for each spit.

Identification of Molluscan Remains

Nomenclature for land Mollusca follows that of Waldèn (1976) and for freshwater Mollusca the list set out by Kerney (1976b). Many of the Dog Hole Fissure specimens are excellently preserved in the calcareous sediments. However, some problems of identification have arisen with the sub-fossil specimens and the modern comparative molluscs because of breakage, fragmentation, and the large numbers of juveniles present which sometimes preclude reliable identification to species level. This is especially the case with the more problematic groups, as represented by the occasional *Pisidium* spp. Most of the unseparated *Oxychilus* sp. probably belong to *Oxychilus cellarius*. The deposits have been separated into a

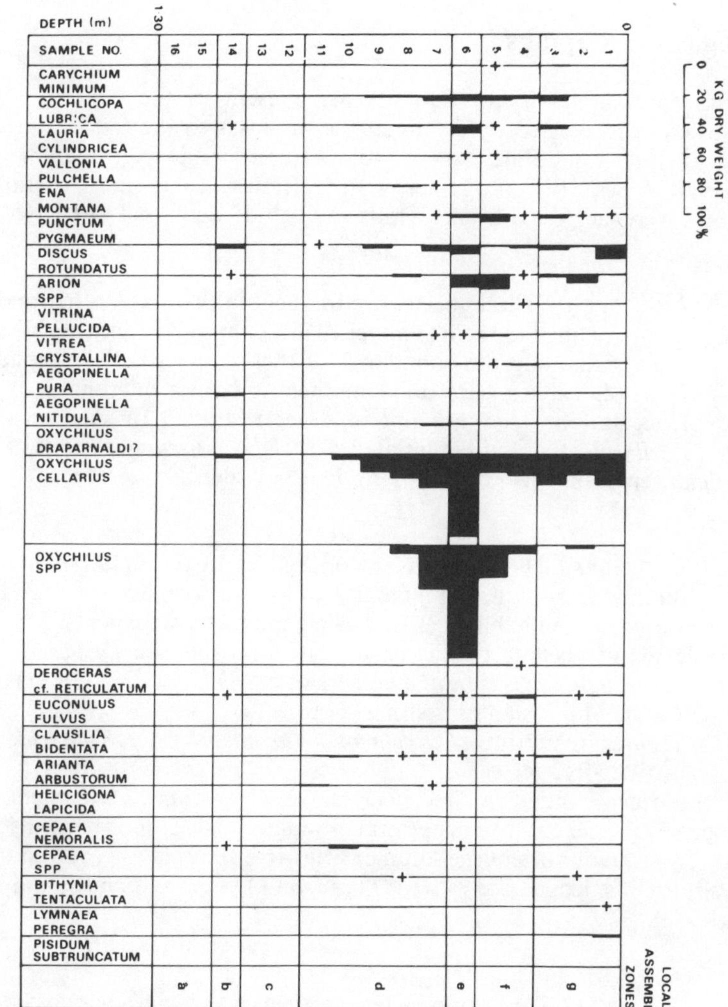

Figure 29. Absolute frequencies of molluscan remains through the Dog Hole Fissure deposits.

series of local molluscan assemblage zones set out in *Table 15*, based on variations in species composition and abundance.

Ecological Groupings

Molluscs from a variety of habitats are present in the deposits. Ecological reconstruction is assisted by ascribing the molluscs to the five broad ecological groupings---the troglophile, 'woodland', 'catholic' and open country groups of Evans and Jones (1973) together with a freshwater group. Several of these groupings were suggested by the Transect Q study described in *Chapter 2*.

Troglophile species These species are frequent in caves and other underground places, but not confined to them (Vandel 1965). Evans and Jones (1973) emphasise the key to understanding the abundance of these species is their capacity to eat flesh as well as vegetable matter, allowing them to occupy microhabitats otherwise devoid of vegetation. They are not however restricted to such environments. *Oxychilus cellarius*, the undifferentiated *Oxychilus, Discus rotundatus* and *Vitrea crystallina*, represent this group in Dog Hole Fissure.

Woodland species The term was introduced by Boycott (1934) and essentially refers to those species requiring moisture and shade, conditions which also occur in some non-woodland habitats as well as woodland environments. Several taxa at Dog Hole Fissure belong to this broad category. *Aegopinella pura, Aegopinella nitidula, Carychium*, are common members of current woodland faunas in the soil leaf litter on the Magnesian Limestone (Transect Q1–3; Q66–8, Chapter 2, *Figures 8 and 9*). Transect Q indicates *Carychium minimum* and *Carychium tridentatum* are rare on the litter-free screes.

On the other hand, *Lauria cylindrica, Ena obscura, Clausilia bidentata* and *Helicogona lapicida* form the rupestral woodland sub-group of Evans and Jones (1973). These favour drier vegetation or litter-free surfaces as occur on tree trunks, stone walls cliffs, ledges and in scree (Transect Q, *Figures 8 and 9*; and Evans and Jones 1973).

'Catholic' species This group includes species which can tolerate a wide variety of habitats ranging from marsh through open environments to closed woodlands. The following taxa in Dog Hole Fissure are attributable to this group—*Cochlicopa lubrica, Punctum pygmaeum, Vitrina pellucida, Euconulus fulvus, Arianta arbustorum, Cepea nemoralis* and *Cepea* sp., and probably members of the slug genera represented here by *Arion* and *Derocers*. Of these taxa, *Cochlicopa lubrica*,

Table 15. Local molluscan assemblage zones recognised in the Dog Hole fissure sequence, Creswell Crags.

Youngest	**Zone g**	*Oxychilus cellarius* (low numbers); *Discus rotundatus* (high numbers); *Cochlicopa, Arion, Punctum, Lauria, Bithynia, Lymnaea, Pisidium.*
	Zone f	*Oxychilus cellarius, Discus* (low numbers), *Cochlicopa, Carychium, Arion, Punctum, Vitrea, Vallonia, Aegopinella pura.*
	Zone e	*Oxychilus* sp. (high numbers), *Discus* (high numbers), *Cochlicopa, Lauria, Punctum, Vallonia, Vitrea, Arion, Clausiliidae, Euconulus, Cepea* sp.
	Zone d	*Oxychilus* sp. (increasing numbers), *Discus, Cochlicopa, Ena, Vitrea, Clausilia, Arianta, Helicogna, Cepea* sp.
	Zone c	no molluscan remains
	Zone b	*Lauria, Discus, Arion, Aegopinella nitidula, Oxychilus cellarius, Euconulus fulvus.*
Oldest	**Zone a**	no molluscan remains

Vitrina pellucida and *Euconulus fulvus* were noted on scree in Transect Q (*Figures 8 and 9*).

'Open Country' species This group includes species which favour more exposed environments lacking marked shade or thick leaf litter from trees or shrubs. *Vallonia pulchella* is the only species attributable to this group in Dog Hole Fissure. This taxon is characteristic of damp grassland or marsh.

Freshwater species *Bithynia tentaculata, Lymnaea peregra* and *Pisidum subtruncatum* are all freshwater species that occur in the current stream and lake at Creswell.

Environmental Reconstruction

The overall pattern of molluscan change is clear in *Figure 29* which indicates an increase in both species abundance and numbers of individuals from spit 14 until spit 6, whereupon both decline. The details of the pattern of change are most reliably inferred from these data which have been standardised to numbers of individuals per species in a standard weight of 1kg of sediment.

The initial sediment occupying spits 15 and 16 appears to derive from a location well removed from soil, vegetation or rock rubble, from which a molluscan population might have been derived by wash or gravity. However, the superjacent spit 14 is characterised by a combination of species—*Lauria cylindracea, Discus rotundatus, Aegopinella nitidula* and *Euconulus*—which together suggest colonisation, or inwash, from woodland with a litter covered soil, associated with drier woody trunks/stems or open rock/scree faces. The small numbers of *Oxychilus* present may have been washed in from these environments or were perhaps attracted by the trapped and decaying small vertebrate remains at this level.

At this time the molluscan fauna appears to have been sealed in by the influx of further sediments from environments lacking molluscan occupants, as previously occurred in spits 15 and 16.

The subsequent consistent increase in numbers and species per 1kg of sediment from spit 9 to spit 1 is extremely important. It matches a similar trend in the vertebrate remains. Initially only three taxa are involved: *Discus rotundatus, Oxychilus cellarius* and *Helicigona lapicida*. This suggests either a primary colonisation, or inwash into the fissure, by a woodland or scree fauna. This environment is similar to that found in spit 14. The consistent rise in numbers of *Oxychilus cellarius* and to a lesser extent of *Vitrea*, suggests the progressive establishment of colonies of these carnivorous species feeding upon the decaying flesh of mammalian remains now accumulating in the fissure.

Several other molluscan taxa appear regularly through these spits, although in relatively low numbers compared to *Oxychilus*. These are *Cochlicopa lubrica, Discus rotundatus, Clausilia bidentata, Arianta arbustorum* and *Cepea* sp. These are all potential members of a scree/rubble fauna occupying the fissure sediments. There is only an occasional indication of the close proximity of woodland—the best indicator *Aegopinella* spp. does not occur. However, some of the specimens of *Lauria, Discus* and *Clausilia* may derive from a wooded habitat.

In the total absence of evidence indicating water or damp conditions in the fissure at this stage, the single shell of *Bithynia tentaculata* is explained here as the result of introduction by birds, or with the mammalian fauna otherwise collecting in the fissure.

The level of carnivorous activity reaches a peak in activity in spit 6, where the major part of the wolf and pig remains occur. The populations of *Cochlicopa, Discus* and *Clausilia bidentata* also achieve substantial numbers here. However from this point, 'carnivorous' activity by molluscs appears to decline. This may be a result of the decaying mammalian remains becoming fully buried in sediment, or an increase in sedimentation rate. At this time some *Oxychilus* or *Vitrea* might have burrowed to reach the buried flesh and hence augmented the numbers of their own species at lower levels.

The two specimens of *Vallonia pulchella* appearing in spits 5 and 6 probably owe their origin to bird transport; there is no supporting evidence of locally increasing surface wetness. In spits 4 and 5, the reappearance of *Aegopinella pura* suggests the proximity of leaf litter and woodland nearby.

The molluscan fauna of spits 1–3 essentially indicates the continuation of the types of micro-habitats found previously in spits 4–6, within and around the fissure. There is one important exception. The molluscan fauna now incorporates a distinct freshwater component. *Lymnaea peregra* is a freshwater species tolerant of such very poor aquatic habitats and might even have been living in the semi-aquatic microhabitat, possibly after introduction by wading birds; *Bithynia tentaculata* and *Pisidium subtruncatum*, although freshwater species, are unlikely to have survived long in this situation after their transport from their more favourable aquatic habitats in the former stream and lake in the Creswell Crags gorge. The deposition of travertine similarly indicates increasing surface wetness, even waterlogging, in the fissure.

The apparent poverty in both numbers of species and individuals in the modern fissure on Transect Q sample Q65, adjacent to the Dog Hole Fissure, *Chapter 2* (*Figures 8 and 9*) is in contrast to the richer fauna of the Dog Hole Fissure sediments. The modern absence at Q65 of *Oxychilus cellarius* is most noticeable, and presumably reflects the absence of flesh-eating opportunities. On the other hand, *Vitrea crystallina* is nowadays fairly abundant at Q65 and across the north-facing scree slopes generally, in contrast with its absence on the south-facing slopes. The reasons for this are unknown, but may also be related to that species' rarity in the Dog Hole Fissure deposits which also face south.

DATING

Radiocarbon Dating

Bulked bone fragments of wolf (*Canis lupus*), red deer (*Cervus elaphus*) and wild pig (*Sus scrofa*) from spits 8–16 were submitted for radiocarbon dating. These gave a radiocarbon age of 9960 ± 140 BP (HAR 4309).

Molluscan Biostratigraphy

Many rock rubble or scree sediments contain a molluscan fauna which considerably post-dates the period of scree deposition—the molluscan fauna falling or burrowing into the deposits (Evans and Jones 1973). The particular circumstances of the Dog Hole Fissure sedimentation and the final sealing with travertine indicate the molluscan fauna is not notably younger than the vertebrate fauna or sediments at this site.

O. cellarius

The presence of species of *Aegopinella* which indicate the presence of woodland together with specimens of *Discus rotundatus, Lauria cylindracea* and *Clausilia bidentata* which may indicate either woodland or scree, suggest that a temperate woodland environment prevailed at the time of deposition. The characteristic cold stage Quaternary molluscan fauna of Britain, dominated by *Pupilla muscorum* (see Kerney 1977a), is not present.

An approximate age for the molluscan fauna and check on the radiocarbon date, may be obtained by reference to the scheme of late-glacial and post-glacial molluscan assemblage zones developed by Kerney (1977b) and Kerney *et al.* (1980). This scheme reflects the recolonisation of southeast England by molluscan species spreading northwards and westwards from their glacial retreats in Europe. The presence of *Oxychilus cellarius* marks the base of Kerney's (1977) zone d which dates to somewhere between 8,470 ± 190 yrs BP (Q 1425) and 7,500 ± 100 yrs BP (St 3410). The base of the molluscan fauna is therefore firmly fixed to the Flandrian, not the Devensian or the Devensian/Flandrian transition *c.* 10,000 bp.

An estimate of minimum age may also be given. The garden snail, *Helix aspersa*, is common in the area today, occurring close to the fissure (*Figure 8*). *Helix aspersa* is an introduced Mediterranean species which seems to have spread across lowland Britain during the Roman period. Its presence defines Kerney's (1977b) molluscan assemblage zone f. Its absence from the sequence at Dog Hole Fissure is taken to indicate a pre-Roman, pre-zone f, date. Unfortunately, because of the topographic setting of the site at the foot of a cliff, it is unlikely to have experienced the consequences of prehistoric woodland clearance and agriculture which generated the open ground faunas defining Kerney's zone e.

Vertebrate Biostratigraphy

Vertebrates recovered from the site are generally comprised of a *warm* stage fauna accumulated in a fairly short period of time (i.e. single individuals penetrate much of the site). Cow (*Bos taurus*), present in spit 2, is not known in the Late Devensian sequences. These data indicate a Flandrian age for the Dog Hole Fissure sediments.

Although many of the vertebrates recorded from the site occur in local Devensian deposits, the marked absence at Dog Hole Fissure of cave hyaena (*Crocuta crocuta*) and reindeer (*Rangifer tarandus*) which are locally known from Late Devensian Z III, suggest the deposits are not of Devensian age.

The radiocarbon date for stratigraphic layer 3a (*c.* 10,000 Late Devensian/Flandrian boundary) appears incompatible with both the molluscan evidence, (even allowing for burrowing and infiltration) and the vertebrate faunal evidence. The latter two data sets suggest mature woodland of Flandrian age. This discrepancy is not unexpected. It is important to note that the sediments and surrounding limestone bedrock of Dog Hole Fissure are porous and carbonate rich. The sealing layer of travertine and sedimentary analyses offer good evidence for water logging and in the upper layers there is travertine deposition. In all probability, flushing of the lower sediments and containing fossils in old carbonate-rich water led to contamination of the skull by 'old' carbon. On the basis of all the biostratigraphic evidence presented above, and the likelihood of contamination, we conclude the radiocarbon date is at least 500 to 1,500 years too old. We therefore conclude that the deposits are Flandrian in age, and younger than *c.* 8,500 years bp.

THE FLANDRIAN DEVELOPMENT OF DOG HOLE FISSURE

These data from the sedimentological and faunal analyses allow the reconstruction of a six stage model of the Flandrian development of the site. This is set out below in *Table 16*.

This sequence has several important implications. The site offers base line data for Flandrian geomorphic and taphonomic processes in the Magnesian Limestone area in particular, and for eastern Britain in general. There are relatively few Flandrian faunal and sedimentological studies of this type. The presence of wolf in post-Devensian deposits is unusual in this region. The beaver remains from the site provide new evidence of its Flandrian occurrence in eastern Britain. It must now be regarded as becoming extinct in the region much later than previously thought likely. The bats, bird and fish remains are the first to be reported from Creswell Crags.

The site's relationship with Dog Hole Cave is important. The presence of the travertine layer at both sites has often in the past been used as a late Devensian stratigraphic horizon. This study demonstrates this travertine development and the hydrological changes were associated with the Flandrian stage. Further, development of travertine is now seen to be probably a very localised development at the site and should not be used as the basis for lithostratigraphical correlations within the Creswell area.

Middle range carnivore activity from the site offers a rare insight into the effect of such predatory activity upon a faunal assemblage. It contrasts quite markedly with well known types of Devensian faunal accumulations which are associated with much larger predators e.g. hyaenas. Such processes are demonstrated in this study to be detectable within faunal assemblages belonging to the Flandrian warm stage by a rigorous analysis of bone fracture and damage patterns. This has been only rarely achieved before.

The palaeoenvironmental evidence from Dog Hole Fissure has been shown to indicate a wider spatial perspective than the confines of the cave; however it has also revealed with precision the series of minor but extremely complex taphonomic and sedimentary events which can take place in a very short period of time. This degree of temporal resolution is uncommon in palaeoecological studies. The combination of geomorphic, sedimentological, vertebrate and molluscan studies described here have also unexpectedly revealed most complex interactions between the wider world and the fissure, and within the fissure:

(i) the two stage disarticulation and movement of the larger vertebrate remains, and subsequent further crushing by further rock movement at the fissure;
(ii) disarticulation patterns which could only take place because of the distinctive pattern of sedimentary infill—yielding distinctive sedimentary fabrics and grain sizes;
(iii) the subsequent colonisation of the corpses of vertebrate and probably invertebrate remains by flesh eating molluscs; and
(iv) the occupation of the site by fox and bats, whilst the fox bred and also introduced gnawed bones on the site.

It has been surprising to establish the extent to which trends in faunal abundance are paralleled by those in the quantity of phosphorus fixed in the fissure sediments. Such sedimentary geochemical studies in this type of context appear therefore to be another means of indirectly assessing faunal abundance by estimating phosphorus deriving from the soft and hard tissues and droppings of animals. The modern transect and fissure study both point out the significance of the transport of aquatic/marsh molluscan remains on the feet of the wading animals, largely birds.

The unusual nature of the site, intermediate between a cave and open ground site, clearly makes them of wider interest than might be suspected. This type of site is open to both external influences and those of the cave environment. If only the associated cave sediments had not been destroyed or lost through poor excavation in the 19th and early 20th centuries, it would have proved possible to explore sedimentary and faunal facies changes from an open into a cave environment. Fortunately the Dog Hole Fissure site itself did not become "extinct" before a rescue dig could be mounted. Such rockfalls are not uncommon. Their frequency in this type of area suggests large quantities of irreplaceable archaeological remains are being lost as a result of natural geomorphic processes.

Perhaps the most interesting aspect of the methodology used in this instance is the enormous complexity revealed on an extremely small site; a complexity not previously realised in excavations of cave sites in Creswell Crags. Individually, the sedimentological, vertebrate or invertebrate analyses were unlikely to have detected the full complexity of the Flandrian history of the site. The implication of the results and methodology adopted in this instance is that selection and testing of sites of specifically different character to those normally excavated may provide a new perspective on both palaeoenvironments and taphonomic processes.

Table 16. Summary of the Flandrian development of Dog Hole Fissure.

Layer	Youngest / Processes
6	occasional residence on the now completely infilled site by rodents and birds — weathering of sediments.
5	travertine — fissure full, formation in waterlogged fissure now almost full of sediment, occasional coarse rock debris collecting; continued fox predation but decreasing biological activity.
4	vertebrate faunal climax, increase in organic matter and phosphorus from faunal remains, low calcium — red fox predation/scavenging and denning.
3b	continued infilling with finer sediments, peak of molluscan faunas, increasing phosphorus enrichment of sediments from decaying faunal remains, damper conditions.
3a	death of *Canis lupus* — post-mortem movements into fissure of skull, upper torso bones, bones lodging at various depths within the fissure, subsequent rock movement and further skull fractures — increase in numbers of other vertebrates, particularly bats, many rodents, birds — molluscan colonisation: (molluscan zone c).
2	infilling of fissure commences with coarse clastic debris — few vertebrates (frog, *Muridae* sp.) and zone b molluscan faunas — connection opened with outside environment — soils etc.
	rockfall, creation of fissure and rock debris, no vertebrate or molluscan faunas, no accumulation in fissure of sediments/soils from the land surface.
1	**Oldest**

CONCLUSIONS

Analyses of the geomorphology, sedimentology and faunal remains of Dog Hole Fissure, Creswell, have revealed a complex history of rock fall, fissure infilling, post-mortem transport of animal remains, and colonisation of the decaying corpses by carnivorous molluscs, the occupation of the site by a fox, and the passive faunal transport of aquatic molluscs to the site by birds. It has provided new Flandrian records for wolf and beaver indicating they became extinct in this area much later than previously believed. The complex history established indicates such fissure traps, lying halfway between cave and open ground sites may provide a new insight on colonisation, extinction, palaeoenvironments and taphonomic processes.

Briggs, D.J., Gilbertson, D.D., Griffin, C.M., Jenkinson, R.D.S., Stebbings, R.E., and Watts, C.M. 1984. Death, Disarticulation and Decay in an Eight Thousand Year Old Rock Fall. Chapter 3 in Jenkinson, R.D.S. and Gilbertson, D.D. *In the Shadow of Extinction: A Quaternary Archaeology and Palaeoecology of the Lake, Fissures and Smaller Caves at Creswell Crags SSSI*. Sheffield: Department of Prehistory and Archaeology, University of Sheffield. Pp. 55 to 74.

CHAPTER 4: STEETLEY QUARRY CAVE: A 'LOST' IPSWICHIAN INTERGLACIAL SITE
and
STEETLEY CAVE: A 5000 YEAR OLD BADGER DEN

with D. Bramwell, K.M. Cartledge, C.M. Griffin, C.O. Hunt and C. Samson.

CONTENTS

Steetley Quarry Cave was both discovered and destroyed approximately 40 years ago. Vertebrate remains preserved from it and reported here include bear (*Ursus arctos*), red deer (*Cervus elaphus*) and horse (*Equus* sp.). The cave deposits are provisionally attributed to the Ipswichian interglacial.

Multi-disciplinary studies of the quite separate Steetley Cave indicate this cave was colonised by badgers approximately 5000 years ago in a forest landscape dominated by *Tilia, Pinus* and *Corylus*. One mesolithic point was found in a position suggesting it was originally lodged in one of the badgers which died in the cave. Increased surface wetness is suggested for several periods of the cave's history. This may have been a factor responsible for its abandonment by badgers.

INTRODUCTION

Many of the caves in the Magnesian Limestone of the Creswell area are poorly known due to the circumstances of their discovery or the haphazard nature of their subsequent exploration. Cave infills dating to the mid-Flandrian stage are especially poorly known. This study reports the results of the recent multi-disciplinary research dealing with palaeontological and archaeological evidence from two caves discovered in Steetley Quarry, located to the south of Worksop (*Figure 4*). One of them, Steetley Quarry Cave, is known only from documentary sources and a small collection of vertebrate bones which have not previously been published. The site itself was destroyed between 1926–39.

A further cave, called Steetley Cave, was discovered in 1976 some distance from the first site. Steetley Cave has been excavated and the results of this work are reported here. The palaeontological evidence indicates the cave was used as a badger den in temperate woodland of lime, oak, pine and hazel. The cave infill dates to a period approximately 5000 years ago.

STEETLEY QUARRY CAVE

The precise location of Steetley Quarry Cave is not known. Documentary evidence indicates it was discovered in 1926 during quarrying operations at Steetley Quarry (SK 560810) near Worksop (Jenkinson 1984). It has proved especially difficult to obtain information about the cave. The description given here is based upon conversation with Mr. Christopher Hedley who joined the Steetley Lime Quarry (now Steetley Minerals Limited) in 1939 and remembers hearing details of the cave. Based upon his account the cave appears to have been located in the 'old quarry' (SK 558811) and was approximately four metres from the quarry top. The extent of the cave is unknown but it is reported to have been approximately three metres in diameter. All trace of the cave was destroyed in subsequent quarrying operations.

A number of fossil bones were discovered in sandy deposits within the cave. Some of these bones were donated in 1926 to Wollaton Hall Museum, Nottingham. It is likely that the extant collection is only a small proportion of the total bones discovered. It is known for instance that a number of bones were kept at the quarry office for some years and that due to their deterioration and friable nature they were eventually discarded (G. Plant *pers. comm.*).

Extant Vertebrate Remains from Steetley Quarry Cave

The extant collection of vertebrate bone from the cave has recently been located and examined. It was evident that not all of the specimens stated to be from the cave are clearly labelled, and an element of doubt must remain as to the provenance of some of these. The total collection numbers 77 bones, of which eight were not identifiable to species level (these are described in *Table 17*).

The vertebrate taxa known from the Steetley Quarry Cave are quite distinct and different from many other faunas known from caves in the Creswell area. Carnivores are evidenced by a single bear (*Ursus arctos*), a rather old individual with osteoarthritis in one foot. Ungulates include red deer (*Cervus elaphus*), a total of three individuals being present, one of which is evidenced by a massacred antler fragment. A single fallow deer (*Dama dama*) is also evidenced by a massacred antler fragment. Other ungulates include a single horse (*Equus* sp.) and four bovids (*Bos* spp.). All the individuals were adults. A single human mandible is also reported from the cave. The mandible appears fully modern. Suspiciously, the style of fossilisation is somewhat different from the rest of the fauna and for the time being it cannot be firmly assigned to the cave.

Table 17. Vertebrate fauna from Steetley Quarry Cave, as located in the Wollaton Hall Museum, Nottingham.

		ANATOMICAL VARIATION																				
		SKULL		MANDIBLE		SEPARATE TEETH		HORNS & ANTLERS		VERTEBRAE		RIBS		SCAPULA		HUMERUS		RADIUS				
		N	%	N	%	N	%	N	%	N	%	N	%	N	%	N	%	N	%			
SPECIES.	Brown Bear U arctos	–	–	1	10.00	3	30.00	–	–	–	–	–	–	–	–	–	–	1	100.00			
	Horse Equus sp	–	–	–	–	–	–	–	–	–	–	–	–	–	–	–	–	–	–			
	Red Deer C elaphus	–	–	–	–	–	–	1	16.67	–	–	–	–	–	–	5	83.33	–	–			
	Fallow Deer C dama	–	–	–	–	–	–	1	100.00	–	–	–	–	–	–	–	–	–	–			
	Deer Cervid sp.	–	–	–	–	–	–	1	16.67	–	–	–	–	–	–	–	–	–	–			
	Bovid Bos sp.	1	2.56	–	–	2	5.13	3	7.69	11	28.21	–	–	2	5.13	6	15.38	2	5.13			
INDE-TERMINATE:	MAMMALIA sp.	–	–	–	–	–	–	–	–	2	16.67	–	–	–	–	–	–	–	–			
TOTAL IDENTIFIED FRAGMENTS		1	1.56	1	1.56	5	7.81	6	9.38	13	20.31	–	–	2	3.13	11	17.19	3	4.69			
TOTAL INDETERMINATE FRAGMENTS		–	–	–	–	–	–	–	–	2	16.67	–	–	–	–	–	–	–	–			
TOTAL FRAGMENTS		–	–	–	–	–	–	–	–	–	–	–	–	–	–	–	–	–	–			
TOTAL INDIVIDUALS		–	–	–	–	–	–	–	–	–	–	–	–	–	–	–	–	–	–			

		ULNA		PELVIS		FEMUR		TIBIA		FIBULA		ASTRAGALUS		CALCANEUM		CUNEIFORMS		METATARSAL METACARPALS		PHALANGES		MISC BONES & FLAKES		TOTAL INDIVIDUALS		TOTAL BONES	
		N	%	N	%	N	%	N	%	N	%	N	%	N	%	N	%	N	%	N	%	N	%	N	%	N	%
SPECIES.	Brown Bear U arctos	–	–	–	–	–	–	–	–	–	–	–	–	–	–	–	–	5	50.00	–	–	–	–	1	8.33	10	100.00
	Horse Equus sp	–	–	–	–	–	–	–	–	2	100.00	–	–	–	–	–	–	–	–	–	–	–	–	2	16.67	2	100.00
	Red Deer C elaphus	–	–	–	–	–	–	–	–	–	–	–	–	–	–	–	–	–	–	–	–	–	–	3	25.00	6	100.00
	Fallow Deer C dama	–	–	–	–	–	–	–	–	–	–	–	–	–	–	–	–	–	–	–	–	–	–	1	8.33	1	100.00
	Deer Cervid sp.	–	–	–	–	–	–	3	50.00	–	–	1	16.67	–	–	–	–	1	16.67	–	–	–	–	1	8.33	6	100.00
	Bovid Bos sp.	1	2.56	1	2.56	1	2.56	1	2.56	–	–	3	7.69	2	5.13	–	–	3	7.69	–	–	–	–	4	33.33	39	99.98
INDE-TERMINATE:	MAMMALIA sp.	–	–	–	–	–	–	–	–	–	–	–	–	–	–	–	–	–	–	–	–	10	83.33	–	–	12	100.00
TOTAL IDENTIFIED FRAGMENTS		1	1.56	1	1.56	1	1.56	2	3.13	2	3.13	4	6.25	2	3.13	–	–	9	14.06	–	–	–	–	–	–	64	84.21
TOTAL INDETERMINATE FRAGMENTS		–	–	–	–	–	–	–	–	–	–	–	–	–	–	–	–	–	–	–	–	10	83.33	–	–	12	15.79
TOTAL FRAGMENTS		–	–	–	–	–	–	–	–	–	–	–	–	–	–	–	–	–	–	–	–	–	–	–	–	76	100.00
TOTAL INDIVIDUALS		–	–	–	–	–	–	–	–	–	–	–	–	–	–	–	–	–	–	–	–	–	–	12	99.99	–	–

Antiquity of Steetley Quarry Cave

The presence of red and fallow deer with a large bovid, possibly *Bison priscus* and the lack of clear Devensian faunas, particularly carnivores, probably indicates that the fauna is interglacial in type, and presumably belongs to the Ipswichian (last) interglacial stage. Supportive evidence for this view exists in that steppe rhinoceros (*Dicerorhinus hemitoechus*) teeth are said to have been found within the cave (Richardson *pers. comm.*) although no trace of the original teeth survive today. Inevitably an element of doubt remains concerning the age of the cave's deposits; a doubt compounded by the fact that nothing of the original cave survives.

STEETLEY CAVE

Steetley Cave was discovered in 1976 during construction work at the Steetley Co. Limited brickworks site at N.G.R. SK 552790. During the construction work an adjacent rock outcrop was partially quarried exposing a small cave (*Figure 30*). The cave is a localised area of phreatic drainage and solution which developed along bedding planes in the Magnesian Limestone. The present length of exposed cave (five metres) terminates at a section of infilling deposits.

The first discovery of the palaeontological specimens made at the cave was by Mr. F. Marsden (Grubert 1976). Subsequent specimens were recovered by R. Paget, R. Richardson and F. Askew (Askew *pers. comm.*). The author's attention was drawn to the cave by Askew who kindly made the faunal material available for study. The specimens reported here are housed in the Creswell Crags Visitor Centre.

Unfortunately, little stratigraphic information was recorded during the earlier excavations. The lack of such details inhibits interpretation of the environmental history represented within the cave. The *in situ* exposures of sediment (*Figures 30–32*) indicate that the internal sediments were fairly shallow and contained a high proportion of limestone clasts. It is clear from examination of the sediments and the contained fauna that the accumulation within the cave occurred within a relatively short timespan. To overcome the problems of interpreting the cave's prehistory the site was re-examined in 1980 with a view to obtaining detailed new information concerning the cave's extent, the nature of the infilling sediments and its associated faunal remains.

This account describes the results of this research and includes a geophysical examination of the cave area, analysis of sediments, archaeology, vertebrate fauna, molluscan and floral remains.

GEOPHYSICAL SURVEY

Prior to the discovery, no obvious entrance to the cave was apparent in the outcrop of Magnesian Limestone. A number of observations suggest that the unlocated original entrance existed to the north of the site. In this region the topographic nature of the outcrop is obscured by extensive industrial development, old quarries and subsequent landscaping. The last of these activities is reported (Plant *pers. comm.*) to have been responsible for the infilling of a small dry valley and heavily fissured limestone outcrop to the north of the site.

The existence of this feature suggested that the original cave entrance might be located here and that the currently exposed cave was the terminus of the cave development. The area between the known cave and the infilled valley is partially covered by a road but also contains a significant area which has not experienced any sort of industrial disturbance in the recent past. This area was examined using geophysical techniques.

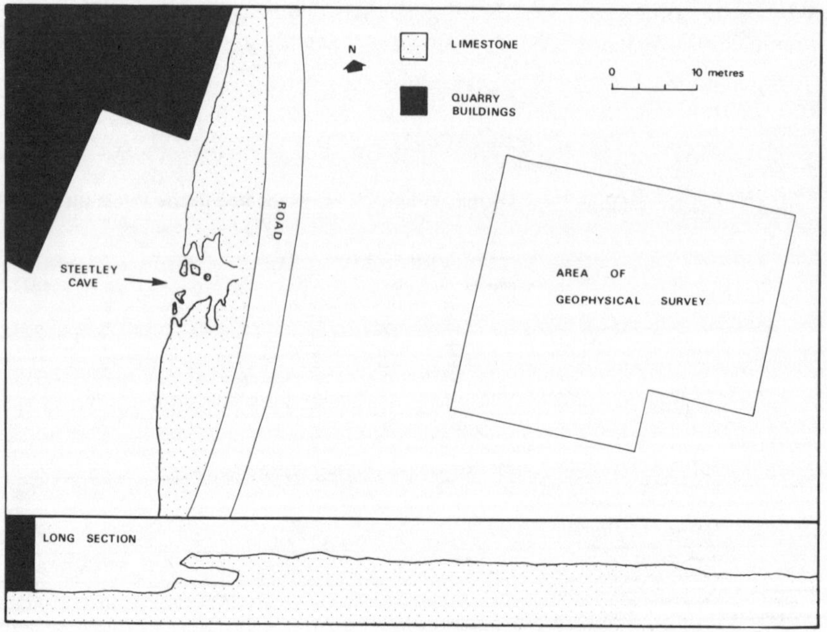

Figure 30. Plan of Steetley Cave showing the ground plan, long section and infilling deposits of the cave.

The purpose of the survey was to determine both the northern extent and locate the original entrance of the cave. The survey was undertaken using a Bradphys III earth-resistance instrument (Aspinall and Pickard 1971). A two-probe electrode configuration (Aspinall and Lynam 1970) with a spacing of 0.5m between the current and potential probes was used throughout the survey. Readings were taken at one metre intervals and the results are given in *Figure 31*.

It can be seen that the geophysical survey located a sizable electrical anomaly. This anomaly is characterised as a low resistance feature occurring within a background of high resistance values. The location and dimensions of this feature are consistent with it being produced by the continuation of the known cave. Experience gained during similar geophysical surveys at Creswell Crags (Samson 1979, Samson and Jenkinson 1979) would suggest that for the cave to produce an anomaly of this intensity it must be situated only a few metres below the ground surface.

The low resistance nature of the feature is indicative of either a subterranean cavity filled with water retentive deposits, or an earth-filled fissure within the rock. As with all geophysical prospection, the precise nature of the anomaly can only be proven by excavation and until this is undertaken the interpretations offered here must remain speculative.

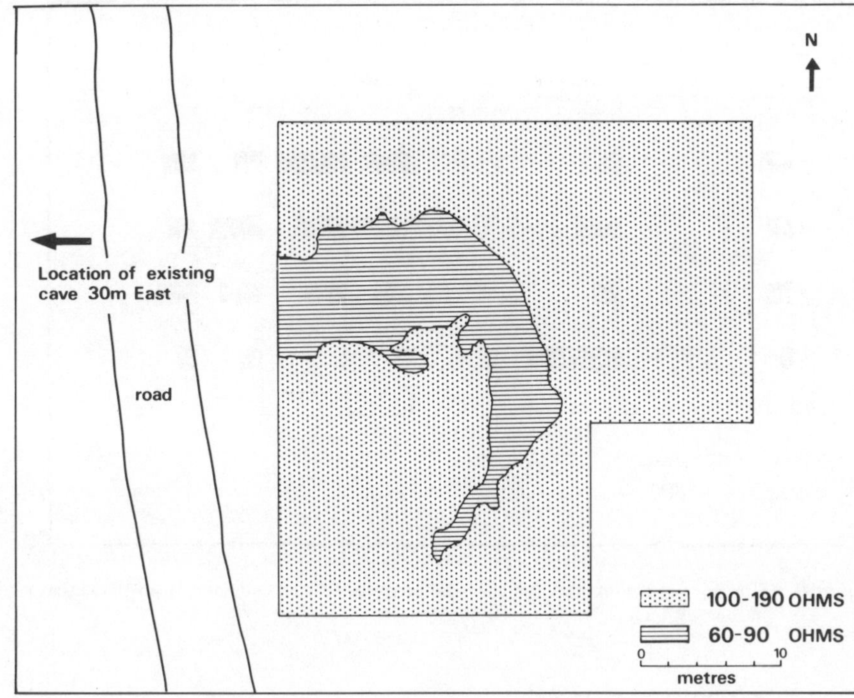

Figure 31. Results of geophysical prospection adjacent to Steetley Cave showing its probable continuation.

SEDIMENTOLOGY

Excavation within the exposed area of the cave revealed sediments which completely infill the rear of the cave. These were sampled and analysed by standard sedimentological methods. The results are given in *Figure 32*.

Results

The small sample size permits only generalisations about the sedimentological characteristics of the samples. Particle size analysis shows that Units 2, 3 and 4 of *Figure 32* are similar. Their mean size ($\bar{x}$) ranges from 3.6 to 4.6∅ and shows a general increase in size down the profile into Unit 1. Sorting is poor throughout the samples but shows some improvement with depth.

The chemical analyses support these generalisations with total carbonate content of Units 2, 3 and 4 falling between 23.7% and 46.2% whereas it is 93.6% in Unit 1. Similarly the organic carbon content ranges from 4.5% to 5.9% in Units 2, 3 and 4; yet is only 2.6% in Unit 1. The phosphorus pattern is similar in that the inorganic phosphorus contents of the upper units are between 180 and 370 mg $P.100g^{-1}$, generally (higher than Unit 4 above 200 mg $P.100g^{-1}$).

Interpretation

The results suggest that Unit 1, the basal layer of the cave, is comprised of Magnesian Limestone that has weathered to a sandy matrix probably with phosphatic minerals such as apatite. The overlying Units 2, 3 and 4 form the cave infill, and have been derived in part from the limestone. The greater proportions of organic phosphorus and organic carbon in the upper layers suggest that the material forming this infill is allochthonous, i.e. derived from sources external to the cave, as well as from the bedrock. Accumulation is probably the result of occupation in the cave, producing debris and other introduced materials. The results also indicate that there has been little or no vertical movement of sediments, since the clay and chemical constituents show a slight decrease with depth, thus suggesting that there has been limited water percolation and solution of the sediments.

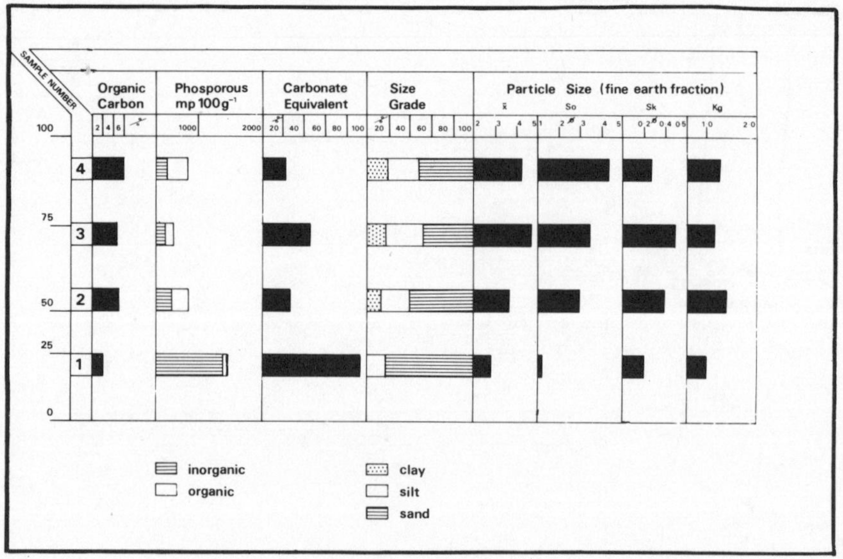

Figure 32. Summary of the textural and chemical properties of the sediments from 1980 excavations in Steetley Cave.

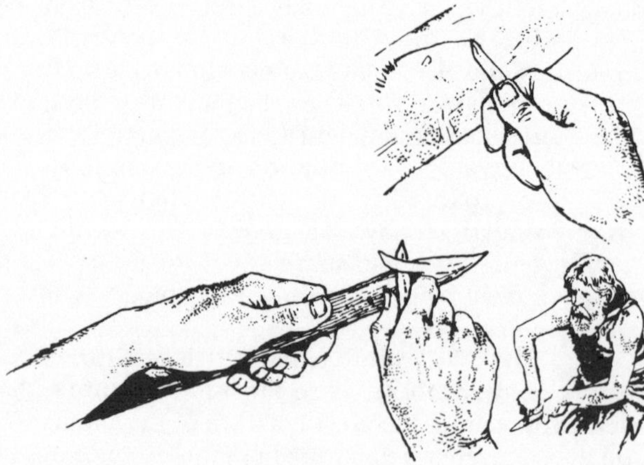

ARCHAEOLOGY

A single geometric microlith (*Figure 33*) was recovered from spit 4, near the roof of the cave, during the 1981 excavation. The microlith is a scalene triangle. It was found over the roof; such a position suggests its location is due to factors other than human use or passage within the cave. A possible explanation of its location is that it was lodged within one of the animals that subsequently died within the cave. The tool was in close association with a badger (*Meles meles*) vertebrae but the latter has no sign of lesions that could have been inflicted during such an event.

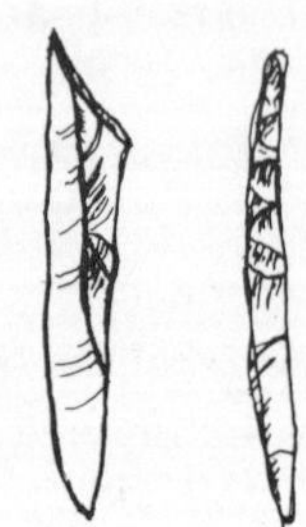

Figure 33. Mesolithic artefact found during the 1981 excavation of Steetley Cave.

VERTEBRATE PALAEOECOLOGY

Vertebrate remains were recovered during the 1976 exploration of the cave (Askew and Richardson *pers. comm.*). In this account, these are considered with those recovered from the spoil of this earlier excavation of the cave in 1980. The total collection consists of 63,178 vertebrate bone fragments which are described in

Table 18. Preservation of the bone was exceedingly good. A significant proportion, 72% of the total remains, allowed identification of mammals to species level and reptiles and amphibians to generic level. Unfortunately the remains in the spoil are unstratified. They were recovered from an infill in the front of the cave which averaged one metre in depth.

The four spit samples removed from *in situ* sediments during the 1980 excavations are described in *Table 19*. Although preservation of the bone was generally good, it was only possible to identify 41% of the total remains.

Large Vertebrates

The larger vertebrates known from the cave include the carnivores wildcat (*Felis sylvestris*), lynx (*Lynx lynx*), badger (*Meles meles*), and red fox (*Vulpes vulpes*), of which badger is the most frequent.

Ungulate species include wild pig (*Sus scrofa*), red deer (*Cervus elaphus*), roe deer (*Capreolus capreolus*), sheep (*Ovis aries*), and cow (*Bos* cf. *primigenious*). Smaller vertebrates include common shrew (*Sorex araneus*), mole (*Talpa europaea*), hedgehog (*Erinacaeus europaeus*) and the rodents red squirrel (*Sciurus vulgaris*), bank vole (*Clethrionmys glareolus*), rat (*Rattus rattus*), and mouse (*Apodemus* sp.). Bird species include tawny owl (*Strix aluco*), wood pigeon (*Columba palumbus*), blackbird (*Turdus merula*), jay (*Garrulus glandarius*) and a corvid. Amphibians represented the most numerous element in the fauna. The 1976 excavation revealed the remains of 2003 individuals and a further 385 individuals are known from the four spits excavated in 1980.

All of the species recorded are characteristic of woodland environment. Many of the smaller vertebrates prefer situations with extensive ground cover and litter. Some of the species (red squirrel and tawny owl) are confined to woodland habitats.

Amphibians

Whilst frog species are known from many caves where they are not necessarily associated with nearby water (Jenkinson 1984), in this instance the numbers of individuals are so great that this fact alone suggests the presence of nearby wet areas, perhaps of open water. The intact, ungnawed state of many of these frog remains argues against their being introduced by a selective predator on frog species. It also suggests actual occupation of the cave by these amphibians.

Analysis of remains from the 1980 samples (*Table 19*) indicates that there are considerable fluctuations in amphibian populations through time. The largest percentage of remains occurred in base spit 1, where 33% of the total amphibian fauna occurs. Spits 2 and 3 show a significant decrease in amphibian remains which only regain their former numbers in the highest level of the cave. It is interesting to speculate upon the origins of these fluctuations. They might be due to local changes in habitat. More likely they may be a direct result of colonisation of the cave by badgers, whereupon the subsequent disturbance would inhibit amphibian activity.

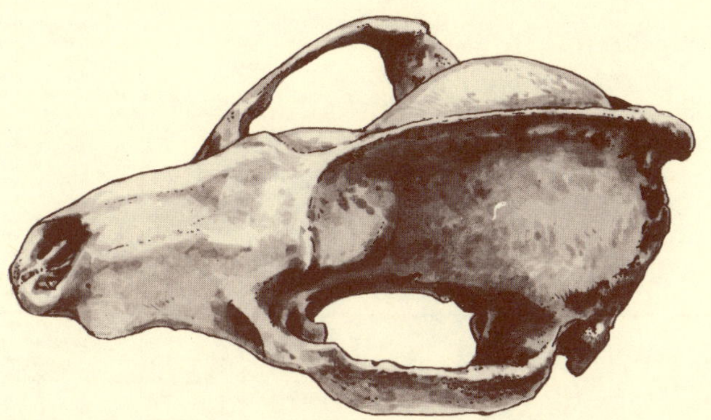

Badger skull

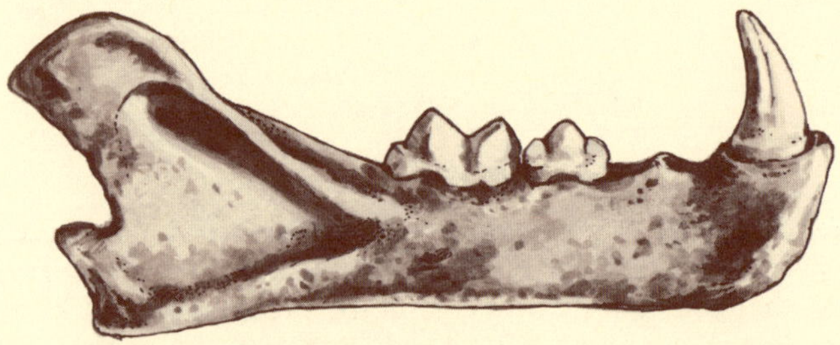

Lynx mandible

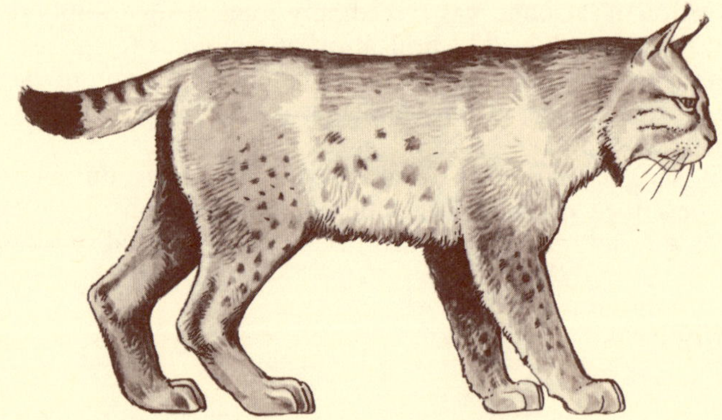

Table 18. Vertebrate fauna recovered from 1976 excavation in Steetley Cave.

ANATOMICAL VARIATION

	SKULL N	SKULL %	MANDIBLE N	MANDIBLE %	SEPARATE TEETH N	SEPARATE TEETH %	HORNS & ANTLERS N	HORNS & ANTLERS %	VERTEBRAE N	VERTEBRAE %	RIBS N	RIBS %	SCAPULA N	SCAPULA %
Common Shrew S. araenus	1	7.69	8	61.54	–	–	–	–	–	–	–	–	–	–
Mole T. europeaus	–	–	6	60.00	–	–	–	–	–	–	–	–	–	–
Hedgehog E. europeus	–	–	–	–	1	10.00	–	–	–	–	–	–	–	–
Wild Cat F. sylvestris	–	–	–	–	–	–	–	–	–	–	–	–	–	–
Northern Lynx F. lynx	–	–	2	33.33	–	–	–	–	–	–	–	–	–	–
Badger M. meles	5	2.62	3	1.57	5	2.62	–	–	13	6.81	21	10.99	4	2.09
Red Fox V. vulpes	–	–	–	–	–	–	–	–	1	4.35	–	–	2	8.70
Wild Pig S. scrofa	12	60.00	4	20.00	–	–	–	–	–	–	–	–	1	5.00
Red Deer C. elaphus	–	–	–	–	–	–	–	–	–	–	–	–	–	–
Roe Deer C. capreolus	2	33.33	–	–	–	–	–	–	–	–	–	–	–	–
Sheep O. aries	5	35.71	–	–	1	7.14	–	–	–	–	–	–	1	7.14
Cow Bos sp.	–	–	–	–	–	–	–	–	1	12.50	1	12.50	–	–
Bank Vole C. glareolus	1	3.57	19	67.86	8	28.57	–	–	–	–	–	–	–	–
Rat R. rattus	1	25.00	–	–	–	–	–	–	–	–	–	–	2	50.00
Mouse Apodemus sp.	4	28.57	7	50.00	3	21.43	–	–	–	–	–	–	–	–
Frog/Toad Rana sp.	1733	3.85	1995	4.43	–	–	–	–	2768	6.15	–	–	2356	5.24
Lizard Lacertidae sp.	–	–	33	100.00	–	–	–	–	–	–	–	–	–	–
INDETERMINATE. PISCES sp.	–	–	11	100.00	–	–	–	–	–	–	–	–	–	–
RODENTIA	22	8.59	5	1.95	106	41.41	–	–	–	–	–	–	8	3.13
MAMMALIA	21	10.14	–	–	5	2.42	–	–	38	18.36	91	43.96	–	–
INDET	–	–	–	–	–	–	–	–	–	–	–	–	–	–
AVES sp.	–	–	–	–	–	–	–	–	–	–	1	4.76	–	–
TOTAL IDENTIFIED FRAGMENTS	1764	3.89	2077	4.58	18	0.04	–	–	2783	6.13	22	0.05	2366	5.21
TOTAL INDETERMINATE FRAGMENTS	43	0.24	16	0.09	111	0.62	–	–	38	0.21	92	0.52	8	0.04
TOTAL FRAGMENTS	1807	2.86	2093	3.31	129	0.20	–	–	2821	4.47	114	0.18	2374	3.76
TOTAL INDIVIDUALS	–	–	–	–	–	–	–	–	–	–	–	–	–	–

	HUMERUS N	HUMERUS %	RADIUS N	RADIUS %	ULNA N	ULNA %	PELVIS N	PELVIS %	FEMUR N	FEMUR %	TIBIA N	TIBIA %	FIBULA N	FIBULA %	ASTRAGALUS N	ASTRAGALUS %
Common Shrew S. araenus	4	30.77	–	–	–	–	–	–	–	–	–	–	–	–	–	–
Mole T. europeaus	2	20.00	–	–	1	10.00	–	–	–	–	1	100.00	–	–	–	–
Hedgehog E. europeus	–	–	–	–	1	10.00	–	–	–	–	–	–	–	–	–	–
Wild Cat F. sylvestris	1	20.00	1	20.00	–	–	2	40.00	1	20.00	–	–	–	–	–	–
Northern Lynx F. lynx	1	16.67	–	–	–	–	–	–	–	–	1	16.67	–	–	–	–
Badger M. meles	40	20.94	7	3.66	14	7.33	13	6.81	27	14.14	22	11.52	–	–	1	0.52
Red Fox V. vulpes	4	17.39	–	–	2	8.70	1	4.35	3	13,04	8	30.43	–	–	–	–
Wild Pig S. scrofa	–	–	–	–	–	–	–	–	–	–	–	–	–	–	–	–
Red Deer C. elaphus	1	50.00	–	–	–	–	–	–	1	50.00	–	–	–	–	–	–
Roe Deer C. capreolus	–	–	–	–	–	–	–	–	–	–	–	–	–	–	1	16.67
Sheep O. aries	1	7.14	–	–	1	7.14	–	–	–	–	–	–	–	–	–	–
Cow Bos sp.	1	12.50	–	–	–	–	–	–	–	–	1	12.50	–	–	–	–
Bank Vole C. glareolus	–	–	–	–	–	–	–	–	–	–	–	–	–	–	–	–
Rat R. rattus	–	–	–	–	–	–	–	–	1	25.00	–	–	–	–	–	–
Mouse Apodemus sp.	–	–	–	–	–	–	–	–	–	–	–	–	–	–	–	–
Frog/Toad Rana sp.	2649	5.89	2363	5.25	–	–	3651	8.11	NOT SEPARATED	NOT SEPARATED	NOT SEPARATED	NOT SEPARATED	NOT SEPARATED	NOT SEPARATED	2801	6.23
Lizard Lacertidae sp.	–	–	–	–	–	–	–	–	–	–	–	–	–	–	–	–
INDETERMINATE. PISCES sp.	–	–	–	–	–	–	–	–	–	–	–	–	–	–	–	–
RODENTIA	22	8.59	4	1.56	19	7.41	20	7.81	31	12.11	16	6.25	–	–	–	–
MAMMALIA	3	1.45	3	1.45	3	1.45	1	0.48	4	1.93	2	0.97	–	–	–	–
INDET	–	–	–	–	–	–	–	–	–	–	–	–	–	–	–	–
AVES sp.	2	9.52	–	–	–	–	–	–	–	–	4	19.05	–	–	–	–
TOTAL IDENTIFIED FRAGMENTS	2704	5.96	2371	5.22	19	0.04	3667	8.08	33	0.07	33	0.07		–	2803	6.17
TOTAL INDETERMINATE FRAGMENTS	27	0.15	7	0.03	22	0.12	21	0.12	35	0.20	22	0.12			–	–
TOTAL FRAGMENTS	2731	4.32	2378	3.76	41	0.06	3688	5.84	68	0.11	55	0.09			2803	4.44
TOTAL INDIVIDUALS	–	–	–	–	–	–	–	–	–	–	–	–	–	–	–	–

	CALCANEUM N	CALCANEUM %	CUNEIFORMS N	CUNEIFORMS %	METATARSAL METACARPALS N	METATARSAL METACARPALS %	PHALANGES N	PHALANGES %	MISC BONES & FLAKES N	MISC BONES & FLAKES %	TOTAL INDIVIDUALS N	TOTAL INDIVIDUALS %	TOTAL BONES N	TOTAL BONES %
Common Shrew S. araenus	–	–	–	–	–	–	–	–	–	–	4	0.19	13	100.00
Mole T. europeaus	–	–	–	–	–	–	–	–	–	–	3	0.14	10	100.00
Hedgehog E. europeus	2	20.00	–	–	–	–	6	60.00	–	–	1	0.05	10	100.00
Wild Cat F. sylvestris	–	–	–	–	–	–	–	–	–	–	2	0.09	5	100.00
Northern Lynx F. lynx	–	–	–	–	–	–	2	33.33	–	–	1	0.05	6	100.00
Badger M. meles	2	1.05	–	–	2	1.05	11	5.76	1	0.52	22	1.06	191	100.00
Red Fox V. vulpes	1	4.35	–	–	–	–	2	8.70	–	–	4	0.19	24	100.01
Wild Pig S. scrofa	–	–	–	–	–	–	3	15.00	–	–	4	0.19	20	100.00
Red Deer C. elaphus	–	–	–	–	–	–	–	–	–	–	:	0.05	2	100.00
Roe Deer C. capreolus	–	–	–	–	1	16.67	2	33.33	–	–	1	0.05	6	100.00
Sheep O. aries	2	14.29	–	–	3	21.43	–	–	–	–	3	0.14	14	99.99
Cow Bos sp.	1	12.50	1	12.50	1	12.50	1	12.50	–	–	1	0.05	8	100.00
Bank Vole C. glareolus	–	–	–	–	–	–	–	–	–	–	11	0.33	28	100.00
Rat R. rattus	–	–	–	–	–	–	–	–	–	–	1	0.05	4	100.00
Mouse Apodemus sp.	–	–	–	–	–	–	–	–	–	–	4	0.19	14	100.00
Frog/Toad Rana sp.	–	–	–	–					24679	54.85	2003	96.34	44995	100.00
Lizard Lacertidae sp.	–	–	–	–	–	–	–	–	–	–	21	1.01	33	100.00
INDETERMINATE. PISCES sp.	–	–	–	–	–	–	–	–	–	–	–	–	11	100.00
RODENTIA	–	–	–	–	–	–	3	1.17	–	–	–	–	256	99.99
MAMMALIA	1	0.48	–	–	4	1.93	8	3.86	23	11.11	–	–	207	99.99
INDET	–	–	–	–	–	–	–	–	17290	100.00	–	–	17290	100.00
AVES sp.	–	–	–	–	8	38.09	1	4.76	5	23.81	–	–	21	99.99
TOTAL IDENTIFIED FRAGMENTS	8	0.02	1	0.01	7	0.02	27	0.06	24680	54.38	–	–	45383	71.84
TOTAL INDETERMINATE FRAGMENTS	1	0.01	–	–	12	0.08	12	0.08	17318	97.37	–	–	17785	28.16
TOTAL FRAGMENTS	9	0.02	1	0.00	19	0.03	39	0.06	41998	66.49	–		63168	100.00
TOTAL INDIVIDUALS	–	–	–	–	–	–	–	–	–	–	2079	100.03	–	–

Table 19. Vertebrate fauna from the 1980 excavation in Steetley Cave.

ANATOMICAL VARIATION	SKULL		MANDIBLE		SEPARATE TEETH		HORNS & ANTLERS		VERTEBRAE		RIBS		SCAPULA		HUMERUS / RADIUS		ULNA		PELVIS	
	N	%	N	%	N	%	N	%	N	%	N	%	N	%	N	%	N	%	N	%
SPIT SPECIES: 1 Badger M meles	–	–	–	–	1	50.00	1	50.00	–	–	–	–	–	–	–	–	–	–	–	–
Frog/Toad Rana sp	19	1.07	121	6.82	–	–	52	2.93	–	–	100	5.64	141	7.95	132	7.44	–	–	201	11.33
Lizard Lacertidae sp	–	–	1	50.00	–	–	–	–	–	–	–	–	1	50.00	–	–	–	–	–	–
INDETERMINATE: FRAGMENTS	–	–	–	–	1	0.03	–	–	–	–	–	–	–	–	–	–	–	–	–	–
TOTAL FRAGMENTS	19	0.37	122	2.37	2	0.04	53	1.03	–	–	100	1.95	142	2.76	132	2.57	–	–	201	3.91
TOTAL INDIVIDUALS	–	–	–	–	–	–	–	–	–	–	–	–	–	–	–	–	–	–	–	–
SPIT SPECIES: 2 Mouse Apodemus sp	–	–	1	25.00	3	75.00	–	–	–	–	–	–	–	–	–	–	–	–	–	–
Frog Rana sp	44	2.98	87	5.90	–	–	75	5.08	–	–	61	4.14	89	6.03	93	6.31	–	–	133	9.02
INDETERMINATE: FRAGMENTS	–	–	–	–	–	–	–	–	–	–	–	–	–	–	–	–	–	–	–	–
TOTAL FRAGMENTS	44	1.54	88	3.07	3	0.10	75	2.62	–	–	61	2.13	89	3.11	93	3.24	–	–	133	4.64
TOTAL INDIVIDUALS	–	–	–	–	–	–	–	–	–	–	–	–	–	–	–	–	–	–	–	–
SPIT SPECIES: 3 Mole T europeus	–	–	–	–	–	–	–	–	–	–	–	–	–	–	–	–	1	100.00	–	–
Frog Rana sp	37	2.79	97	7.30	–	–	118	8.89	–	–	61	4.59	90	6.78	75	5.65	–	–	110	8.28
Lizard Lacertidae sp	–	–	1	50.00	–	–	–	–	–	–	1	50.00	–	–	–	–	–	–	–	–
INDETERMINATE: FRAGMENTS	–	–	–	–	8	0.54	–	–	–	–	–	–	–	–	–	–	–	–	2	0.14
TOTAL FRAGMENTS	37	1.32	98	3.50	8	0.29	118	4.21	–	–	62	2.21	90	3.21	75	2.67	1	0.04	112	3.99
TOTAL INDIVIDUALS	–	–	–	–	–	–	–	–	–	–	–	–	–	–	–	–	–	–	–	–
SPIT SPECIES. 4 Frog Rana sp	36	2.56	95	6.77	–	–	62	4.42	–	–	55	3.92	118	8.40	94	6.70	–	–	160	11.40
Lizard Lacertidae sp	–	–	–	–	–	–	–	–	–	–	–	–	–	–	–	–	–	–	–	–
Fish Pisces sp	–	–	1	100.00	–	–	–	–	–	–	–	–	–	–	–	–	–	–	–	–
INDETERMINATE: FRAGMENTS	–	–	–	–	12	0.47	–	–	–	–	–	–	2	0.08	1	0.04	1	0.04	2	0.08
TOTAL FRAGMENTS	36	0.91	96	2.44	12	0.30	62	1.58	–	–	55	1.40	120	3.05	95	2.41	1	0.03	162	4.12
TOTAL INDIVIDUALS	–	–	–	–	–	–	–	–	–	–	–	–	–	–	–	–	–	–	–	–
TOTAL EXCAVATED FRAGMENTS	–	–	–	–	–	–	–	–	–	–	–	–	–	–	–	–	–	–	–	–

ANATOMICAL VARIATION	FEMUR		TIBIA		FIBULA		ASTRAGALUS		CALCANEUM		CUNEIFORMS / METATARSAL METACARPALS		PHALANGES		MISC BONES & FLAKES		TOTAL INDIVIDUALS		TOTAL BONES	
	N	%	N	%	N	%	N	%	N	%	N	%	N	%	N	%	N	%	N	%
SPIT SPECIES: 1 Badger M meles	–	–	–	–	–	–	–	–	–	–	–	–	–	–	–	–	1	0.88	2	100.00
Frog/Toad Rana sp	–	–	–	–	–	–	207	11.67	–	–	–	–	–	–	801	45.15	111	98.24	1774	100.00
Lizard Lacertidae sp	–	–	–	–	–	–	–	–	–	–	–	–	–	–	–	–	1	0.88	2	100.00
INDETERMINATE: FRAGMENTS	–	–	–	–	–	–	–	–	–	–	–	–	2	0.06	3360	99.91	–	–	3363	100.00
TOTAL FRAGMENTS	–	–	–	–	–	–	–	–	–	–	–	–	2	0.04	4161	80.94	–	–	5141	100.01
TOTAL INDIVIDUALS	–	–	–	–	–	–	–	–	–	–	–	–	–	–	–	–	113	100.00	–	–
SPIT SPECIES: 2 Mouse Apodemus sp	–	–	–	–	–	–	–	–	–	–	–	–	–	–	–	–	1	1.33	4	100.00
Frog Rana sp	–	–	–	–	–	–	108	7.32	–	–	–	–	–	–	785	53.22	74	98.67	1475	100.00
INDETERMINATE: FRAGMENTS	–	–	–	–	–	–	–	–	–	–	–	–	–	–	1387	100.00	–	–	1387	100.00
TOTAL FRAGMENTS	–	–	–	–	–	–	108	3.77	–	–	–	–	–	–	2172	75.79	–	–	2866	100.01
TOTAL INDIVIDUALS	–	–	–	–	–	–	–	–	–	–	–	–	–	–	–	–	75	100.00	–	–
SPIT SPECIES: 3 Mole T europeus	–	–	–	–	–	–	–	–	–	–	–	–	–	–	–	–	1	1.37	1	100.00
Frog Rana sp	–	–	–	–	–	–	88	6.63	–	–	–	–	–	–	652	49.10	71	97.26	1328	100.01
Lizard Lacertidae sp	–	–	–	–	–	–	–	–	–	–	–	–	–	–	–	–	1	1.37	2	100.00
INDETERMINATE: FRAGMENTS	1	0.07	–	–	–	–	–	–	–	–	–	–	–	–	1462	99.25	–	–	1473	100.00
TOTAL FRAGMENTS	1	0.04	–	–	–	–	88	3.14	–	–	–	–	–	–	2114	75.39	–	–	2804	100.01
TOTAL INDIVIDUALS	–	–	–	–	–	–	–	–	–	–	–	–	–	–	–	–	73	100.00	—	–
SPIT SPECIES. 4 Frog Rana sp	–	–	–	–	–	–	107	7.62	–	–	–	–	–	–	677	48.22	129	98.47	1404	100.01
Lizard Lacertidae sp	–	–	–	–	–	–	–	–	–	–	–	–	–	–	1	100.00	1	0.76	1	100.00
Fish Pisces sp	–	–	–	–	–	–	–	–	–	–	–	–	–	–	–	–	1	0.76	1	100.00
INDETERMINATE: FRAGMENTS	–	–	1	0.04	–	–	–	–	–	–	–	–	–	–	2510	99.25	–	–	2529	100.00
TOTAL FRAGMENTS	–	–	1	0.03	–	–	107	2.72	–	–	–	–	–	–	3188	81.02	–	–	3935	100.01
TOTAL INDIVIDUALS	–	–	–	–	–	–	–	–	–	–	–	–	–	–	–	–	131	99.99	–	–
TOTAL EXCAVATED FRAGMENTS	–	–	–	–	–	–	–	–	–	–	–	–	–	–	–	–	–	–	14 746	–

Origins of the Vertebrate Fauna

The origin of bone fragments for larger species is most likely the result of two types of events:

(i) occupation of the cave by badgers;
(ii) scavenging by lynx and fox.

The carnivore remains, particularly those of badger, are derived from individuals of all ages. For badger, 36% of the individuals are foetal. Few of the carnivore bones are broken, most are complete, and have no trace of gnawing or teeth marks. Both of these observations suggest cave residence by badgers.

Ungulate species known from the 1976 spoil are typically represented by manus and pes parts and few of these are undamaged (*Table 18*). It is likely that their presence within the cave is due to scavenging activity by the carnivores, particularly lynx and fox.

The vertebrate fauna indicates that the sediments collected in a temperate interglacial climate, probably the present Flandrian warm stage.

MOLLUSCAN PALAEOECOLOGY

Molluscan remains were collected from the 1980 excavations in Steetley Cave and analysed as described in *Chapter 3*. The majority of identifications are based upon identifiable apices; shell fragments were assigned to taxonomic groups and their frequency noted (*Table 20*). The total number of specimens found was very low, as was the range of species. Preservation of larger taxa was poor, as the shells appeared to have been crushed, with only smaller, flatter species such as *Oxychilus* and *Discus* surviving intact.

Analysis

Detailed ecological reconstruction based upon these results is not possible owing to the limited numbers of specimens recovered. The species found are all land snails and many are fairly ubiquitous, to be found in a range of habitats including damp rocks and screes. *Oxychilus cellarius* in particular can be found in caves and as a carnivorous snail its presence might indicate that some form of carrion was being consumed.

Table 20. Molluscs recovered from the 1980 excavation in Steetley Cave.

Sample	Spit 4	Spit 1	1976 spoil
Species			
Cochlicopa lubrica (Müller)	1		
Discus rotundatus (Müller)	1		4
Oxychilus cellarius (Müller)	5		1
Zonitidae (fragments)	+	+	+
Clausilia spp.	3		1
Cepaea sp.	1	1	4
Cepaea (fragments)	+	+	+

Oxychilus, Discus rotundatus and the Clausiliidae are all temperate species, suggesting the climate was not markedly colder than prevails today. *Discus rotundatus* together with members of the Clausiliidae family are usually taken as evidence of temperate woodland, but like *Oxychilus* may have been actually occupying the cave. This molluscan fauna provides one measure of the age of this cave's deposits. Dr. M.P. Kerney (1977) has identified the age at which various molluscan species recolonised the British Isles from their retreats in southern Europe in which they lived during the most recent period of extensive glaciation in Britain, approximately 20,000–14,000 years ago. The presence of *Oxychilus cellarius* suggests the deposits collected more recently than 8,400 years ago; the lack of the nowadays ubiquitous 'Roman' snail—*Helix aspersa*—indicates accumulation took place before the Roman period. The period of cave deposit formation is therefore seen to belong to an interglacial period, quite probably the present Flandrian interglacial stage.

PALYNOLOGY AND ALGAL MICROFOSSILS

Methods

Four samples, from 0.0m, 0.60m, 0.77m and 1.05m were boiled in KOH, sieved over 10 micron nylon mesh to remove clay, and swirled on a watch glass to remove silt and sand, as described more fully in Hunt (1984). 150–250 pollen grains were counted from each sample. Algal microfossils were also counted. The results were calculated as percentages of total Quaternary pollen and spores (*Figure 34*).

Palaeoecology

The counts from the samples from 0.0, 0.6 and 0.77m suggest that the vegetation outside the cave was woodland, dominated by *Tilia* (lime), *Pinus* (pine) and *Corylus* (Hazel). The count from the sample from 1.05m shows an increase in pollen of Gramineae (grasses). This suggests a break in the woodland canopy, which might have been due to the fall of a nearby tree or the product of clearance by man.

The very high counts of *Tilia* pollen, especially in the two lower samples, are anomalous, since this tree is a very low producer of pollen. It is unlikely that the *Tilia* pollen is over-represented by differential weathering, since all the pollen in the samples was well preserved. It is possible that the *Tilia* pollen was concentrated in the cave in the dung of herbivores, since *Tilia* has nutritious foliage (Pennington 1974:75). Alternatively, badgers might have brought *Tilia* branches into the cave as bedding.

Marsh species are more common in the samples from 0.6, 0.77 and 1.05m than in the sample from 0.0m. *Alnus*, a tree characteristic of damp ground, is present in the sample from 0.77m, as are the marsh cryptogams *Lycopodium* and *Sphagnum*. The high counts of algal microfossils, especially in the sample from 0.77m, suggests at least seasonal, standing water in the cave; the peak of reworked pre-Quaternary spores in the sample from 0.77m may reflect transport into the cave by running water. Since conditions both inside and outside the cave became wetter, it is suspected that climatic factors (increased precipitation or reduced evaporation) are responsible, rather than some local hydrological change.

The high counts of fern spores are typical of cave deposits (Campbell 1977, Gale and Hunt in prep.), probably because of the suitability of the cave-mouth environment for the growth of ferns (Lloyd 1977).

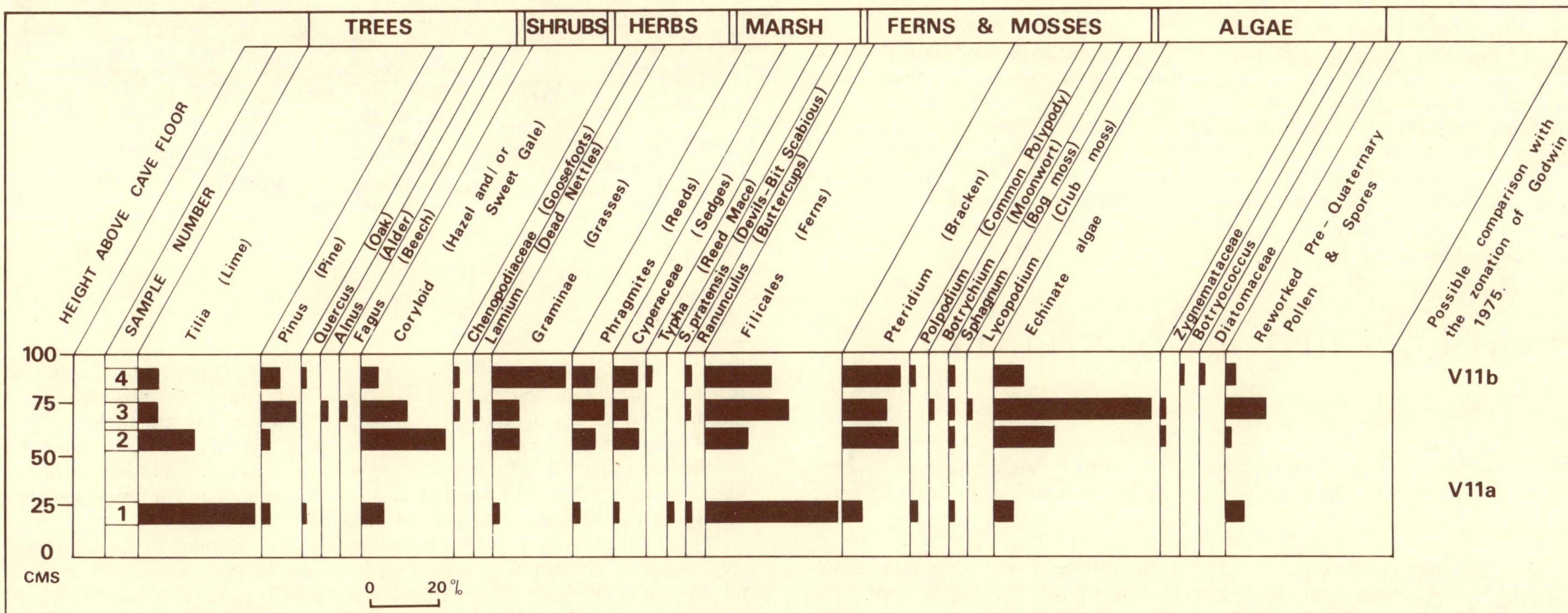

Figure 34. Pollen diagram showing the frequency of plant species recovered from 1981 excavations at Steetley Cave.

Pre-Quaternary Spores and Pollen

Most of the pre-Quaternary species are derived from Carboniferous rocks. They are mostly attributable to the genus *Lycospora*. Pollen grains of the genera *Classopollis, Araucariacites* and *Cerebropollenites* are derived from Mesozoic deposits. It is probable that these species have been reworked into the cave from some type of nearby glacial deposit. The local Magnesian limestone is usually barren of pollen and spores, so the absence of Permian species is not surprising.

Dating

No pollen diagrams have yet been constructed for local Flandrian deposits, hence biostratigraphic correlation or dating are necessarily tentative. The tree-dominated pollen diagram suggests a mid-Flandrian date, and the presence of *Tilia* suggests a date of Godwin's (1975) Zone VIc or later (*Tilia* is not known in the U.K. before Zone VIc in the Flandrian). If the increase in Gramineae pollen in sample 1 indicates clearance, this would be assigned to Godwin's Zone VIIb. It is thus probable that the section was laid down in a relatively short time around 5000 years bp (*c.* 3000 yrs bc).

In brief, the plant microfossils reflect a lime-pine-hazel woodland, with possible signs of clearance at the top of the pollen diagram. The composition of this woodland cover is notably different to that found in the area today (*Chapter 2*). There was a peak of wetness in sample 3 from 0.77m, probably caused by climatic factors. The deposit is about 5000 years old, and has been substantially influenced by badger denning.

FLANDRIAN HISTORY OF STEETLEY CAVE

Analysis of the resistivity survey, sediments, vertebrate bones, molluscs and pollen from the excavations within Steetley Cave suggest a sequence of Flandrian events.

Oldest

1. The accumulation of poorly sorted sediments derived from *in situ* weathering of the bedrock in the near empty cave rear. It is likely that the cave entrance detected by geophysical methods was open at this time.
2. Colonisation of the cave by badgers and the introduction of increased quantities of organic remains resulting in the higher levels of phosphorus detected in the sediments. Badgers, who go to great lengths to find suitable bedding material in these habitation areas, were no doubt introducing vegetable matter from the surrounding woodland which was dominated by *Tilia, Pinus* and *Corylus*. The presence nearby of a marsh area is indicated by amphibian remains and by marsh plant species. Finds of algal fossils indicate that conditions in the cave during this period were damp and at times probably pools of standing water were present inside the cave.
3. Eventually, the activity of badgers transporting sediment into the cave on their feet, coupled with natural erosion of the limestone bedrock, had almost entirely filled the area available. At this time human activity in the area is indicated by the presence of a Mesolithic point, most likely lodged in one of the badgers which subsequently died in the rear of the cave. Finally, the infilled cave became unsuitable for badger occupation.

DISCUSSION

This palaeoecological and geomorphological research at Steetley Cave provides useful evidence of Flandrian warm stage developments which are poorly understood at other sites. From the palaeontological viewpoint this cave provides a well stratified occurrence of a pollen zone VIc–VIIb vertebrate and molluscan fauna. Of particular note in this respect are the species badger (*Meles meles*), lynx (*Lynx lynx*), wildcat (*Felis sylvestris*), red squirrel (*Sciurus vulgaris*), and roe deer (*Capreolus capreolus*) which are otherwise poorly documented during this period. Some of these species are also recorded from the Early Flandrian at Dog Hole Fissure (*Chapter 3*).

Pollen, spores and algal microfossils recovered from the cave provide an insight into local vegetational development during the mid-Flandrian. The derivation of pre-Quaternary pollen and spores from earlier deposits is demonstrated; these offer the possibility of locating sources for the cave sediments. The algal microfossils indicate that the cave environment was very moist at times.

The results of the sedimentary analyses to detect geomorphological processes prevalent in a cave during the Flandrian, underlines the need to elucidate environmental conditions at work within particular cave types. In this case the stability of geomorphological events contrasts with the processes known from the Dog Hole Fissure site, which is of broadly similar age.

Bramwell, D., Cartledge, K.M., Gilbertson, D.D., Griffin, C.M., Hunt, C.O., Jenkinson, R.D.S. and Samson, C. 1984. Steetley Quarry Cave: A 'Lost' Interglacial Site and Steetley Cave: A 5000 year old Badger Den. Chapter 4 in Jenkinson, R.D.S. and Gilbertson, D.D. *In the Shadow of Extinction: A Quaternary Archaeology and Palaeoecology of the Lake, Fissures and Smaller Caves at Creswell Crags SSSI.* Sheffield: Department of Prehistory and Archaeology, University of Sheffield. Pp. 75 to 88.

PART III MIGRATION, COLONISATION AND EXTINCTION AT CRESWELL CRAGS

CHAPTER 5: THE BIRDS OF BRITAIN: WHEN DID THEY ARRIVE?

with D. Bramwell

CONTENTS

Fossil bird faunas from Devensian and early Flandrian deposits in the Creswell Crags Caves are described. The nature of the recolonisation of mainland Britain by birds is discussed. The bird fossils from Pin Hole Cave and Robin Hood's Cave demonstrate that a remarkably diverse avifauna was present in the last cold stage, particularly during its closing phases. The arctic/tundra-type avifaunas which dominated the Devensian were replaced by a woodland bird fauna during its closing episodes. The more limited evidence from early Flandrian deposits suggests a continued shift towards dominance by woodland species. This contrasts with recent discussions which suggest that the recolonisation of mainland Britain by woodland bird species took place during the Flandrian *not* in the final episodes of the Devensian.

INTRODUCTION

Late Quaternary bird fossils have been recovered from a number of localities in Britain, particularly from caves with deposits dating to the Devensian Cold Stage, i.e. approximately 80–10,000 years bp (Bramwell 1960). Despite the relative abundance of such evidence, few attempts have been made at reconstructing the bird geography of the Quaternary in Europe. Initial studies by Stresemann (1948), Clark (1948), Moreau (1954) and Bramwell (1960) provided a basis of interpretation of European bird geography during the Late Pleistocene.

Moreau (1954:430) suggested that a rich bird fauna was present in the sub-arctic summers which were characteristic of much of the Devensian cold stage in northern Europe. These faunas were thought not to contain arboreal species. The appearance of arboreal species in mainland Britain has been suggested to date from the appearance of woodland during the early Flandrian, *not earlier than 8–10,000 years bp* (Moreau 1954, Yalden 1982).

This paper reports recent work on a large collection of fossil bird bones from Devensian sediments within the Creswell Crags caves. The new evidence suggests that these traditional views of the recolonisation of mainland Britain by woodland birds may need to be reviewed.

FOSSIL LOCALITIES

A significant quantity of bird fossils were recovered from the Creswell Caves by Armstrong (1926, 1929, 1940) and earlier workers (Mello 1875, 1876; Dawkins 1876). Often bird remains were abundant, but much material remains undescribed and uninterpreted. In his Pin Hole Cave studies, Armstrong recorded all excavated items in two dimensions, the details being marked upon the specimens. A number of attempts have been made since Armstrong's death to interpret his excavations—notably by Kitching (1963) and Campbell (1977). Both of these authors expressed doubts on the accuracy of Armstrong's records. Recent archival research by Jenkinson (1984) established the exact nature of the excavation and recording methods used by Armstrong. This development has subsequently allowed a full review of his work in the cave (Jenkinson 1984) and has both clarified the age of the deposits and underlined the importance of the site for British Late Quaternary vertebrate studies. Important bird faunas are also known from Robin Hood's Cave (*Figure 35*), in Jenkinson (1984) and from the work of Campbell (1969) who dealt with late-Devensian deposits.

Preliminary analysis of the bird remains recovered by Armstrong was undertaken by Newton (unpublished) at the British Museum (Natural History), and subsequently by Bramwell who has recently completed the identification of all recorded bird bones from the caves. The other specimens included in this study have been recovered from recent excavations in Steetley Cave and Dog Hole Fissure (*Chapters 3 and 4*).

All extant specimens discussed in this study are currently housed in either the University of Manchester Museum or the Creswell Crags Visitor Centre. Avifauna nomenclature follows that set out by Gruson (1976).

Pin Hole Cave

This small cave is located within the northern outcrop of the Creswell gorge (*Figure 5*). It was first described by Mello (1875) whose excavations were confined to a small trench in the entrance area. Examination of the cave by Armstrong (1928) showed that the cave was more extensive than previously assumed. Armstrong subsequently undertook a prolonged campaign of excavations from 1924 and sporadically until 1935 and published a number of excavation accounts before his death in 1959 (Armstrong 1926, 1929). Interpretation of Armstrong's excavation has been confused by a misunderstanding of his recording techniques.

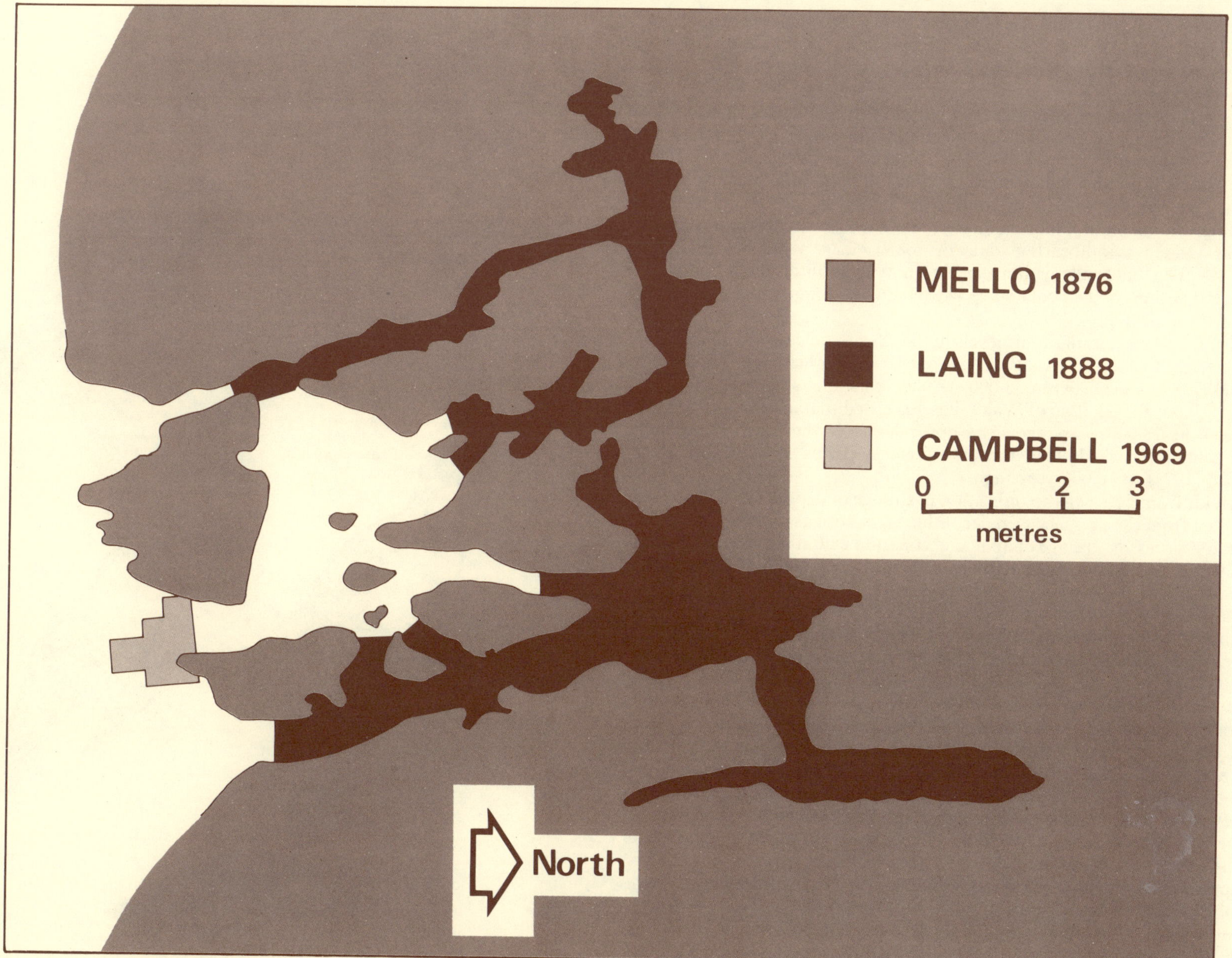

Figure 35. Ground plan of Robin Hood's Cave showing excavated areas.

This problem has been reviewed by Jenkinson (1984) who noted that Armstrong's excavation could be separated into twenty 0.30m levels in the cave. Using his records, a large number of Armstrong's original finds from the cave can be assigned to these levels.

The cave is well known for its evidence of palaeolithic human occupation which includes at least two separate middle palaeolithic and two upper palaeolithic industries.

The presence of middle palaeolithic artefacts in stratigraphic levels 8–13 demonstrate that these deposits date to an early period in the last cold stage or earlier. A single fragment of reindeer (*Rangifer tarandus*) antler from stratigraphic level 12 has yielded a radiocarbon date of 38850±2500 years BP (Scott and Hughes 1981). This date falls within the Upton Warren interstadial complex, a warmer period within the last cold stage where summer temperatures sometimes approached those of today.

The age of the higher stratigraphic levels in the cave is indicated by the presence of upper palaeolithic artefacts of early upper palaeolithic type, thought by Campbell (1977) to date between 38,000–18,000 years ago. Jacobi (1980), in his study of the Upper Palaeolithic of Wales, has suggested that artefacts of this type date between 30–28,000 years ago. The upper levels of the cave, stratigraphic levels 1–4, contain a backed blade industry of later upper palaeolithic type, dated by Campbell (1977) to 10,000 years ago.

Although far from perfect as an indication of the age of deposits in this cave, the ages suggested from the presence of palaeolithic stone tool assemblages provide a framework for discussing the age of animal occupation within the cave. These data suggest that the cave has deposits dating to the early (levels 20–14), mid (8–13) and late parts of the last cold stage in Britain.

Vertebrate fossil bones from the cave were initially reported by Jackson (1962) and Kitching (1963), and these have been reviewed by Campbell (1977). A total of 22,516 vertebrate specimens from the cave have recently been re-examined by Jenkinson (1984).

The list of vertebrates from the cave is extensive and is dominated by large cold stage species of Devensian age (Jenkinson 1984). The rich bird fauna component has recently been identified by Bramwell. The results of this analysis are set out in *Table 25*, and *Figures 36* and *37*, where the 102 recorded bird species are plotted according to the twenty 0.30m thick layers excavated by Armstrong. The recently obtained evidence used to date these sequences is also summarised in *Table 25*.

It can be seen in these tables of fossil bird finds that relatively large numbers of individuals are recorded for kestrel (*Falco tinnunculus*), red grouse (*Lagopus lagopus*), ptarmigan (*Lagopus mutus*), skylark (*Alauda arvensis*), jackdaw (*Corvus monedula*), blackbird (*Turdus merula*), redwing (*Turdus iliacus*) and songthrush (*Turdus philomelos*). Many remaining species are known in only low numbers or as single individuals. Of particular note is the more or less continuous presence of the Galliformes, red grouse (*Lagopus lagopus*) and ptarmigan (*Lagopus mutus*). Falcons are also continuously present, particularly kestrel (*Falco tinnunculus*) with

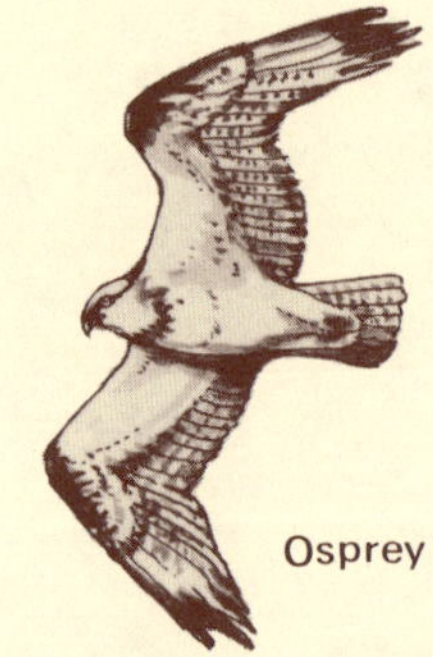

Osprey

Golden Eagle

Ptarmigan

Woodpecker

Goldeneye

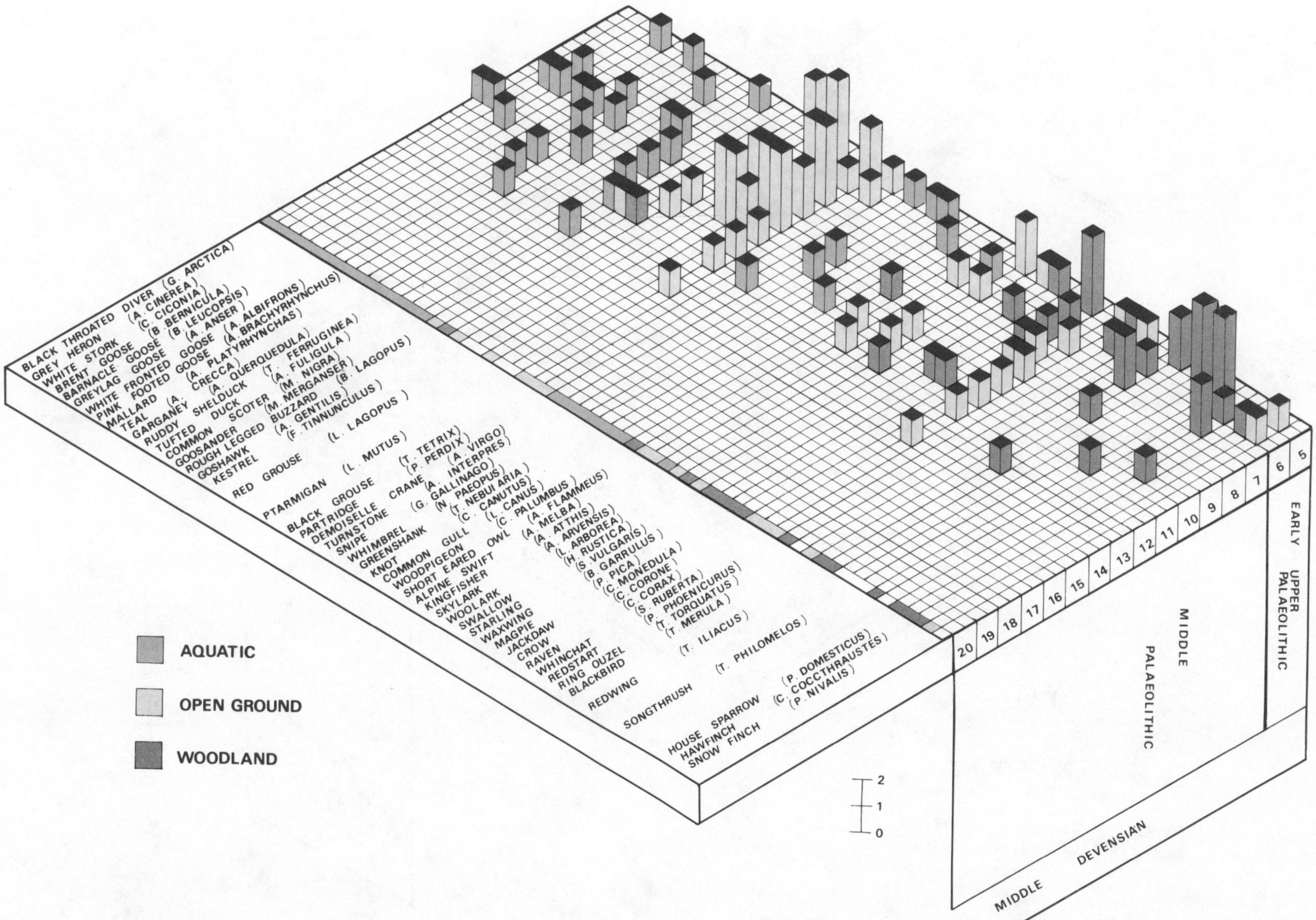

Figure 36. Diagram showing the frequency of Mid Devensian birds and their habitats from Pin Hole Cave.

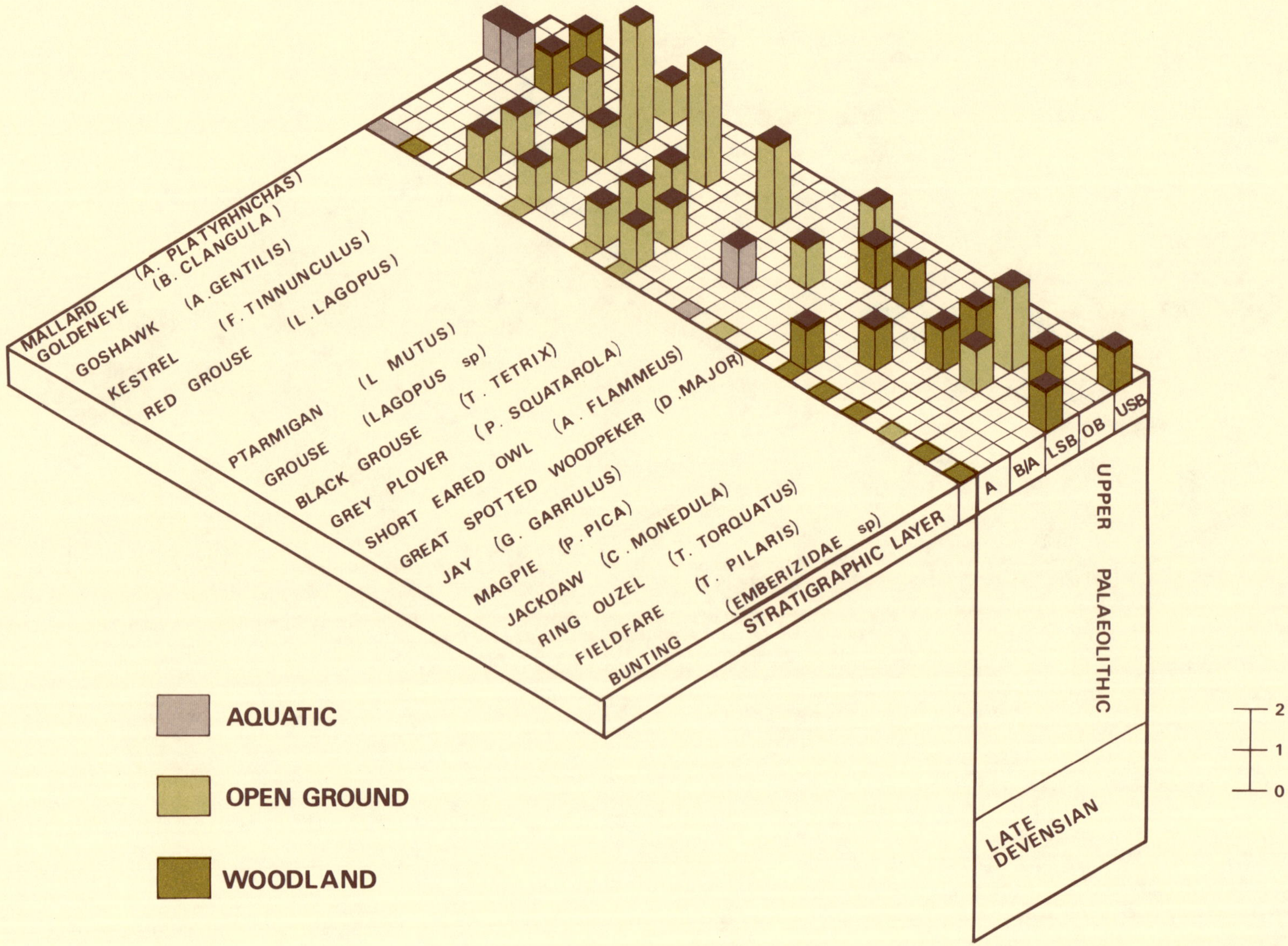

Figure 37. Diagram showing the frequency of Late Devensian birds from their habitats from Pin Hole and Robin Hood's Cave.

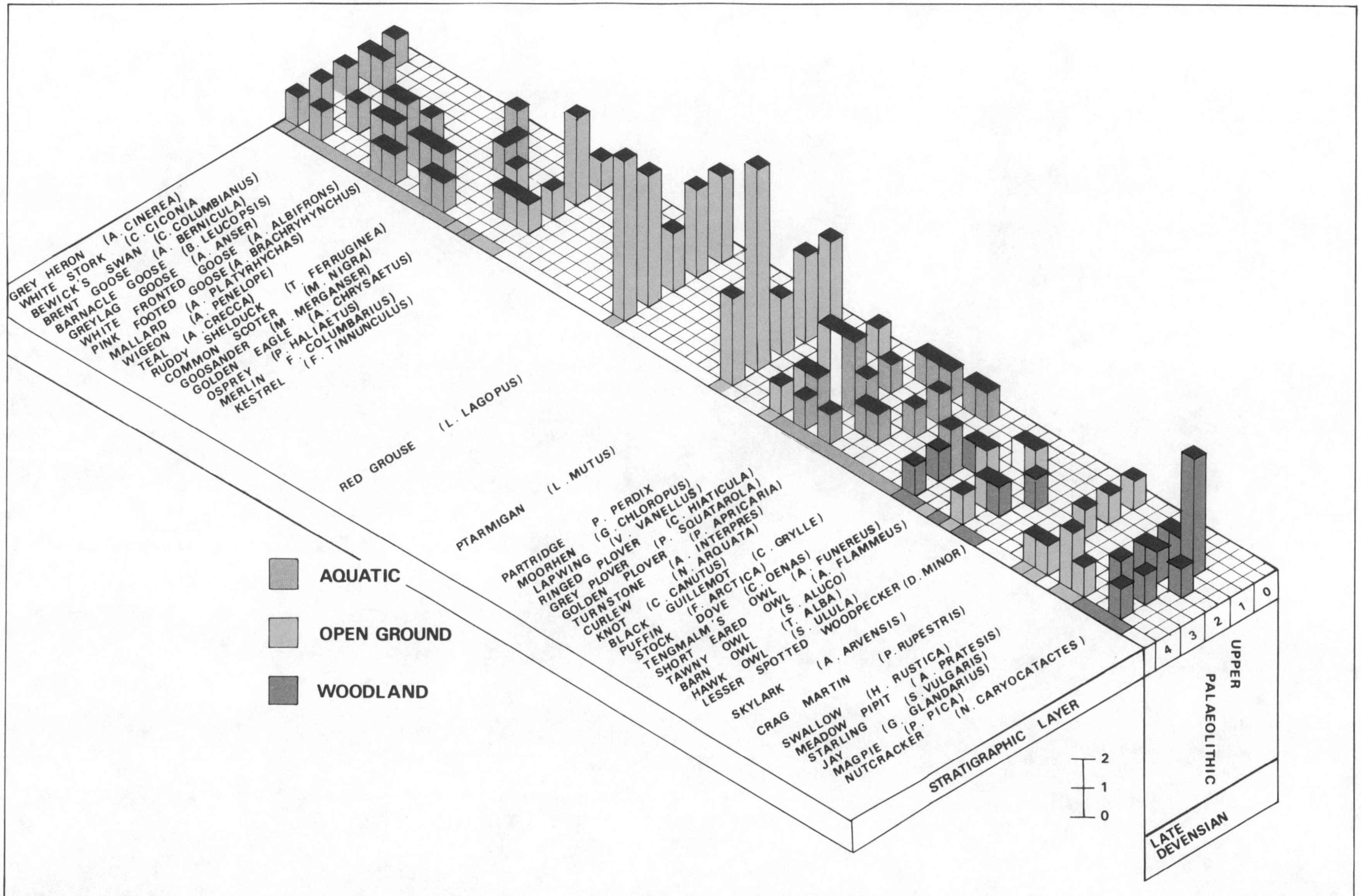
GREY HERON (A. CINEREA)
WHITE STORK (C. CICONIA
BEWICK'S SWAN (C. COLUMBIANUS)
BRENT GOOSE (B. BERNICULA)
BARNACLE GOOSE (B. LEUCOPSIS)
GREYLAG GOOSE (A. ANSER)
WHITE FRONTED GOOSE (A. ALBIFRONS)
PINK FOOTED GOOSE (A. BRACHRYHYNCHUS)
MALLARD (A. PLATYRHYCHAS)
WIGEON (A. PENELOPE)
TEAL (A. CRECCA)
RUDDY SHELDUCK (T. FERRUGINEA)
COMMON SCOTER (M. NIGRA)
GOOSANDER (M. MERGANSER)
GOLDEN EAGLE (A. CHRYSAETUS)
OSPREY (P. HALIAETUS)
MERLIN F. COLUMBARIUS)
KESTREL (F. TINNUNCULUS)
RED GROUSE (L. LAGOPUS)
PTARMIGAN (L. MUTUS)
PARTRIDGE P. PERDIX
MOORHEN (G. CHLOROPUS)
LAPWING (V. VANELLUS)
RINGED PLOVER (C. HIATICULA)
GREY PLOVER (P. SQUATAROLA)
GOLDEN PLOVER (P. APRICARIA)
TURNSTONE (A. INTERPRES)
CURLEW (N. ARQUATA)
KNOT (C. CANUTUS)
BLACK GUILLEMOT (C. GRYLLE)
PUFFIN (F. ARCTICA)
STOCK DOVE (C. OENAS)
TENGMALM'S OWL (A. FUNEREUS)
SHORT EARED OWL (A. FLAMMEUS)
TAWNY OWL (S. ALUCO)
BARN OWL (T. ALBA)
HAWK OWL (S. ULULA)
LESSER SPOTTED WOODPECKER (D. MINOR)
SKYLARK (A. ARVENSIS)
CRAG MARTIN (P. RUPESTRIS)
SWALLOW (H. RUSTICA)
MEADOW PIPIT (A. PRATESIS)
STARLING (S. VULGARIS)
JAY (G. GLANDARIUS)
MAGPIE (P. PICA)
NUTCRACKER (N. CARYOCATACTES)
AQUATIC
OPEN GROUND
WOODLAND
STRATIGRAPHIC LAYER
0 1 2 3 4
UPPER PALAEOLITHIC
LATE DEVENSIAN
2
1
0

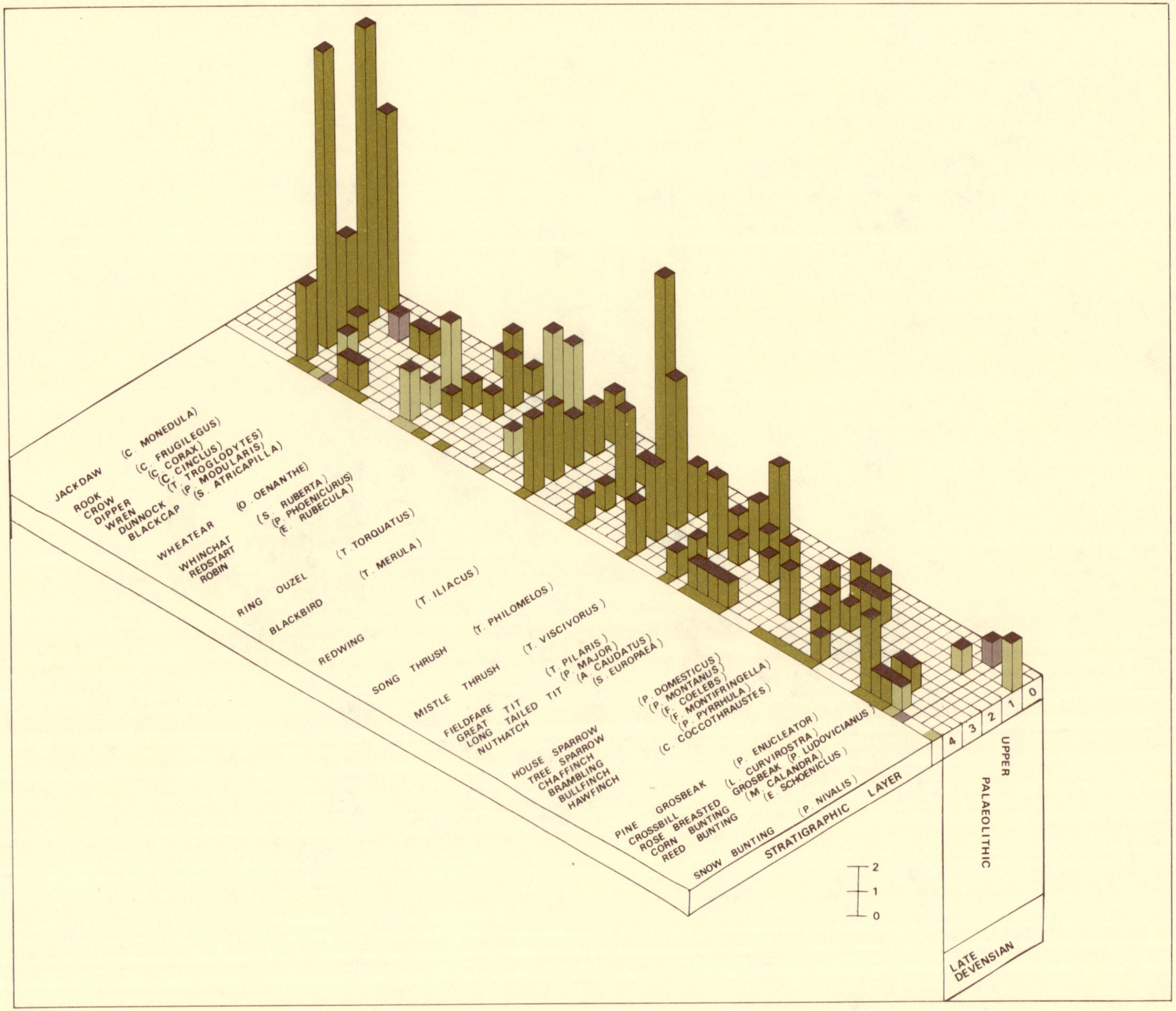

JACKDAW (C. MONEDULA)
ROOK (C. FRUGILEGUS)
CROW (C. CORAX)
DIPPER (C. CINCLUS)
WREN (T. TROGLODYTES)
DUNNOCK (P. MODULARIS)
BLACKCAP (S. ATRICAPILLA)
WHEATEAR (O. OENANTHE)
WHINCHAT (S. RUBERTA)
REDSTART (P. PHOENICURUS)
ROBIN (E. RUBECULA)
RING OUZEL (T. TORQUATUS)
BLACKBIRD (T. MERULA)
REDWING (T. ILIACUS)
SONG THRUSH (T. PHILOMELOS)
MISTLE THRUSH (T. VISCIVORUS)
FIELDFARE (T. PILARIS)
GREAT TIT (P. MAJOR)
LONG TAILED TIT (A. CAUDATUS)
NUTHATCH (S. EUROPAEA)
HOUSE SPARROW (P. DOMESTICUS)
TREE SPARROW (P. MONTANUS)
CHAFFINCH (F. COELEBS)
BRAMBLING (F. MONTIFRINGELLA)
BULLFINCH (P. PYRRHULA)
HAWFINCH (C. COCCOTHRAUSTES)
PINE GROSBEAK (P. ENUCLEATOR)
CROSSBILL (L. CURVIROSTRA)
ROSE BREASTED GROSBEAK (P. LUDOVICIANUS)
CORN BUNTING (M. CALANDRA)
REED BUNTING (E. SCHOENICLUS)
SNOW BUNTING (P. NIVALIS)
STRATIGRAPHIC LAYER
4 3 2 1 0
UPPER PALAEOLITHIC
LATE DEVENSIAN
2
1
0

Crossbill

isolated occurrences of golden eagle (*Aquila chrysaetos*), rough-legged buzzard (*Buteo lagopus*), goshawk (*Accipiter gentilis*), osprey (*Pandion haliaetus*) and merlin (*Falco columbarius*). The anseriformes are also present throughout most of the succession. With the exception of mallard (*Anas platyrhynchos*), there is considerable variation in species present through time.

It is clear from this analysis and the chronology set out in *Table 25* that these avian families have been present throughout the greater part of the Mid and Late Devensian and were particularly numerous in the Late Devensian. This trend is not seen for other species, such as the passeriformes, which occur frequently within the cave sediments. It can be seen that passeriform numbers and species have increased considerably in the youngest deposits within the cave, which are dated to the Late Devensian (Jenkinson 1984).

Robin Hood's Cave

This site is one of the largest and most complex caves in the Creswell gorge (*Figures 5 and 35*) and consists of at least four large chambers with a number of subsidiary passages. Most of the palaeontological investigations within it took place during the nineteenth century. Extensive excavations in the western area of the cave are reported by Mello (1875, 1876) and in the eastern and rear areas by Laing (1889). More recent excavations were undertaken by Campbell (1969) in the western talus area of the cave.

Large numbers of vertebrate remains were recovered by the nineteenth century excavators, especially from the western area of the cave. The vertebrate faunas were reported by Dawkins (1876) and were recently reviewed in Jenkinson (1984). The vertebrate fauna includes mammal species typical of Devensian cold stage deposits. It is dominated by cave hyaena (*Crocuta crocuta*), wolf (*Canis lupus*), brown bear (*Ursus arctos*), woolly rhinoceros (*Coelodonta antiquitatus*), mammoth (*Mammuthus primigenious*), horse (*Equus* sp.), bison (*Bos* sp.), reindeer (*Rangifer tarandus*) and giant deer (*Megaloceros giganteus*). The evidence available from Robin Hood's Cave provides a relatively well dated example of a diverse avian fauna (*Table 21*) with woodland species which date from the Late Devensian. The faunas are demonstrably earlier than the widely canvassed Flandrian dates for the recolonisation of Britain by woodland species postulated in Moreau (1954) and Yalden (1982).

Dog Hole Fissure

Table 22 describes the early mid-Flandrian avian bone material in respect of the five stratigraphic layers recognised in the Dog Hole Fissure excavation (*Chapter 3*). The table shows that only passeriform species are represented. It includes: great tit (*Parus major*), long tailed tit (*Aegithalos caudatus*), flycatcher (*Muscicapidae* sp.), blackcap (*Sylvia atricapilla*), redstart (*Phoenicurus phoenicurus*), redpoll (*Acanthis flammea*), fieldfare (*Turdus pilaris*), blackbird (*Turdus merula*), and jackdaw (*Corvus monedula*).

This avian fauna would not be out of place in the hazel/pine dominated woodland of the early Flandrian as described in Godwin (1975). It contrasts quite markedly with the earlier mid and late Devensian faunas set out in this paper. Despite the highly unusual nature of this fissure site, which could have affected the range of species present, some species known to be numerous in earlier faunas are notably absent.

Table 21. The bird species, recorded by minimum number of individuals from J.B. Campbell's excavation in Robin Hood's Cave.

STRATIGRAPHIC LAYER	Mallard (*Anas cf platyrhynchos*)	Golden eye (*Bucephala clangula*)	Goshawk (*Accipiter gentilis*)	Kestrel (*Falco tinnunculus*)	Red grouse (*Lagopus lagopus*)	Ptarmigan (*Lagopus mutus*)	Grouse (*Lagopus sp.*)	Black Grouse (*Tetrao tetrix*)	Grey plover (*Pluvialis cf squatoroia*)	Short-eared owl (*Asio flammeus*)	Great spotted woodpecker (*Dendrocopos cf major*)	Jay (*Garrulus cf glandarius*)	Magpie (*Pica cf pica*)	Jackdaw (*Corvus monedula*)	Ring ouzel (*Turdus cf torquatus*)	Turdus cf pilaris	Emberizidae sp.
USB	-	-	1	-	1	-	1	-	-	1	-	-	-	-	-	-	1
OB	1	1	1	1	3	3	-	1	-	-	1	1	-	1	2	1	-
LSB	-	-	-	-	1	1	-	-	-	1	-	-	-	1	1	-	1
B/A	-	-	-	1	1	-	1	-	1	-	-	-	1	-	-	-	-
A	-	-	-	1	1	1	1	-	-	-	-	1	-	-	-	-	-
TOTAL BONES	1	1	2	4	6	6	4	1	1	4	1	2	1	2	3	1	2

Table 22. The bird species, recorded by minimum number of individuals from the 1978 excavation of Dog Hole Fissure.

STRATIGRAPHIC LAYERS	SPIT	Parus major (Great tit)	Aegithalos caudatus (Long-tailed tit)	Muscipapidae sp.	Sylvia atricapilla (Blackcap)	Phoenicurus phoenicurus (Redstart)	Acanthis flammea (Redpoll)	Turdus iliacus (Redwing)	Turdus pilaris (Fieldfare)	Turdus merula (Blackbird)	Corvus monedula (Jackdaw)	Passerine sp.
6	1	-	-	-	-	-	-	-	-	1	1	-
5	2	-	-	-	-	-	-	-	-	-	-	-
4	3	1	1	-	1	1	-	-	1	-	-	-
	4	-	-	-	-	-	1	-	-	-	-	-
	5	-	-	-	-	-	-	-	-	-	-	1
3b	6	-	-	-	-	-	-	-	-	-	-	1
	7	-	-	-	-	-	-	-	-	-	-	1
	8	-	-	1	-	-	-	-	-	-	-	-
3a	9	-	-	-	-	-	-	1	-	-	-	-
	10	-	-	-	-	-	-	-	-	-	-	-
	11	-	-	-	-	-	-	-	-	-	-	-
	12	-	-	-	-	-	-	-	-	-	-	-
2	13	-	-	-	-	-	-	-	-	-	-	-
	14	-	-	-	-	-	-	-	-	-	-	-
	15	-	-	-	-	-	-	-	-	-	-	-
	16	-	-	-	-	-	-	-	-	-	-	-
TOTAL BONES		1	1	1	1	1	1	1	1	1	1	3

Steetley Cave

Analysis of faunal remains from the Steetley cave described in Chapter 4 suggests that its main use was as a badger den approximately 5,000 years ago. The number of avian fossils known from the cave is small but these include a humerus, ulna and tibiatarsus of tawny owl (*Strix aluco*), a sternum, coracoid and scapula of wood pigeon (*Columba palumbus*), a tibiatarsus of blackbird (*Turdus merula*), a humerus which compares well to that of jay (*Garrulus glandarius*), and a corvid scapula.

The species present suggest a woodland environment, and this corroborates the pollen evidence which suggests a Lime (*Tilia* sp.), Pine (*Pinus* sp.) and Hazel (*Corylus* sp.) dominated woodland. Many of the avian bones are likely to owe their origin within the cave to predation and scavenging by foxes.

WHEN DID BRITISH BIRDS ARRIVE?

The fossil evidence of birds set out for these four caves provides a rare opportunity to examine the way in which birds colonised Britain. These events can be considered separately for the Mid-Devensian and Late Devensian cold stage and the Flandrian warm stage.

Mid-Devensian Occupants

The evidence for birds during this period comes from Pin Hole Cave. In this cave the lowest levels (20–14) remain undated and are devoid of bird bones. The earliest evidence for bird species is found in layers 14 to 7. These levels are shown by Jenkinson (1984) to date to the 'Upton Warren interstadial complex' of Coope, Morgan and Osbourne (1971) on the basis of a radiocarbon date on a reindeer (*Rangifer tarandus*) antler. The radiocarbon estimation of $38{,}850 \pm 2500$ years (Scott and Hughes 1981) falls within this warm interlude.

The bird species known from these levels are set out in *Figure 36*, where their habitat preferences are shown. It is clear from this figure that the bird fauna is varied. Duck and geese species, present at this time, suggest the presence of nearby open stretches of water. Some species, especially red grouse (*Lagopus lagopus*) and ptarmigan (*Lagopus mutus*), indicate open ground. The presence in levels 4–6 of species which today prefer woodland habitats indicates there may have been small areas of scrub vegetation either in or near the Creswell gorge.

Late Devensian Occupants

Knowledge of Late Devensian avifaunas is much better than that for earlier periods and separate faunas are known from Pin Hole Cave and Robin Hood's Cave (*Figure 37*). In Pin Hole Cave, the upper stratigraphic levels (1–4) are attributable to the Late Devensian *c.* 13,000–10,000 years BP on the basis of the association with a backed blade industry of Later Upper Palaeolithic type, dated by Campbell (1969) to *c.* 10,000 years bp. Examination of the associated avifaunas indicates that while many taxa known from the Middle Devensian continue with these later levels, there is also a trend towards an increasing number of other taxa. The duck and geese species now include the barnacle goose (*Branta leucopsis*), pink-footed goose (*Anser brachyrhynchus*), wigeon (*Anas penelope*), ruddy shelduck (*Tadorna ferruginea*). New additions to the falcons include osprey (*Pandion haliaetus*) and merlin (*Falco columbarius*) and although grouse and ptarmigan remain numerous, the galliformes now also include black grouse (*Tetrao tetrix*) and partridge (*Perdix perdix*). Members of the Charadriiformes display a dramatic increase in numbers, best illustrated in the upper stratigraphic levels of Pin Hole Cave and new species include lapwing (*Vanellus vanellus*), grey plover (*Pluvialis squatorola*), golden plover (*Pluvialis apricaria*), turnstone (*Arenaria interpres*), curlew (*Numenius arquata*), common gull (*Larus canus*), black guillemot (*Cepphus grylle*) and puffin (*Fratercula arctica*). These developments in the Creswell region must be in response to the local development of streams and lakes nearby in this period.

Owl species, particularly those presently associated with coniferous forest cover, also now appear and species include Tengmalm's owl (*Aegolius funereus*), barn owl (*Tyto alba*) and hawk owl (*Survia ulula*). It is clear from the presence of lesser spotted woodpecker (*Dendrocopos minor*) and large numbers of Passeriform species that the presence of woodland during the late Devensian facilitated the rapid diversification of the avifauna. Woodland species now known to be present during this latest phase include meadow pipit (*Anthus pratensis*), starling (*Sturnus vulgaris*), magpie (*Pica pica*), nutcracker (*Nucifraga caryocatactes*), jackdaw (*Corvus monedula*), rook (*Corvus frugilegus*), wren (*Troglodytes troglodytes*), dunnock (*Prunella modularis*), blackcap (*Sylvia atricapilla*), wheatear (*Oenanthe oenanthe*), robin (*Eritchacus rubecula*), ring ouzel (*Turdus torquatus*), redwing (*Turdus iliacus*), fieldfare (*Turdus pilaris*), great tit (*Parus major*), long tailed tit (*Aegithalos caudatus*), nuthatch (*Sitta europaea*), tree sparrow (*Passer montanus*), chaffinch (*Fringella coelebs*), brambling (*Fringella montifringella*), bullfinch (*Pyrrhula pyrrhula*), hawfinch (*Coccothraustes coccothraustes*), pine grosbeak (*Pinicola enucleator*), crossbill (*Loxia curvirostra*), rose breasted grosbeak (*Pheuticus ludovicianus*), corn bunting (*Miliaria calandra*), reed bunting (*Emberiza schoeniclus*) and snow bunting (*Plectrophenax nivalis*).

The presence of woodland species dating before the end of the last cold stage is confirmed by the presence of such species in Robin Hood's Cave sediment dated to Godwin's (1975) pollen zone III by Campbell (1969, Table 30).

Flandrian Occupants

Unfortunately, the record available from the beginning of the present interglacial is incomplete. No avifaunas are known as yet from sites in the Creswell area which clearly date to Godwin's (1975) pollen zone IV. Evidence from Dog Hole Fissure dating to post 8,400 yrs BP (*Chapter 3*), shows a dominance by woodland species, particularly redstart (*Phoenicurus phoenicurus*) and redpoll (*Acanthis flammea*). Deposits from Steetley Cave (*Chapter 4*) dated to Godwin's (1975) pollen zone VIIA (the Atlantic), include tawny owl (*Strix aluco*), wood pigeon (*Columba palumbus*), blackbird (*Turdus merula*) and jay (*Garrulus garrulus*), all woodland species which equate well with the pollen evidence for lime-pine-hazel dominated woodland.

CONCLUSIONS

The analysis of fossil avian faunas from the Creswell Crags Caves discussed in this paper has drawn upon a number of lines of evidence and attempted to construct a coherent account of avian colonisation of the Creswell area during the Devensian cold stage.

The palaeontological sequence from Pin Hole Cave and Robin Hood's Cave demonstrate that a remarkably diverse avifauna was present during the mid Devensian and particularly during the Upton Warren interstadial complex. The presence of arboreal taxa is especially interesting since these were previously widely regarded as not colonising Britain until the Flandrian. The evidence from these caves dramatically improves our understanding of avifaunas for this period.

Changes in the composition of avifauna are noted. Of particular note is the change from an arctic/tundra type fauna during parts of the mid- and late-Devensian to a woodland fauna during the closing stages of the late-Devensian. Evidence for very early Flandrian avifaunas in the Creswell caves suffers from the limited numbers of fossil localities known, but such faunas are seen to support the evidence available from the late Devensian of a shift toward dominance by woodland species. Therefore we conclude that woodland bird faunas were well established at Creswell in the early and mid Flandrian. Current views on the date of the colonisation of Britain by arboreal bird taxa appear to be in need of revision. Similarly these data also indicate that current views on the extinction of the earlier cold stage bird fauna need to be re-evaluated.

Jenkinson, R.D.S. and Bramwell, D. 1984. The Birds of Britain: When Did they Arrive? Chapter 5 in Jenkinson, R.D.S. and Gilbertson, D.D. *In the Shadow of Extinction: A Late Quaternary Archaeology and Palaeoecology of the Lake, Fissures and Smaller Caves at Creswell Crags SSSI.* Sheffield: Department of Prehistory and Archaeology, University of Sheffield. Pp. 89 to 99.

CHAPTER 6: CHANGES IN EUROPEAN GEESE AND DUCK MIGRATION PATTERNS DURING THE QUATERNARY

with S.A. Sutherland

CONTENTS

This paper deals with the problem of when the present patterns of bird migration evolved in northwestern Europe. The most common explanation is that they evolved in the Flandrian. However, examination of the remains of fossil geese from Pleistocene cave deposits in Europe and Africa suggests that the directions, routes and distance of geese migrations were already established in the Pleistocene. Nevertheless, recent modifications in these migration patterns are detectable. These may be due to the impact of glaciers and changes in the climate, topography and sea level.

INTRODUCTION

Modern ornithological studies have demonstrated widespread and variable migratory movement amongst avian species. Some species are shown to be migratory in the sense that all, or most, individuals make regular seasonal movements between breeding and wintering ranges. There are two general explanations of the origins of these migration patterns, i.e. the origins of the distances, distances and routes travelled. These explanations are outlined below.

The Flandrian Model

The recent history of this form of migratory movement has been discussed by Moreau (1954), Mayr and Meise (1980) and Curry-Lindhal (1981). These studies suggest that modern European avian migration patterns originated during the Flandrian warm stage, and developed following the last (Devensian) cold stage during which the areas available for birds would have been reduced due to extensive ice cover in northern latitudes. Following the retreat of the glaciers, birds could extend their way northwards, colonising land as it became available.

This model was inferred from present avian distributions, the assumption being that current wintering ranges help indicate the general direction from which the original extension of ranges occurred. Few attempts have been made to test this hypothesis using the fossil records for bird distribution which are available from Quaternary sites such as the Creswell Crags caves. The concessionary view is that such evidence throws little light upon the subject, chiefly because of the supposed incompleteness of the palaeontological evidence.

Alternative Hypothesis—The Pleistocene Inheritance Model

In fact there is not the dearth of avian fossil data often assumed by ornithologists. Relevant palaeontological evidence to test the above model is available from a number of European Quaternary sites shown in *Figure 38* and *Table 23*.

If, as seems to be suggested by ornithologists, the distance and orientation of migratory movement of geese were established as late as during the Flandrian, one would anticipate geese populations being confined to northern Europe during the Pleistocene. The alternative view is that migration patterns were already well established in the late Pleistocene and that ranges have simply shifted north during the Flandrian. A test of both ideas would be to examine whether or not it is possible to identify, from Pleistocene *cold stage* sites:

1) former breeding grounds around the northern limit of the unglaciated part of Europe, and
2) evidence of wintering range primarily within North Africa and the Mediterranean. If, in addition, current migration routes do 'preserve' earlier established patterns, then
3) there should be some trace of geese in the rest of Europe, and
4) implicit from their modern distribution, there should be few species within the greater part of the U.S.S.R. and Central Asia.

The species of goose discussed here are: Barnacle goose (*Branta leucopsis*), Greylag goose (*Anser anser*), Brent goose (*Branta bernicla*), White-fronted goose (*Anser albifrons*), Lesser white-fronted goose (*Anser erythropus*), Bean goose (*Anser fabalis*) and Pint-footed goose (*Anser brachyhynchus*). These species typically breed in the Arctic (to Boreal) zone and winter in temperate to warm temperate zones. The Greylag is an exception, breeding in warmer Boreal to temperate zones and wintering in temperate to warm temperate zones.

FOSSIL FAUNAS

The location of fossil bearing localities with evidence for geese are set out in *Figure 38*. *Table 23* lists these localities according to the age of deposits represented. The majority of sites are caves, except where stated otherwise and these can usefully be discussed for each species.

a) *Branta leucopsis* (Barnacle goose). The earliest record of this species in Britain dates to the Hoxnian warm stage from Barnfield Pit, Swanscombe. This specimen was originally identified as *Branta* sp. by Swinton (1964). It was re-identified by Harrison (1979) as *Branta* cf. *leucopsis*, and comes from the Middle Gravel (*Homo* level) E. The only other British find comes from the late Pleistocene levels of Chelm's Combe, Cheddar (Jackson 1926). Many of the European records date from the early part of this century and may require authentication. Bate (1915–16) recorded one or two bones in the Mousterian deposits at St. Brelade's Bay, Jersey, and from four sites in Malta. It may have been found at Forbe's Quarry, Gibraltar (Lambrecht 1933) and, according to Blanc (1920), it was common in the Final Gravettian levels of Grotta Romanelli (Italy). More reliable records come from France, the Aurignacian-Solutrean levels of Pair-non-Pair à Marcamps, Magdalenian VI deposits at Le Morin à Pessac-sur-Dordogne (Mourer-Chauvire 1975), and the Oldest Dryas at Meiendorf, Germany. Citing Blanc's data, Mourer-Chauvire (1975) suggested the possibility of Barnacle goose wintering in the central Mediterranean during the colder phases of the Pleistocene.

b) *Branta bernicla* (Brent goose). This species is slightly more common in the fossil record of both Britain and Europe. Eight bones have been identified from Pin Hole Cave, Creswell Crags, and at least five fragments at Tornewton Cave, South Devon (Otter and Hyaena strata), (Harrison 1980). An early report of this species from Walthamstow must be treated with caution as a similar record was recently re-identified as *Anser anser* (Greylag goose) by Harrison (1980).

Branta bernicla occurs with Barnacle goose at St. Brelade's Bay, Jersey (Bate 1915), and two of the Malta sites (Bate 1916). One secure record from Italy dates to the Upper Palaeolithic levels of Arene Candide (Cassoli 1980), and the species is common to the Final Gravettian at Grotta Romanelli (Blanc 1920). Further Italian finds were made in the Middle Pleistocene deposits at Loreto a Venose, and at the sites of Grotta del Fossellone, Malagrotto, Grotta dei Giganti, and Cardamone (*Figure 39*). Interesting finds are from Denmark where Winge (1903) records the species from five archaeological sites, the most numerous occurrence being at Gudumlund. All of these sites are of Mesolithic age.

c) *Anser anser* (Greylag goose). This species is one of the earliest geese recorded in Britain, with a fragment from West Runton, East Anglia (Upper Forest Bed Series of the Lower Pleistocene) (Harrison 1980). Ipswichian occurrences are known from dated finds from Ilford and Grays (Harrison 1980). The majority of fossil greylag geese in Britain date to the Later Devensian and are known from Walthamstow, Ravencliffe Cave, Kirkdale Cave (Harrison 1980) and Langwith Cave (Newton, in Mullins 1913). The location of these sites is shown in *Figure 38*. A juvenile bone from Pin Hole Cave, Creswell Crags is tentatively referred to this species. Occurrences in Europe include the sites of St. Acheul (Milne-Edwards 1867–71), Lespugue (Saint Perier, France 1927); Kesslerloch and Schweizersbild, Magdalenian sites in Switzerland (Stehlin and Studer 1918); Upper Palaeolithic levels at Grotta Romanelli (Blanc 1920) and Colombi (Regalia 1907) in Italy, the sites of Predmost, Ludmirau, Certova, Balcarova and possibly more, in Czechoslovakia (Capek 1910), Takacs-Menyhert Cave (Kraszna-Kanal sediment) in Hungary; Schusterlucke in Austria and in Germany the site of Ulm, Schelklingen and Weimar-Taubach (Lambrecht 1933). More recently Villalta (1964) has listed greylag goose from late palaeolithic levels at Santimamine, Spain. Other recent records include Fuchsen-Teufelslucken in Austria (Soergel 1966), and from France two individuals in Magdalenian levels at Rond due Barry à Sinzelles and Aurignacian-Solutrean levels in Pair-non-Pair à Marcamps, one individual at Soulabé à Montseron (Mourer-Chauvire 1975). Heinrich (1977) identified *Anser anser vel fabalis* from Weichselian deposits at Pisede bei Malchin in northern Germany. Greylag goose is the only goose species recorded from any of the Pleistocene sites listed by Burcak-Abramovich (1975) in the U.S.S.R. It has been found at only two of these, one being in the Crimea and one in Moldavia.

Flandrian records include those from Vardo, Norway (Christiani 1929), Hohen Viecheln in north Germany (Soergel 1961), and sites in Denmark (Winge 1903).

d) *Anser albifrons* (White-fronted goose). This species is recorded from the Late Pleistocene of North Africa at Waddi Kubbaniya, Nubia (*Figure 38*). Uncertain identifications include either White-fronted goose (*Anser albifrons*), or Pink-footed goose (*Anser brachyrhynchus*) and a clavicle of either White-fronted goose (*Anser albifrons*) or Brent goose (*Branta bernicla*) are known from Pin Hole Cave, Creswell Crags. Newton (in Mullins 1913) identified this species at Langwith and Ightham fissure. Kent's Cavern may also have Late Pleistocene finds of this species (Harrison 1980). Ipswichian and Hoxnian locations include Ilford and Barnfield Pit, Swanscombe (Harrison 1979, Swinton 1964). In the rest of Europe it has a temporally and spatially scattered distribution, from the Middle-Upper Pleistocene of Binagady in the Crimea, Acheulean and pre-Mousterian levels at Torre in Pietra, Epigravettian levels at Grotta Romanelli (Blanc 1920) in Italy and Late Weichselian deposits at Pisede bei Malchin (Heinrich 1977), Remetehegy (Janossy 1979) and Certova dira (Capek 1910). Mesolithic occurrences include Hohen Viecheln and Fuchsen-Teufelslucken (Soergel 1961, 1966), Arene Candide (Cassoli 1980), and Devencze Cave (Janossy 1979). In North Africa this species is recorded at Wadi Kubbaniya (Nubia) in deposits circa 17–18,000 years old and later records exist for *Anser anser, Anser albifrons* and *Branta ruficollis* (Red-breasted goose) which are depicted in Egyptian art of the 6th Dynasty (Ballmann 1980).

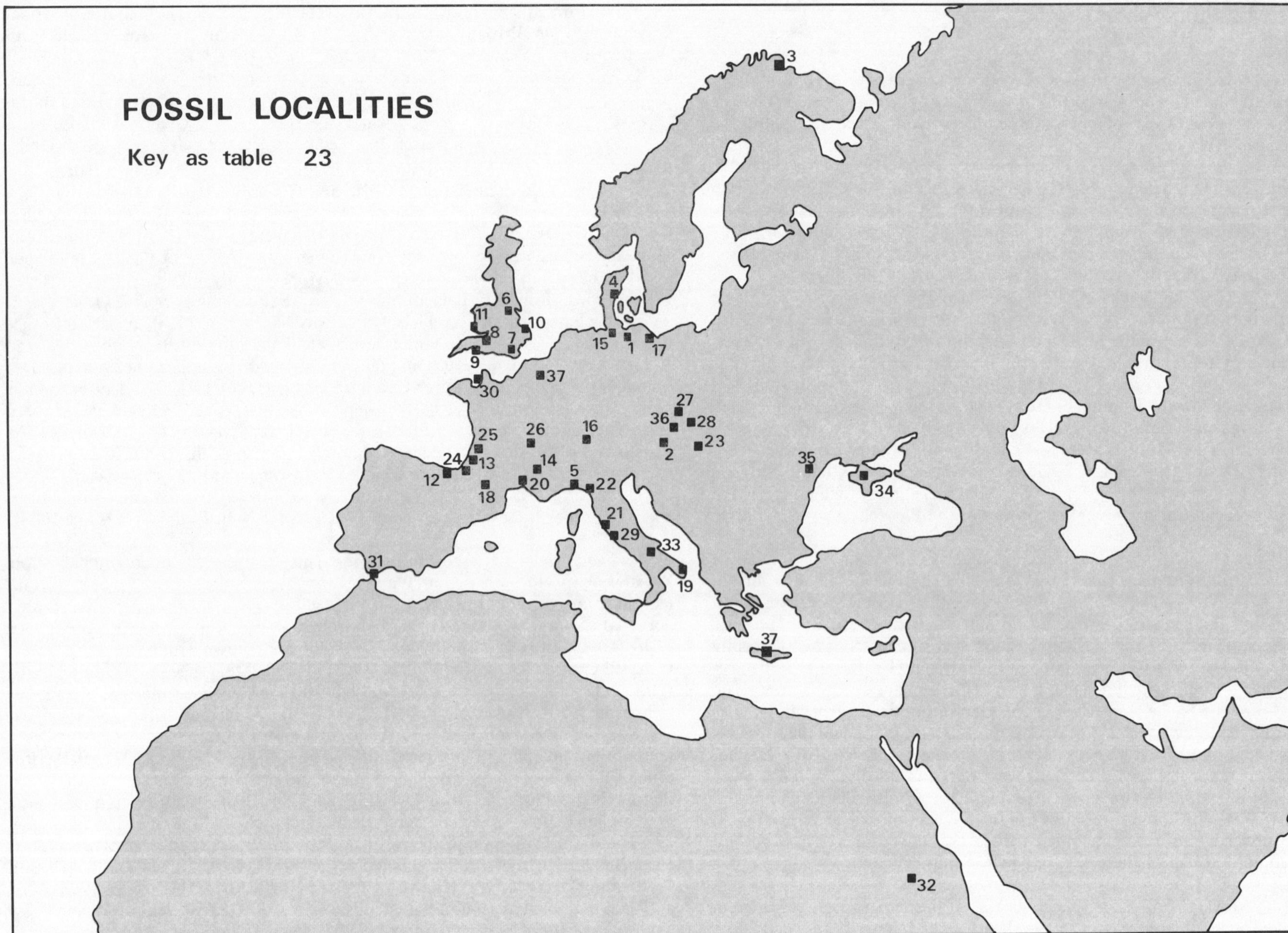

Figure 38. European fossil localities of Quaternary duck and geese remains.

Table 23. Quaternary age fossil localities with evidence for duck and geese species.

Flandrian

	1. Hohen Viecheln (Germany)	2. Fuchsen-Teufelslucken (Austria)	3. Vardo (Norway)	4. Danish middens	5. Arene Candide (Italy)
Barnacle goose (*Branta leucopsis*)					
Brent goose (*Branta bernicla*)				■	
Greylag goose (*Anser anser*)	■		■	■	
White-fronted goose (*Anser albifrons*)	■	■			■
Lesser white-fronted goose (*Anser erythropus*)		■			
Bean goose (*Anser fabalis*)	■	■			
Pink-footed goose (*Anser brachyrhynchus*)					
Anseriform egg shells					
Goosander sp. (*Mergus connectens n.s.p.*)					

Devensian

	6. Ravencliffe (UK)	7. Walthamstow (UK)	6. Kirkdale (UK)	6. Langwith (UK)	6. Pin Hole (UK)	8. Chelm's Combe (UK)	8. Soldier's Hole (UK)	7. Ightham (UK)	9. Kents Cavern (UK)	12. Santimamine (Spain)	13. Le Morin (France)	14. Rond du Barry (France)	15. Meiendorf (Germany)	16. Kesslerloch (Switzerland)	16. Schweizersbild (Switzerland)	17. Pisede bei Malchin (Germany)	2. Fuchsen-Teufelslucken (Austria)	18. Soulabe a Montseron (France)	2. Schusterlucke (Austria)
Barnacle goose (*Branta leucopsis*)					■	■	■				■		■						
Brent goose (*Branta bernicla*)						■													
Greylag goose (*Anser anser*)	■	■	■	■	■					■		■		■	■	■	■	■	■
White-fronted goose (*Anser albifrons*)				■?				■	■							■			
Lesser white-fronted goose (*Anser erythropus*)							■												
Bean goose (*Anser fabalis*)																			
Pink-footed goose (*Anser brachyrhynchus*)					■														
Anseriform egg shells					■														
Goosander sp. (*Mergus connectens n.s.p.*)																			

	19. Grotta Romanelli (Italy)	5. Arene Candide (Italy)	21. Palidoro (Italy)	22. Colombi (Italy)	23. Remetehegy (USSR)	34. Merzin (USSR)	24. Isturitz (France)	25. Pair-non-Pair (France)	26. Les Fees (France)	27. Predmost (Czech.)	27. Ludmirau (Czech.)	27. Balcarova (Czech.)	28. Certova (Czech.)	29. Torre in Pietra (Italy)	30. St. Brelade's Bay (Channel Isles)	31. Forbe's Quarry (Gibraltar)	32. Wadi Kubbaniya (Egypt)	36. Stranska Skala (Czech.)	37. Simonelli Cave (Crete)
Barnacle goose (*Branta leucopsis*)	■							■							■	■			
Brent goose (*Branta bernicla*)	■	■													■				
Greylag goose (*Anser anser*)	■							■		■	■	■	■						
White-fronted goose (*Anser albifrons*)	■				■		■						■	■			■		■
Lesser white-fronted goose (*Anser erythropus*)	■																		
Bean goose (*Anser fabalis*)	■		■?											■					
Pink-footed goose (*Anser brachyrhynchus*)									■						■				
Anseriform egg shells							■												
Goosander sp. (*Mergus connectens n.s.p.*)																		■	

Ipswichian / Mid. Pleistocene / Lower Pleistocene

	Ipswichian: 7. Ilford (UK)	7. Grays (UK)	11. Bacon Hole (UK)	7. Barnfield Pit (UK)	Mid. Pleistocene: 33. Loreto a Venosa (Italy)	25. Abri Suard (France)	20. Mas Rambault (France)	Lower Pleistocene: 10. West Runton (UK)	35. Moldavia (USSR)	34. Crimea (USSR)	9. Tornewton (UK)
Barnacle goose (*Branta leucopsis*)				■							
Brent goose (*Branta bernicla*)					■						■
Greylag goose (*Anser anser*)	■	■						■	■	■	
White-fronted goose (*Anser albifrons*)	■			■							
Lesser white-fronted goose (*Anser erythropus*)							■				
Bean goose (*Anser fabalis*)			■								
Pink-footed goose (*Anser brachyrhynchus*)											
Anseriform egg shells						■					
Goosander sp. (*Mergus connectens n.s.p.*)											

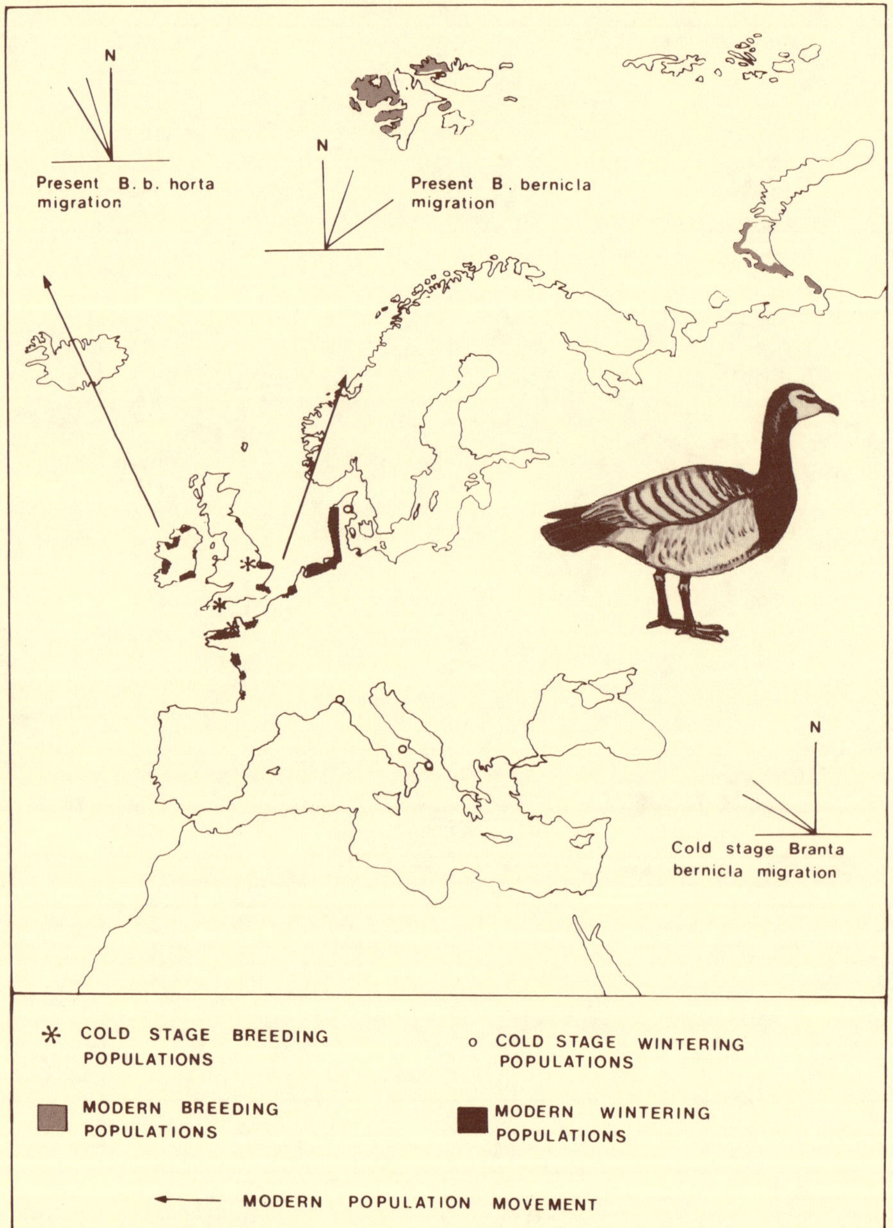

Figure 39. Current warm stage and last cold stage migratory movements of Barnacle geese.

e) *Anser erythropus* (Lesser white-fronted goose). This species has not been found in sites in northern Europe, but appears to be represented further south in Britain in Late Pleistocene levels at Soldier's Hole, Mendip. Blanc (1920) records finds at Romanelli in the Final Epigravettian. Soergel has recorded two fragments from subfossil deposits at Fuchsen-Teufelslucken. A coracoid fragment which compares well to those of this species was recovered from Middle Pleistocene levels at Mas Rambault à Frontigna in France (Mourer-Chauvire 1975). Lesser white-fronted goose may also occur in the Kermanshah Valley (Iran) during the Sarab phase (post 8000 BC).

f) *Anser fabalis* (Bean goose). The only record in Britain for this species is from last interglacial levels in Bacon Hole, Gower (Harrison 1977). At Torre in Pietra (Cassoli 1980) the species occurs in 'pre-Mousterian levels'. Late Pleistocene occurrences include those from Palidoro (Cassoli 1980), Grotta Romanelli (Blanc 1920), Terramare and Colombi in Italy, Bivak cave in Hungary (Janossy 1979), and Predmost in Czechoslovakia (Capek 1910). Mesolithic occurrences include Fuchsen-Teufelslucken in Austria and Hohen Viecheln in Germany (Soergel 1966, 1961) and Pilisszanto in Hungary.

g) *Anser (fabalis) brachyrhynchus* (Pink-footed goose). Six bones of this species are known from Creswell Crags. An occurrence at Ravencliffe Caves has been re-identified as *Anser anser* by Harrison (1980). Bate (1915–16) records fragments from the Mousterian levels of St. Brelade's Bay, Jersey, and Mourer-Chauvire (1975) lists this species at Les Fees à Chatelperron (Perigordian), and Abri Suard à la Chaise (Middle Pleistocene) in France. A more doubtful record in need of authentication, is from Upper Palaeolithic levels in Grotta Romanelli (Regalia 1907).

During the original excavations in Pin Hole Cave, Creswell Crags, Armstrong (1928) recorded five complete anseriform eggs, found *in situ*. Recent re-analysis of the palaeontological collection from this cave (Jenkinson 1984) records a further 179 anseriform egg fragments, all dating to the Last Cold Stage and being particularly common in deposits thought to date to the Upton Warren Interstadial. Anseriform egg shell fragments are also reported from Crimean sites, particularly Mezin (Shovkoplyas 1965) in association with Upper Palaeolithic artefact industries dating to the last Cold Stage.

Further indirect evidence is known from the Mid-Pleistocene deposits at Stranska Skala in Czechoslovakia (Janossy 1979). At this site over 700 fossil bones of adult Goosander (*Mergus connectens* sp.) have been identified. Although this species is not a goose, its presence in these deposits is useful in that no juvenile birds are recorded, identifying this population as a wintering one.

QUATERNARY CHANGES IN GEESE MIGRATION AREAS

Several aspects of modern geese distribution and migratory patterns are relevant to a full understanding of Quaternary migration systems. The total zone of present migratory movement recorded for the geese species discussed here extends between latitudes 82°N and 30°N. This modern distribution is more northerly than that recorded for Pleistocene populations which are seen to be distributed between latitudes 53°N–25°N (*Table 23*). The palaeontological evidence clearly indicates that a northward shift in the familiar area for these species has taken place since the latter part of the Pleistocene.

Breeding

The differentiation of breeding and wintering areas and the orientation of movement are also important aspects of modern geese migration patterns. It is likely that in geese wintering areas the population would be composed entirely of adult birds. Breeding areas can conversely be recognised from the greater range of individual birds and particularly the presence of juveniles. In theory these different areas (characterised by differences in the population age-structure of the geese) ought to be recognised in the fossil record.

Migration Range: Distance and Orientation

For modern populations, the average distance separating the breeding and wintering areas is extremely variable for each species. The distance for each species are as follows:

Branta leucopsis	16–2,400 kilometres
Branta bernicla	24–2,800 kilometres
Anser albifrons	24–3,200 kilometres
Anser erythropus	20–2,400 kilometres
Anser fabalis	16–2,000 kilometres
Anser brachyrhynchus	16–2,400 kilometres

It can be seen that for most of these species the distance travelled is over 1500 kilometres. The distance for *Anser anser* is omitted from this list as the distances separating its breeding and wintering grounds vary greatly.

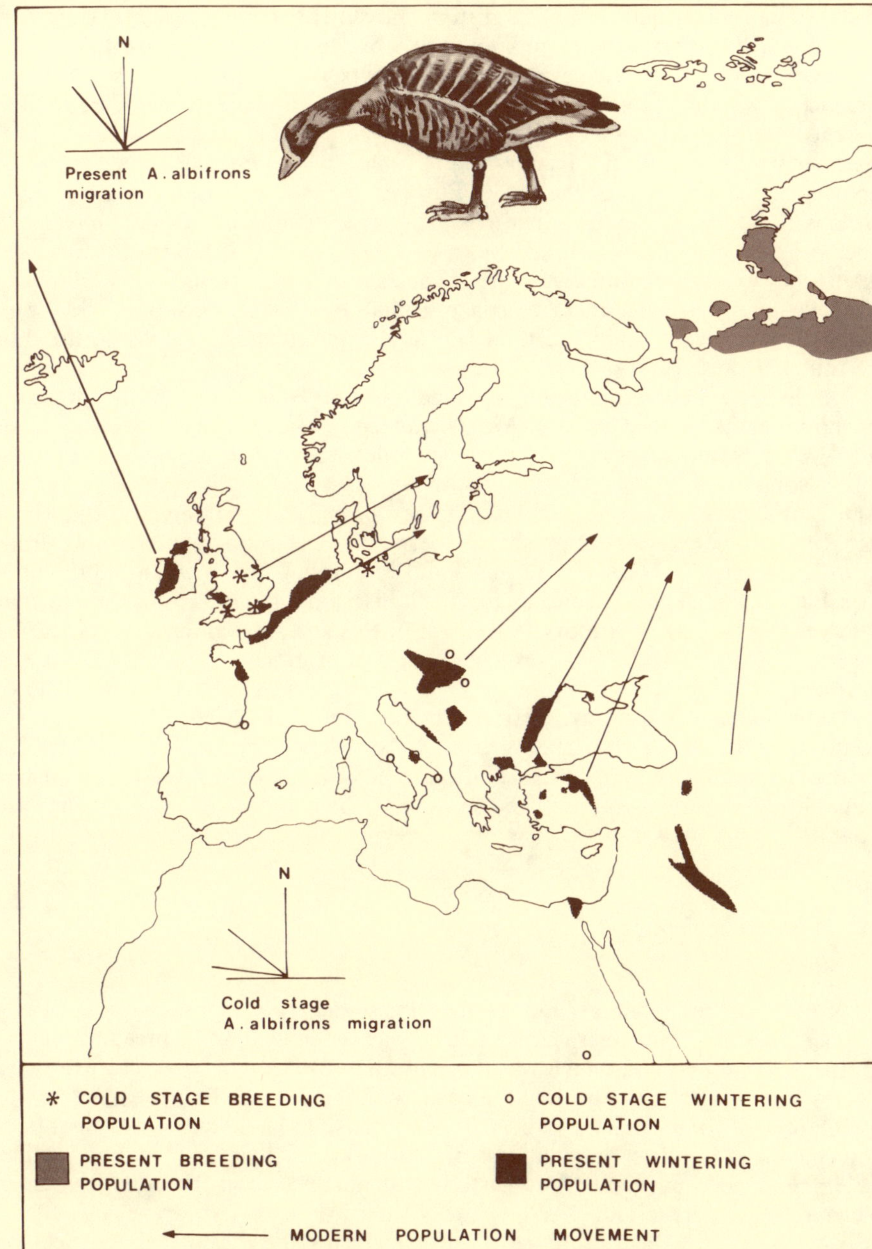

Figure 40. Current warm stage and last cold stage migratory movements of White-fronted goose.

The dominant orientation of migratory movement is northeasterly. However, smaller breeding populations are known to move northwest. The fossil data may also be examined to provide evidence of these type of movements in the past. The presence of breeding populations in more northerly latitudes can be inferred by the presence of duck egg shell fragments and juvenile bones from Pin Hole Cave, Creswell Crags and from Mezin in the Crimea, where egg shell fragments are reported. Fossil records for the rest of Europe are firstly well to the south and are composed entirely of adult individuals. The large sample of *Mergus connectens*, albeit a goosander (i.e. duck!) and not a goose (Janossy 1979), bone for Stranska Skala all of which are adult and which must therefore be a wintering population is of particular note. This evidence suggests that Pleistocene breeding areas were present in southern Britain and the Crimea, and that wintering areas occurred to the south of these locations.

The distance between breeding grounds at Pin Hole Cave to the probable wintering areas in the central Mediterranean suggests that the distance of migratory movement was of the same order as that exhibited by modern populations.

One of the clearest examples is that of *Anser albifrons* (*Figure 40*), which displays the greatest present movement between areas and which is known from Wadi Kubbaniya in Nubia (wintering?) and Pin Hole Cave (breeding) during the Late Pleistocene. These locations are 4800kms apart, a similar distance to that observed for modern migratory movement of this species. Similar differences can be demonstrated for *Branta bernicla*. It is to be anticipated that, despite the distances involved for each species, the areas between seasonal ranges would have few individuals present. It is important to note that the Pleistocene sites known from large areas of Central and Western Europe have not produced evidence of fossil geese populations. The distribution of fossil records for geese is therefore similar to that known today in the sense that the areas of their occurrence are separated by an area in which few or no geese occur.

CONCLUSIONS

In summary, the evidence suggests that Pleistocene geese fossils occur in two distinct regions—a northern area, which was associated with breeding, and a southern wintering area which was concentrated around the Mediterranean.

It is also clear from the fossil record that there have been changes in the orientation of migratory movement between these areas. Analyses of migratory movements of modern populations of geese species have shown two distinct orientations to movement, northeastern and northwestern. The distribution of Pleistocene wintering and breeding areas outlined in this study suggest that a northwesterly migration route was prevalent during the Pleistocene, particularly during its closing stages. These changes are shown schematically in *Figure 41*.

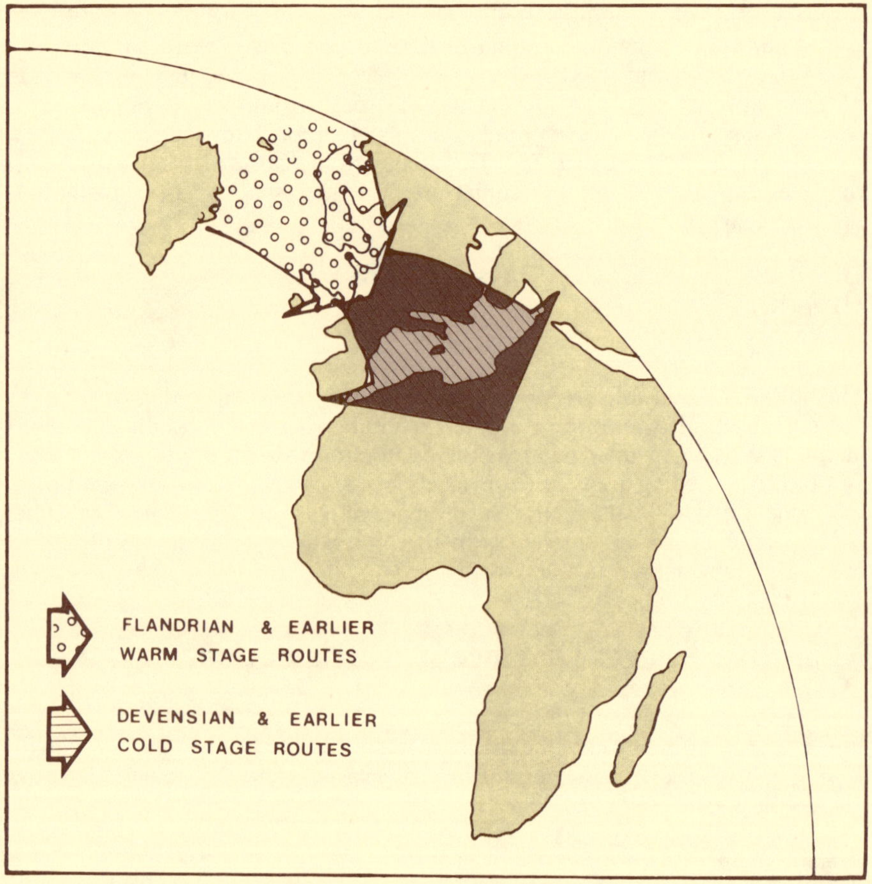

Figure 41. The suggested model for warm and cold stage geese migratory movements.

This observation implies that the modern orientations of migratory movements for some species have their origins in the Pleistocene. However, it is also clear from comparison of modern and Pleistocene migration route orientation that the northeasterly route, used by some modern geese populations, is an innovation of the Late Pleistocene and presumably developed in response to environmental factors, particularly the presence of remnant ice to the north and northeast of breeding range areas. Implicit in this suggestion is the presence of fewer sub-groups within Pleistocene populations than those present in modern populations.

This study of fossil bird remains suggests that geese migration patterns were well established *prior* to the Flandrian. Breeding and wintering areas have shifted in a generally northern direction as land became available and changing environmental conditions dictated a move for geese species in order to remain in their preferred habitat and chosen niche in the late Pleistocene.

Distance and direction of migration appears to have largely been maintained for many species. Interfering with these processes is the presence of natural barriers, particularly mountainous areas, glaciated regions and climatic regimes all of which appear to have affected a change in the pattern of movement. This study demonstrates the recent nature of changes in the direction of migration routes from northwesterly in the Pleistocene to the present day northeasterly routes. These may be due in part to the presence of natural barriers.

Although geese remains are relatively rare in the fossil record, this study notes that there is not the dearth of evidence suggested by ornithologists. The evidence that is available from Quaternary sites confirms the hypothesis that significant changes have taken place in the migratory patterns of geese. Precise dating of changes in migration patterns remains difficult but the evidence available suggests that, rather than the assumed Flandrian age, many significant changes have taken place during the Late Pleistocene in Europe.

Jenkinson, R.D.S. and Sutherland, S. 1984. Changes in European Geese and Duck Migration Patterns During the Quaternary. Chapter 6 in Jenkinson, R.D.S. and Gilbertson, D.D. *In the Shadow of Extinction: A Late Quaternary Geology and Palaeoecology of the Lake, Fissures and Smaller Caves at Creswell Crags SSSI*. Sheffield: Department of Prehistory and Archaeology, University of Sheffield. Pp. 101 to 109.

CHAPTER 7: A RAPID BUT SHORT LIVED COLONISATION OF THE BRITISH ISLES BY THE NORTHERN LYNX

by R.D.S. Jenkinson

CONTENTS

This paper reviews the importance of the northern lynx (*Lynx lynx* L.) as a component of the Devensian and early Flandrian fauna of the British Isles. Consideration of the reliability of the evidence concerning the antiquity and environmental context of previous finds suggests a brief invasion of the British Isles in the late Devensian and/or the early Flandrian, followed by local extinction.

INTRODUCTION

Recent studies of the history of vertebrate faunas during the Pleistocene and Flandrian periods within the British Isles by Yalden (1982) and Stuart (1983) have included little information on occurrences of the northern lynx (*Lynx lynx* L.). This is a particularly interesting carnivore. A study by Guggisberg (1975) has suggested that the northern lynx became extinct in Britain during the Devensian cold stage. In contrast, this powerfully built, medium sized cat has enjoyed a vast European distribution during the Flandrian period. At this time the species displayed a marked preference for old, high-timbered forests, particularly those with dense undergrowth (Guggisberg 1975). The intensification of forestry-based industries coupled with uncontrolled hunting are widely recognised as significant causes of the modern decline in northern lynx populations.

Its status in fossil vertebrate faunas within the British Isles has received little attention since the work of Dawkins (1866) and Jackson (1931), who noted that the species occurred in deposits which would now be attributed to the Devensian cold stage. This implied appearance in the British Isles of this woodland species within Devensian deposits, characterised by their shrub and tundra vegetation, is intriguing.

The contradictory nature of the fossil evidence and modern distribution of this species can be reconciled in two ways. First, the modern lynx populations presently living in tundra might have adapted to woodland biomes during the early Flandrian. The second possibility is that the distribution of lynx was indeed confined to former woodland areas and their apparent association with Devensian cold stage vertebrate faunas may be the result of a misunderstanding of the fossil evidence.

This study reviews the fossil evidence for northern lynx from fifteen British localities including Creswell Crags in order to define its recent temporal and spatial distribution, and to test the hypothesis that such a distribution is linked to the development of Flandrian woodland biomes.

THE FOSSIL EVIDENCE

A major drawback in any consideration of fossil and sub-fossil lynx in Britain is that many specimens have been recovered from caves where primitive excavation techniques and subsequent lack of detailed reporting impedes a clear understanding of the stratigraphic relationship between faunal assemblages. This problem is aggravated by the frequent lack of independent dating evidence. The fifteen fossil occurrences of northern lynx discussed in this study can be considered in respect of associated faunal and artefactual assemblages from which they were recovered, aided in some instances by independent dating evidence.

Table 24 sets out the Quaternary vertebrate faunas which provide evidence for lynx. These are listed according to reported age, the Devensian localities being dated upon the basis of apparent associations with Pleistocene mammals: i.e. hyaena (*Crocuta crocuta*), lion (*Felis leo*), and woolly rhinoceros (*Coelodonta antiquitatis*).

It is highly probable that 'mixing' with earlier Devensian fossil material has taken place at some of these localities. Remains from Banwell Cave, Mendip, for instance, are thought to have been washed into the cave and are therefore not *in situ* (Davies 1922). Those remains from Langwith Cave, Derbyshire, are derived from a poorly excavated site (Mullins 1913). Northern lynx remains from the sites of Aveline's Hole, Mendip (Davies 1922) and Victoria Cave, Yorkshire (Jackson 1938) are seemingly more reliably dated in that they were recovered from horizons containing Later Upper Palaeolithic artefact assemblages. This technology was shown by Campbell's (1977) radiocarbon dates to be confined to the Late Devensian pollen zones II–III of Godwin (1975).

Of the remaining fossil localities, where there is no association with Early and Mid-Devensian vertebrates or palaeolithic artefact assemblages, *post quem* dates are indicated by other elements of the vertebrate fauna. For example, the vertebrate faunas at Lynx Cave, Staffordshire (Jackson 1962), Kinsey Cave, Yorkshire (Jackson 1932), and Inchnadamff, Sutherland (Peach and Horne 1917), include *Rangifer tarandus*, a Devensian species that is known from radiocarbon

Table 24. Fossil localities with vertebrate faunas which include Northern Lynx within the British Isles.

	E. europaeus	*S. araneus*	*T. europaea*	*C. crocuta*	*F. sylvestris*	*L. lynx*	*F. leo*	*G. gulo*	*M. putorius*	*M. meles*	*C. lupus*	*V. vulpes*	*U. arctos*	*L. lutra*	*C. antiquitatis*	*Equus* sp.	*S. scrofa*	*C. elephas*	*A. alces*	*C. capreolus*	*R. tarandus*	*Bos* sp.	*S. vulgaris*	*C. glareolus*	*A. terrestris*	*L. lemmus*	*D. torquatus*	*Lepus* sp.	*O. pusilla*	*F. tinnunculus*	*L. mutus*	*Lagopus* sp.	*L. canus*	*S. aluco*	*C. palumbus*	*T. merula*	*G. garrulus*	*C. corax*	*C. monedula*	*Rana/Bufo* sp.
LATE GLACIAL																																								
Banwell cave				■		■	■	■			■	■	■		■						■	■																		
Langwith cave	■	■	■		■	■			■	■	■	■	■	■		■	■	■		■	■	■	■	■	■	■	■	■			■	■		■	■	■				■
Avelines hole						■			■			■	■			■		■								■	■	■	■		■	■								
Victoria cave						■				■		■	■					■																						
FLANDRIAN																																								
Cales Dale cave					■	■				■	■	■										■		■	■			■		■		■	■					■	■	■
Lynx Cave (Clwyd) (layer A)	■					■				■		■					■	■		■	■?	■?					■?	■								■				
Lynx Cave (Clwyd) (layer C)						■						■								■		■			■															
Moughton Fell cave						■						■	■			■												■												
Kinsey cave						■					■		■								■	■																		
Teesdale fissure						■				■	■	■					■	■			■	■																		
Lynx cave (Staffs)						■			■		■	■										■																		
Yew Tree cave						■					■	■					■			■																				
Robin Hood's cave					■	■				■	■	■	■			■		■	■	■		■																		
Steetley cave	■	■	■		■	■				■							■	■		■		■	■	■				■						■	■	■	■			■
Neale's cave						■																																		
Gop cave						■																																		
Inchnadamff						■								■			■				■																■			
Kilgreany cave						■																																		

dating to have survived into the Younger Dryas i.e. Late Devensian pollen zone III of Godwin (1975), at Dead Man's Cave (Mellars 1969) and Gough's Cave (Jacobi 1980).

Similarly, the presence of *Equus* sp. along with northern lynx at Moughton Fell Cave, Yorkshire (Jackson 1931) and Robin Hood's Cave, Creswell (Laing 1889) suggests an early Flandrian *post quem* date for the lynx horizons at these localities. The available evidence suggests that horse survived the Devensian and lingered into the pollen zone IV of Godwin (1975) (Bramwell 1973, Wiijnagaarden-Bakker 1974). The vertebrate fauna from Neale's Cave, Devonshire was dated by Neale and Sutcliffe (in Jackson 1962) to the Mesolithic.

Vertebrate remains including Lynx from Steetley Cave, Creswell, are independently dated by the presence of a mesolithic artefact and pollen to zone VIIa–VIIb of the Godwin (1975) pollen sequence (*Chapter 4*).

A near complete skull and mandible from Yew Tree Cave, Nottinghamshire (Ransom 1866) were the first specimens of northern lynx to be described from a British locality (Dawkins and Sandford 1866). Precise dating of the vertebrate fauna from this site remains problematic. However, analysis of the preserved specimens from this excavation shows that the associated remains include those of *Canis lupus, Vulpes vulpes, Sus scrofa*, and *Capreolus capreolus* (Jenkinson 1984). Notably absent from the vertebrate fauna is any trace of earlier Devensian species which are known in considerable quantities from nearby sites. Roe deer (*Capreolus capreolus*) is known from Flandrian but not Devensian deposits in the region. Its occurrence with *Lynx lynx* establishes the fauna as one which cannot be demonstrated to be older than the Flandrian.

Further specimens were discovered by Laing (1889) in the rear of Robin Hood's Cave, Creswell. The two mandibles, maxilla and radius, occurring beneath a flowstone in the western area of the cave, were originally described as *Felis brevirortris* (Croizet and Jobert 1828) by Stewart (in Laing 1889). The original specimens have unfortunately been lost since the excavations, but the detailed description given by Stewart indicates that, although large, they fall within the size range for modern *Lynx lynx* and are smaller than the size range reported by Kurten (1978) for *Lynx issiodorensis* (Croizet and Jobert 1828).

The age of deposits containing a juvenile mandible of lynx from Kilgreany Cave, County Waterford have been subject to much discussion (Jackson 1962, Savage 1966), particularly as the occurrence of Pleistocene species at this site have important implications for our understanding of Midlandian (last cold stage) colonisation of Ireland by vertebrates. These authors conclude that the earliest demonstrable sequence within the cave is of Neolithic age but there remains a possibility that Late Devensian/Flandrian deposits once existed within it (Jackson 1962).

It can be seen from this description of fossil occurrences of northern lynx that, with the exception of the remains from Victoria Cave, each occurrence is either of established Flandrian age or represents a locality from which both Devensian and Flandrian vertebrates are known.

DISCUSSION

The significance of this observation is that of the fifteen fossil occurrences of northern lynx in the British Isles, many are from localities not demonstrably older than the Flandrian. Of the remaining localities, three have suffered either geomorphological disturbance of deposits, or were too poorly excavated to be confident of association between other elements of the vertebrate fauna or artefacts.

This analysis shows that it cannot be demonstrated that northern lynx occurs in association with Early and Mid-Devensian vertebrates, or at any site earlier than the Late Devensian (pollen zones II–III). The evidence from Steetley Cave, Creswell, suggests a *post quem* date for northern lynx in Britain of Godwin's (1975) pollen zone VIIa during the Flandrian.

These observations have a number of implications for our understanding of the species colonisation by, and subsequent extinction of, this species within the British Isles. It is likely that the appearance of the species is associated with the development of regional temperate forest biotypes particularly during the Early Flandrian. The apparent occurrence of the species in late Devensian contexts and its apparent associations with palaeolithic assemblages must be treated with suspicion and need testing through rigorous stratigraphic investigations combined with radiocarbon dating.

Our understanding of the antiquity of the colonisation of the British Isles by this species is complicated by the rapid rise in sea level during the early Flandrian. This problem is particularly acute when considering its occurrence in Ireland. If the colonisation by the northern lynx was associated with the development of temperate woodland, this must imply colonisation during the Littletonian, (i.e. post 10,000 bp in Ireland) not conceivably before the Boreal, and prior to the flooding of the land connection which is dated by Cullingford, Caseldine and Gotts (1980) to 7500 years bp.

The strong association of this species with Devensian survivors (e.g. horse and reindeer) at Dead Man's Cave (Mellars 1969, Jacobi 1980) and Dog Hole Fissure, Creswell (Chapter 3) suggests that the temporal distribution of the northern lynx is mainly confined to the Late Devensian and the Early Flandrian. At maximum, it extends to Godwin's (1975) pollen zone VIIa.

The absence of northern lynx from localities with horizons younger than pollen zone VIIa may be important, especially in view of the widespread evidence for woodland clearance toward the end of the Atlantic. This phenomenon may be a major factor accounting for the extinction of this species in mainland Britain. At Steetley Cave, Creswell, palaeobotanical studies indicate that a woodland biotype, favoured by lynx, is followed by a dramatic increase in *Gramineae* pollen in Godwin's (1975) pollen zone VIIb, and may be indicative of woodland clearance. Lynx extinction might therefore be due to woodland burning by human groups during the closing stages of the Mesolithic.

CONCLUSIONS

Although a relatively rare fossil, this study notes the importance of the northern lynx as a constituent of Late Devensian and Flandrian vertebrate faunas. Analysis of the fossil evidence suggests that the species colonisation of Britain was relatively rapid and short-lived. The precise nature of such a temporally restricted distribution requires further definition, in view of the importance of migration, colonisation and extinction in palaeontological studies. A priority for further study of this species in Britain must be the application of rigorous stratigraphic studies and absolute dating methods to fossil material from Late Devensian contexts.

Jenkinson, R.D.S. 1984 A Rapid but Short Lived Colonisation of the British Isles by the Northern Lynx. Chapter 7 in Jenkinson, R.D.S. and Gilbertson, D.D. *In the Shadow of Extinction: A Late Quaternary Archaeology and Palaeoecology of the Lake, Fissures and Smaller Caves at Creswell Crags SSSI.* Sheffield: Department of Prehistory and Archaeology, University of Sheffield. Pp. 111 to 115.

CHAPTER 8: VERTEBRATE SPECIES TURNOVER RATES AT CRESWELL CRAGS, 70,000 TO 9,000 b.p.

by R.D.S. Jenkinson

CONTENTS

This study reports the development of an index of vertebrate faunal turnover rates appropriate to cave faunal studies. Variations in the value of this index are shown to be parallel to trends in species diversity and population numbers.

INTRODUCTION

Most studies of Quaternary vertebrate faunas concentrate on information that can be derived from a knowledge of the types of species found, the habitats they represent, and the evidence of antiquity these indicate. However, there are other ways of approaching palaeontological data. One of these is to examine 'constancy' and 'inconstancy' of the faunas found in the archaeological layers. These ideas concern the frequency to which a species detected in one level can be found in the next level. Where there is a high rate of turnover of species from one layer to the next (i.e. a species tends to occur at one level but *not* the next) there can be said to be a high level of inconstancy. The converse, where species are uniformly present from one level to the next, is said to have a high level of constancy. In ecological terms, the ideas of constancy and inconstancy reflect the stability of the plant or animal populations in an area. Many modern ecosystems have been classified according to the stability (constancy) of their populations through time. This study is concerned with applying the concepts of constancy to the evidence provided from studies of the vertebrate faunas from successive levels excavated from Pin Hole Cave, Creswell, by Armstrong (1928). An examination of the species found (*Table 25*) indicates that there is a predominance of cold stage species present—e.g. brown bear (*Ursus arctos*), mammoth (*Mammuthus primigenius*), reindeer (*Rangifer tarandus*). Consequently to help interpret the Creswell archaeological faunas it is worthwhile briefly examining the stability or constancy of modern arctic ecosystems. The major studies by Ives and Barry (1974), Remmert (1980) and Tierzen (1978) are especially useful in this context. In brief, many arctic terrestrial ecosystems experience considerable fluctuations through time of both the numbers of species present and the number of individuals present. By definition they are 'inconstant' systems.

Despite the presence of these major fluctuations, they are, overall, rather 'deficient' in species—they are species-poor. However, modern research in arctic environments has also shown that this property of repeated change within a small pool of species does confer advantages on the arctic ecosystem. Such 'inconstant' systems are seen to be remarkably resilient to 'ecological catastrophes' such as fire, disease, avalanche etc.

This situation is in contrast to the more stable populations of 'constant' ecosystems. Forest ecosystems are typically more stable and 'constant' than those of the high arctic. The rate of the local arrivals and local disappearances of species is relatively lower in forests. 'Constant' ecosystems are typical of more equable climates and environments. Not surprisingly, they are also characterised by much larger numbers of species per unit area of ground. Consequently, these observations on stability and change offer insights into the character of past ecosystems and environments.

This paper describes an index which can be used to quantify species turnover, i.e. the relative degree of constancy—displayed by faunas from successive layers of cave deposits. The levels of constancy determined may then be compared with the results of more conventional analyses of the faunas in order to identify whether or not the fossil faunas appear to show the relationships between constancy, faunal species diversity and environmental severity described above.

AN INDEX OF CHANGE FOR FOSSIL FAUNAS

A key factor allowing an analysis of vertebrate faunal change is the design of a uniform means of calculating vertebrate faunal turnover rates which is applicable to fossil vertebrate faunas. This can be achieved by evaluating the difference in species and their frequency in the faunas recovered from successive levels on archaeological and palaeontological sites. For such palaeontological collections

Table 25. The minimum number of individuals of vertebrate species recovered from Pin Hole Cave by A.L. Armstrong

SPECIES	STRATIGRAPHIC LAYER 0	1	2	3	4	5	6	7	8	9	10	11	12	13	14	15	16	17	18	19	20
INSECTIVORA:																					
Erinaceus europaeus (Hedgehog)	3	-	-	-	1	-	-	-	-	-	-	-	-	-	-	-	-	-	-	-	-
Sorex minutus (Pygmy shrew)	-	-	-	2	-	-	-	-	-	-	-	-	-	-	-	-	-	-	-	-	-
Sorex araneus (Common shrew)	-	-	-	1	-	-	1	-	-	-	-	-	-	-	-	-	-	-	-	-	-
Talpa europaea (Mole)	-	1	-	1	-	-	1	-	-	-	-	-	-	-	-	-	-	-	-	-	-
CHIROPTERA:																					
Rhinolophus hipposideros (Lesser horseshoe bat)	11	11	14	14	4	4	2	-	-	-	-	-	-	-	-	-	-	-	-	-	-
Myotis daubentoni (Water bat)	-	2	-	1	-	-	-	-	-	-	-	-	-	-	-	-	-	-	-	-	-
Myotis mystacinus (Whiskered bat)	4	-	2	3	-	3	-	-	-	-	-	-	-	-	-	-	-	-	-	-	-
Myotis nattereri (Natterers bat)	-	3	2	5	2	-	-	-	-	-	-	-	-	-	-	-	-	-	-	-	-
Plecotus auritus (Long eared bat)	1	2	-	1	1	-	-	-	-	-	-	-	-	-	-	-	-	-	-	-	-
Barbastella barbastella (Barbastelle bat)	2	1	-	-	-	-	-	-	-	-	-	-	-	-	-	-	-	-	-	-	-
Pipistrellus pipistrellus (Common bat)	-	1	-	-	-	-	-	-	-	-	-	-	-	-	-	-	-	-	-	-	-
Nyctalus leisleri (Leisler's bat)	-	1	-	1	-	-	-	-	-	-	-	-	-	-	-	-	-	-	-	-	-
CARNIVORA:																					
Crocuta crocuta (Cave hyaena)	-	2	4	3	3	4	3	6	5	4	4	11	5	1	1	1	1	-	1	-	-
Felis sylvestris (Wild cat)	1	1	1	1	1	-	-	1	-	-	-	-	-	-	-	-	-	-	-	-	-
Felis leo (Cave lion)	-	1	1	1	1	-	-	1	1	3	2	1	1	1	-	-	1	-	-	-	-
Mustela putorius (Polecat)	-	1	-	1	1	-	1	1	2	1	-	1	-	-	-	-	-	-	-	-	-
Mustela erminea (Stoat)	-	1	1	2	-	1	-	1	-	-	-	1	1	-	-	-	-	-	-	-	-
Mustela nivalis (Weasel)	1	-	-	-	-	1	-	-	-	-	-	-	-	-	-	-	-	-	-	-	-
Meles meles (Badger)	1	2	2	1	1	1	-	1	1	-	-	3	-	-	-	-	-	-	-	-	-
Canis lupus (Wolf)	1	1	1	3	3	2	3	3	2	1	1	2	2	1	1	1	-	-	-	-	-
Vulpes vulpes (Red fox)	1	1	3	5	18	3	-	4	4	5	2	3	2	1	-	1	-	-	-	-	-
Ursus arctos (Brown bear)	1	2	2	3	3	3	2	2	2	1	1	4	1	1	-	1	-	-	-	-	-
PROBOSCIDEA:																					
Mammuthus primigenius (Woolly mammoth)	-	-	2	1	1	-	1	4	1	2	1	2	3	1	-	1	-	-	-	-	-
PERISSODACTYLA:																					
Coelodonta antiquitatis (Woolly rhinoceros)	2	1	2	3	2	3	4	2	3	4	2	5	2	1	1	1	-	-	-	-	-
Equus sp. (Horse)	3	2	2	2	2	2	5	4	3	3	2	10	6	3	1	1	-	-	1	-	-
ARTIODACTYLA:																					
Sus scrofa (Wild pig)	-	2	1	-	-	-	1	-	-	-	-	1	-	-	-	1	-	-	-	-	-
Megaloceros giganteus (Giant deer)	-	-	1	-	1	-	1	1	1	1	1	1	1	-	-	-	-	-	-	-	-
Rangifer tarandus (Reindeer)	2	5	14	17	12	17	9	7	7	6	4	13	4	1	1	1	1	-	-	1	-
Bos	1	1	1	1	1	1	2	1	1	1	1	2	1	1	-	1	1	-	-	-	-
RODENTIA:																					
Sciurus vulgaris (Red squirrel)	-	1	-	-	-	-	-	-	-	-	-	-	-	-	-	-	-	-	-	-	-
Muscardinus avellanarius (Dormouse)	-	1	-	-	1	-	-	-	-	-	-	-	-	-	-	-	-	-	-	-	-
Clethrionomys glareolus (Bank vole)	4	4	-	3	-	1	1	-	-	-	-	-	-	-	-	-	-	-	-	-	-
Arvicola terrestris (Water vole)	1	-	1	-	1	-	1	2	-	2	-	1	1	-	-	-	-	-	-	-	-
Microtus arvalis (Common vole)	-	7	-	-	1	-	-	-	-	-	-	2	-	-	2	-	-	-	-	-	-
Microtus agrestis (Field vole)	-	1	-	-	-	-	-	-	-	-	-	-	-	-	-	-	-	-	-	-	-
Microtus oeconomus (Root vole)	-	2	-	2	2	2	-	-	-	-	-	5	1	-	-	-	-	-	-	-	-
Microtus gregalis (Gregarious vole)	-	1	1	1	2	-	-	1	-	3	-	3	4	1	-	-	-	-	-	-	-
Lemmus lemmus (Norway lemming)	-	4	6	5	3	22	21	7	2	7	37	36	39	1	-	-	-	-	-	-	-
Dicrostonyx torquatus (Arctic lemming)	7	29	18	38	6	36	23	5	2	10	33	24	19	1	1	-	-	-	-	-	-
Apodemus flavicollis (Yellow -necked field mouse)	-	3	4	1	1	-	-	-	1	-	-	2	1	-	-	-	-	-	-	-	-
Mus musculus (House mouse)	-	-	-	-	-	-	-	-	-	-	-	-	-	-	-	-	-	-	-	-	-
Rattus rattus	-	1	-	-	-	-	1	-	-	-	-	1	-	-	-	-	-	-	-	-	-

SPECIES	0	1	2	3	4	5	6	7	8	9	10	11	12	13	14	15	16	17	18	19	20
	STRATIGRAPHIC LAYER																				
LAGOMORPHA:																					
Lepus timidus (Mountain hare)	1	2	4	3	2	3	2	1	1	1	-	1	1	-	-	-	-	-	-	-	-
GAVIIFORMES (DIVERS):																					
Gavia arctica (Black -throated diver)	-	-	-	-	-	-	-	-	-	-	-	-	1	-	-	-	-	-	-	-	-
CICONIIFORMES (HERONS):																					
Ardea cinerea (Grey heron)	1	1	1	1	-	-	-	1	-	-	-	-	1	-	-	-	-	-	-	-	-
Ciconia ciconia (White stork)	-	1	-	-	-	-	-	-	-	1	-	-	-	-	-	-	-	-	-	-	-
ANSERIFORMES (GEESE & DUCKS):																					
Cygnus columbianus (Bewick's swan)	-	-	-	-	1	-	-	-	-	-	-	-	-	-	-	-	-	-	-	-	-
Branta bernicla (Brent goose)	-	-	-	1	-	-	-	-	1	1	-	-	-	-	-	-	-	-	-	-	-
Branta leucopsis (Barnacle goose)	-	-	1	-	-	1	-	-	-	-	-	-	-	-	-	-	-	-	-	-	-
Anser anser (Greylag goose)	-	-	1	1	-	-	-	-	-	1	-	-	-	-	-	-	-	-	-	-	-
Anser albifrons (White fronted goose)	-	-	-	1	-	-	-	-	-	1	-	-	-	-	-	-	-	-	-	-	-
Anser brachyrhynchus (Pink footed goose)	-	-	1	-	1	1	-	-	1	-	1	1	-	1	-	-	-	-	-	-	-
Anas platyrhynchos (Mallard)	-	-	-	1	1	-	-	-	-	1	-	-	-	-	1	-	-	-	-	-	-
Anas penelope (Wigeon)	-	-	-	1	-	-	-	-	-	-	-	-	-	-	-	-	-	-	-	-	-
Anas crecca (Teal)	1	-	-	1	-	-	-	-	-	-	-	1	-	-	-	-	-	-	-	-	-
Anas querquedula (Garganey)	-	-	-	-	-	-	1	-	-	-	-	-	-	-	-	-	-	-	-	-	-
Tadorna ferruginea (Ruddy shelduck)	-	-	-	-	1	-	-	-	1	-	-	-	-	-	-	-	-	-	-	-	-
Aythya fuligula (Tufted duck)	-	-	-	-	-	-	1	-	-	-	-	-	-	-	-	-	-	-	-	-	-
Melanitta nigra (Common scoter)	-	1	-	-	1	-	-	-	-	1	-	1	1	-	-	-	-	-	-	-	-
Mergus merganser (Goosander)	-	-	2	-	-	1	-	-	-	-	-	1	-	-	1	-	-	-	-	-	-
FALCONIFORMES (HAWKS & FALCONS):																					
Aquila chrysaetos (Golden eagle)	-	-	1	-	-	-	-	-	-	-	-	-	-	-	-	-	-	-	-	-	-
Buteo lagopus (Rough -legged buzzard)	-	-	-	-	-	-	-	-	-	-	-	1	-	-	-	-	-	-	-	-	-
Accipiter gentilis (Goshawk)	-	-	-	-	-	-	-	-	-	-	-	1	-	-	-	-	-	-	-	-	-
Pandion haliaetus (Osprey)	-	-	-	1	-	-	-	-	-	-	-	-	-	-	-	-	-	-	-	-	-
Falco columbarius (Merlin)	-	-	-	1	-	-	-	-	-	-	-	-	-	-	-	-	-	-	-	-	-
Falco tinnunculus (Kestrel)	1	3	1	1	-	2	-	1	1	-	1	-	1	-	-	-	-	-	-	-	-
GALLIFORMES (GROUSE):																					
Lagopus lagopus (Red grouse)	3	3	2	4	5	3	2	-	-	1	3	-	-	-	-	-	-	-	-	-	-
Lagopus mutus (Ptarmigan)	3	3	2	7	3	2	1	3	2	3	1	1	1	-	1	-	-	-	-	-	-
Tetrao tetrix (Black grouse)	-	1	1	1	-	-	1	-	-	-	-	-	-	-	-	-	-	-	-	-	-
Perdix perdix (Partridge)	1	2	2	1	1	1	1	-	-	-	-	-	-	-	-	-	-	-	-	-	-
GRUIFORMES (CRANES):																					
Anthropoides virgo (Demoiselle crane)	-	-	-	-	-	-	-	-	-	-	-	-	1	-	-	-	-	-	-	-	-
Gallinula chloropus (Moorhen)	-	-	-	1	-	-	-	-	-	-	-	-	-	-	-	-	-	-	-	-	-
CHARADRIIFORMES (WADERS, GULLS & AUKS):																					
Vanellus vanellus (Lapwing)	-	-	-	1	1	-	-	-	-	-	-	-	-	-	-	-	-	-	-	-	-
Charadrius hiaticula (Ringed plover)	-	1	-	-	-	-	-	-	-	-	-	-	-	-	-	-	-	-	-	-	-
Pluvialis squatorola (Grey plover)	1	-	1	2	1	-	-	-	-	-	-	-	-	-	-	-	-	-	-	-	-
Pluvialis apricaria (Golden plover)	1	-	-	1	-	-	-	-	-	-	-	-	-	-	-	-	-	-	-	-	-
Arenaria interpres (Turnstone)	1	-	-	1	-	1	-	-	-	-	-	-	-	-	-	-	-	-	-	-	-
Gallinago gallinago (Snipe)	-	-	-	-	-	-	-	-	-	1	1	-	-	-	-	-	-	-	-	-	-
Numenius arquata (Curlew)	-	1	1	-	-	-	-	-	-	-	-	-	-	-	-	-	-	-	-	-	-
Numenius phaeopus (Whimbrel)	-	-	-	-	-	1	-	-	-	-	-	-	-	-	-	-	-	-	-	-	-
Tringa negularia (Greenshank)	-	-	-	-	-	1	-	-	-	-	-	-	-	-	-	-	-	-	-	-	-
Calidris canutus (Knot)	1	-	-	-	-	-	-	-	-	-	-	1	-	-	-	-	-	-	-	-	-
Stercorarius sp. (Skua)	-	-	-	-	1	-	-	-	-	-	-	-	-	-	-	-	-	-	-	-	-
Larus canus (Common gull)	-	-	-	-	-	-	1	-	-	-	-	-	-	-	-	-	-	-	-	-	-

	STRATIGRAPHIC LAYER																				
SPECIES	**0**	**1**	**2**	**3**	**4**	**5**	**6**	**7**	**8**	**9**	**10**	**11**	**12**	**13**	**14**	**15**	**16**	**17**	**18**	**19**	**20**
Cepphus grylle (Black guillemot)	1	-	-	-	-	-	-	-	-	-	-	-	-	-	-	-	-	-	-	-	-
Fractercula arctica (Puffin)	-	-	1	-	-	-	-	-	-	-	-	-	-	-	-	-	-	-	-	-	-
COLUMBIFORMES (PIGEONS & DOVES):																					
Columba oenas (Stock dove)	-	-	-	1	1	-	-	-	-	-	-	-	-	-	-	-	-	-	-	-	-
Columba palumbus (Woodpigeon)	-	-	-	-	-	-	-	-	-	-	1	-	-	-	-	-	-	-	-	-	-
STRIGIFORMES (OWLS):																					
Aegolius funereus (Tengmalm's owl)	-	-	1	-	-	-	-	-	-	-	-	-	-	-	-	-	-	-	-	-	-
Asio flammeus (Short eared owl)	-	-	1	-	-	2	-	-	-	-	-	-	1	-	-	-	-	-	-	-	-
Strix aluco (Tawny owl)	-	1	-	-	-	-	-	-	-	-	-	-	-	-	-	-	-	-	-	-	-
Tyto alba (Barn owl)	-	1	-	1	1	-	-	-	-	-	-	-	-	-	-	-	-	-	-	-	-
Survia ulula (Hawk owl)	-	-	-	1	-	-	-	-	-	-	-	-	-	-	-	-	-	-	-	-	-
APODIFORMES (SWIFTS):																					
Apus melba (Alpine swift)	-	-	-	-	-	-	-	1	-	-	-	1	-	-	-	-	-	-	-	-	-
CORACIIFORMES (KINGFISHERS):																					
Alcedo atthis (Kingfisher)	-	-	-	-	-	-	1	-	-	-	-	-	-	-	-	-	-	-	-	-	-
PICIFORMES (WOODPECKERS):																					
Dendrocopos minor (Lesser spotted woodpecker)	-	-	-	1	-	-	-	-	-	-	-	-	-	-	-	-	-	-	-	-	-
PASSERIFORMES (PERCHING BIRDS):																					
Alauda arvensis (Skylark)	1	1	1	2	1	2	-	1	-	-	1	-	1	-	-	-	-	-	-	-	-
Lullula arborea (Woodlark)	-	-	-	-	-	-	-	-	-	-	-	1	-	-	-	-	-	-	-	-	-
Ptynoprogne rupestris (Crag Martin)	-	-	-	-	1	-	-	-	-	-	-	-	-	-	-	-	-	-	-	-	-
Hirundo rustica (Swallow)	-	1	-	1	2	2	-	-	-	-	-	-	-	-	-	-	-	-	-	-	-
Anthus pratensis (Meadow pipit)	-	-	-	-	1	-	-	-	-	-	-	-	-	-	-	-	-	-	-	-	-
Sturnus vulgaris (Starling)	3	1	1	1	-	1	-	1	-	-	-	-	-	-	-	-	-	-	-	-	-
Bombycilla garrulus (Waxwing)	-	-	-	-	-	-	-	-	-	-	-	-	1	-	-	-	-	-	-	-	-
Garrulus glandarius (Jay)	-	1	1	-	-	-	-	-	-	-	-	-	-	-	-	-	-	-	-	-	-
Pica pica (Magpie)	-	1	-	1	1	-	-	-	-	-	-	-	1	-	-	-	-	-	-	-	-
Nucifraga caryocatactes (Nutcracker)	-	-	1	-	-	-	-	-	-	-	-	-	-	-	-	-	-	-	-	-	-
Corvus monedula (Jackdaw)	8	12	4	12	3	3	1	1	1	-	-	-	-	-	-	-	-	-	-	-	-
Corvus frugilegus (Rook)	-	-	1	-	-	-	-	-	-	-	-	-	-	-	-	-	-	-	-	-	-
Corvus corone (Crow)	-	-	-	-	-	-	-	-	1	1	-	-	-	-	-	-	-	-	-	-	-
Corvus corax (Raven)	-	-	-	1	-	-	-	1	-	1	1	1	1	-	1	-	-	-	-	-	-
Cinclus cinclus (Dipper)	-	1	-	-	-	-	-	-	-	-	-	-	-	-	-	-	-	-	-	-	-
Troglodytes troglodytes (Wren)	-	-	-	-	1	-	-	-	-	-	-	-	-	-	-	-	-	-	-	-	-
Prunella modularis (Dunnock)	1	-	-	-	1	-	-	-	-	-	-	-	-	-	-	-	-	-	-	-	-
Sylvia Atricapilla (Blackcap)	-	1	-	-	-	-	-	-	-	-	-	-	-	-	-	-	-	-	-	-	-
Oenanthe oenanthe (Wheatear)	-	-	3	1	2	-	-	-	-	-	-	-	-	-	-	-	-	-	-	-	-
Saxicola ruberta (Whinchat)	1	-	-	-	-	1	-	-	-	-	-	-	-	-	-	-	-	-	-	-	-
Phoenicurus phoenicurus (Redstart)	2	-	1	1	-	1	1	-	-	-	-	-	-	-	-	-	-	-	-	-	-
Erithacus rubecula (Robin)	1	2	1	-	-	-	1	-	-	-	-	-	-	-	-	-	-	-	-	-	-
Turdus torquatus (Ring ouzel)	3	4	-	1	-	-	1	-	-	-	-	-	-	-	-	-	-	-	-	-	-
Turdus merula (Blackbird)	2	2	1	3	3	-	1	2	-	-	-	-	-	-	-	-	-	-	-	-	-
Turdus iliacus (Redwing)	1	1	3	1	1	2	-	-	-	1	-	-	-	1	-	-	-	-	-	-	-
Turdus philomelos (Song thrush)	-	2	7	3	2	3	4	-	-	-	-	-	1	-	-	-	-	-	-	-	-
Turdus viscivorus (Mistle thrush)	-	1	3	1	1	-	1	2	-	-	-	-	-	-	-	-	-	-	-	-	-
Turdus pilaris (Fieldfare)	3	2	3	-	1	-	-	-	-	-	-	-	-	-	-	-	-	-	-	-	-
Parus major (Great tit)	-	1	-	-	1	-	-	-	-	-	-	-	-	-	-	-	-	-	-	-	-
Aegithalos caudatus (Long tailed tit)	-	-	-	-	1	-	-	-	-	-	-	-	-	-	-	-	-	-	-	-	-
Sitta europaea (Nuthatch)	-	1	1	-	1	-	-	-	-	-	-	-	-	-	-	-	-	-	-	-	-
Passer domesticus (House sparrow)	-	1	-	2	-	-	-	-	-	-	1	-	-	-	-	-	-	-	-	-	-
Passer montanus (Tree sparrow)	1	-	-	-	-	-	-	-	-	-	-	-	-	-	-	-	-	-	-	-	-

	STRATIGRAPHIC LAYER																				
SPECIES	**0**	**1**	**2**	**3**	**4**	**5**	**6**	**7**	**8**	**9**	**10**	**11**	**12**	**13**	**14**	**15**	**16**	**17**	**18**	**19**	**20**
Fringella coelebs (Chaffinch)	-	-	1	-	-	-	-	-	-	-	-	-	-	-	-	-	-	-	-	-	-
Fringella montifringella (Brambling)	1	1	-	1	-	-	-	-	-	-	-	-	-	-	-	-	-	-	-	-	-
Pyrrhula pyrrhula (Bullfinch)	-	1	1	-	-	-	-	-	-	-	-	-	-	-	-	-	-	-	-	-	-
Coccothraustes coccothraustes (Hawfinch)	-	1	-	-	1	-	1	-	-	-	-	-	-	-	-	-	-	-	-	-	-
Pinicola cf enucleator (Pine grosbeak)	-	-	-	-	3	-	-	-	-	-	-	-	-	-	-	-	-	-	-	-	-
Loxia curvirostra (Crossbill)	-	-	-	1	1	-	-	-	-	-	-	-	-	-	-	-	-	-	-	-	-
Pheuticus ludovicianus (Rose breasted grosbeak)	-	-	-	1	1	-	-	-	-	-	-	-	-	-	-	-	-	-	-	-	-
Miliaria calandra (Corn bunting)	-	1	-	1	-	-	-	-	-	-	-	-	-	-	-	-	-	-	-	-	-
Emberiza schoeniclus (Reed bunting)	1	-	-	-	-	-	-	-	-	-	-	-	-	-	-	-	-	-	-	-	-
Plectrophenax nivalis (Snow bunting)	2	-	-	-	-	1	1	-	-	-	-	-	-	-	-	-	-	-	-	-	-
Carduelis chloris (Greenfinch)	-	1	-	1	-	-	-	-	-	-	-	-	-	-	-	-	-	-	-	-	-
Carduelis cannabina (Linnet)	-	-	-	-	-	-	-	1	-	-	-	-	-	-	-	-	-	-	-	-	-
AMPHIBIA:																					
Rana sp. (Frog/Toad)	47	53	21	104	98	4	3	7	-	-	1	3	4	3	-	-	-	-	-	-	-
PISCES:																					
Salmo sp. (Salmon)	-	-	-	-	1	1	-	-	-	-	-	-	-	-	-	-	-	-	-	-	-
Thymallus thymallus (Grayling)	-	-	-	1	2	-	1	1	1	1	6	1	1	-	-	-	-	-	-	-	-
Esox lucius (Pike)	-	-	1	-	1	1	1	-	2	3	1	5	3	-	-	-	-	-	-	-	-
Leuciscus cephalus (Chub)	-	-	-	-	-	1	-	-	-	-	-	-	-	-	-	-	-	-	-	-	-
Cyprinid sp. (Carp)	-	-	1	-	-	-	-	-	1	-	-	1	-	-	-	-	-	-	-	-	-
Perca sp. (Perch)	-	-	-	1	-	-	-	1	-	-	-	-	-	-	-	-	-	-	-	-	-
Platichthys flesus (Flounder)	-	-	1	-	-	-	-	-	-	-	-	-	-	-	-	-	-	-	-	-	-

the species present in any one level or horizon can be described in two ways: 'originating species', i.e. those present in a particular level but not present in the underlying level. A second description is that of 'extinction' where a species present in one level is absent in the overlying level. Neither of these descriptions necessarily records the first appearance or last presence of any of the species being considered. These measures may be combined in the index of faunal turnover rates set out below. It is based on the numbers of species and minimum numbers of individuals for each level.

This index is defined:

$$\frac{TS}{TI} \times \frac{Jo/Io}{Je/Ie} \%$$

where J = species, I = minimum numbers of individuals, o = originating species, e = extinct species, TS = total species present in the unit and TI = Total individuals present in the unit.

CASE STUDY: PIN HOLE CAVE

This site has been excavated by Mello (1875) and Armstrong (1928), and reviewed by Jenkinson (1984). Recent re-analysis of the excavators' records at Pin Hole Cave has clarified the stratigraphic relationships of previous finds in this cave and allowed for the separation of vertebrate remains according to twenty-one stratigraphic layers each of 0.30m thickness (Jenkinson 1984). From a total of 22,516 bone fragments, identified to 166 species, it has been possible to separate 15,315 vertebrate bones into twenty separate horizons (Jenkinson 1984).

The species present within the cave are listed in *Table 25*. These are shown against the minimum number of individual estimations within each stratigraphic layer. Many of these species are common in Late Pleistocene sediments, particularly cave hyaena (*Crocuta crocuta*), wolf (*Canis lupus*), brown bear (*Ursus arctos*), mammoth (*Mammuthus primigenius*), woolly rhinoceros (*Coelondonta antiquatis*), giant deer (*Megaloceros giganteus*) and reindeer (*Rangifer tarandus*). An unusual aspect of the cave is the preservation of large quantities of remains of smaller vertebrates. The evidence of birds, fish and amphibians is also of particular note.

Figure 42 illustrates the quantity of vertebrate bone species and minimum numbers of individuals for each stratigraphic layer of the cave. Examination of this figure and table shows that there was an overall trend towards a larger, more diverse, vertebrate community in the higher levels of the cave sediments. Nevertheless it is also clear that many minor fluctuations occurred within this predominantly cold stage fauna. An independent measure of the variety of habitats near the cave during the various stages of its infilling is provided in *Figure 43*: tree dwellers, burrowers, wholly or partially aquatic species occur, as do species characteristic of grass-steppe plains and tundra.

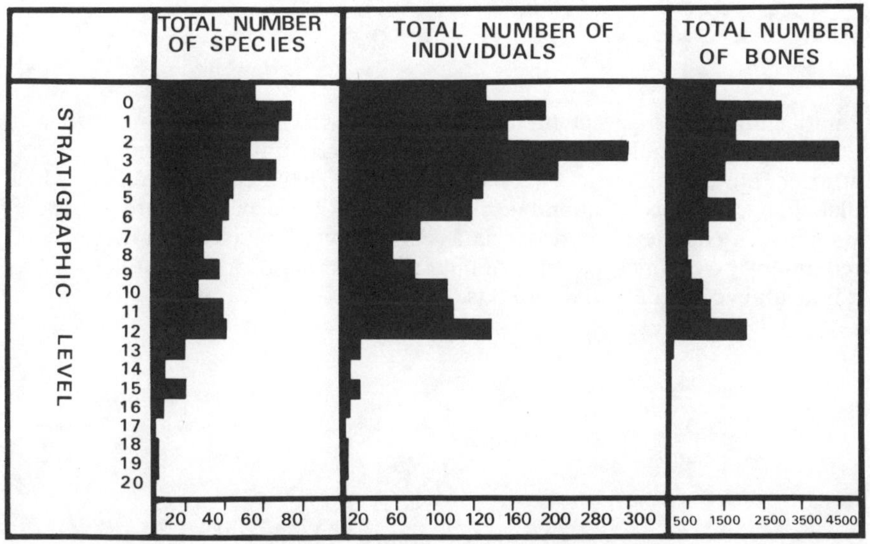

Figure 42. The frequency of vertebrate bones, species and minimum numbers of individuals for Pin Hole Cave.

VERTEBRATE FAUNAL TURNOVER RATES

Figure 44 presents a plot of the constancy of cave faunas through the Pin Hole Cave sequence. Stratigraphic layers 13–16, and to a lesser extent 8–9 and 1–2 show a high degree of turnover (i.e. inconstancy). The intervening levels display a high degree of constancy—stability—in the vertebrate faunas. In summary, the actual sequence identified in these terms is:

base of cave sediments (levels 13–16) high turnover—(inconstancy); levels 10–12—constancy; levels 8–9—inconstancy; levels 5–7—constancy; level 4—slight rise in inconstancy; level 3—constancy; level 2—inconstancy; level 1—constancy.

A comparison of these data with that on habitat diversity and overall species numbers reveals the broadly sympathetic relationships between trends that was anticipated from study of the modern ecological survey.

These results may be interpreted in two ways. First, they do appear to make ecological sense; there are no inherent reasons why species turnover rates in past arctic ecosystems should behave differently to those obtained in modern ecological surveys. However, it is also the case that any loss or gain of a species in a fauna with a very small number of species is likely to result in a large percentage change. In this case, rapid change identified would be the result of sample size as well as ecological factors. However, there is no reason to suppose that the change produced by the loss of one species in a small fauna, should not normally be cancelled out by the equally small gain of a further species.

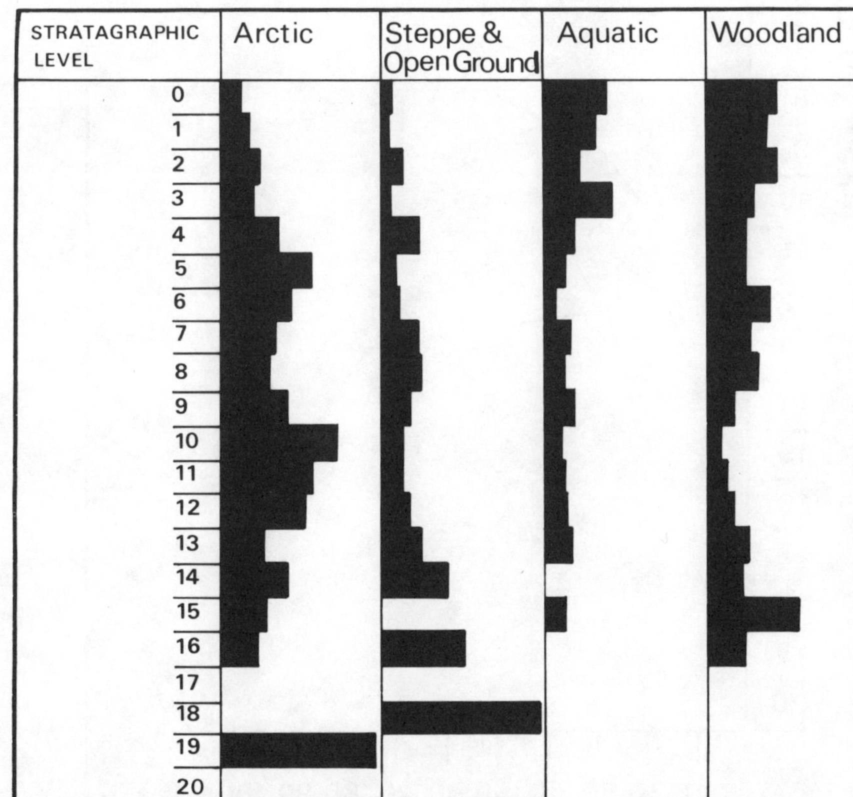

Figure 43. Diagrams showing habitats indicated by the minimum number of individual vertebrate species from Pin Hole Cave.

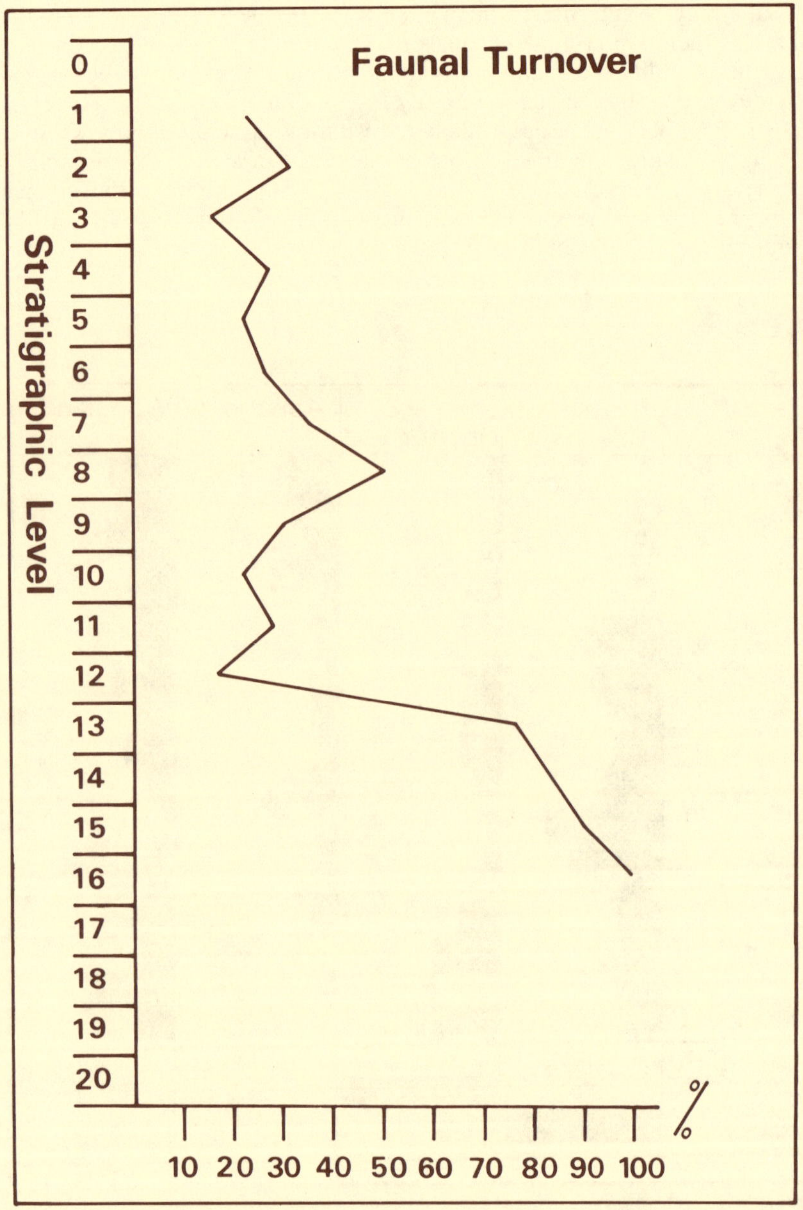

Figure 44. Changes in faunal turnover rates calculated for Pin Hole Cave.

CONCLUSIONS

This initial analysis suggests that presently available data on cave faunas at Creswell is appropriate for analysis with this relatively unusual method. Patterns in turnover rate through time have been detected. They occur at levels in which parallel changes in species abundance and habitats happen. In future the use of more sophisticated indexes on better data sets may reveal much closer insights into past community dynamics, patterns of migration, colonisation and extinction, and environmental constraints and habitats.

Jenkinson, R.D.S. 1984 Vertebrate Species Turnover Rates at Creswell Crags, 70,000 to 9,000 b.p. Chapter 8 in Jenkinson, R.D.S. and Gilbertson, D.D. *In the Shadow of Extinction: A Late Quaternary Geology and Palaeoecology of the Lake, Fissures and Smaller Caves at Creswell Crags SSSI*. Sheffield: Department of Prehistory and Archaeology, University of Sheffield. Pp. 117 to 124.

CHAPTER 9: CONCLUSIONS

Many inter-related themes can be detected in the preceding chapters. The saddest concern the appalling loss of archaeological evidence and the degradation of the archaeological record that has plagued Creswell Crags. Against this picture of early, genteel exploitation and ineptitude, the work of Leslie Armstrong stands out in sharp contrast. His work and records can still be studied; his finds can be examined in Museum collections. The activities of too many of his contemporaries and predecessors have resulted in the extinction of far too much of the archaeological legacy of Creswell Crags.

The present studies have also emphasised the significance of change. Change is recognisable at many different scales of time and space. The small fissure by Dog Hole Cave has emphasised the remarkable variety and speed with which animal species can take advantage of an opportunity for a home, or a carcass to consume.

The evidence from the Creswell Cave deposits is also allowing a fuller and more accurate picture of much larger scale colonisation and migration across the British Isles. The date of the arrival of our bird faunas appears to be notably older than previously thought. These large-scale movements reflect major fluctuations in climate. These same fluctuations which offered opportunity to many species also posed a threat to the survival of others. Numerous taxa were able to survive the extremes of arctic climates of the last cold stage by occupying refuges in Mediterranean or African lands. These data from Creswell form important components of an attempt to understand how the behaviour of migratory bird species altered in response to these climatic stresses.

For many species, the opportunity to migrate did not result in their survival. Extinction was the principal threat faced by the fauna at Creswell Crags. The threat derived from climatic or human pressures. The causes of the extinction of the well known Pleistocene mammals, e.g. mammoth, dirk-toothed cat, at Creswell remains unclear. However the new studies from Creswell, by providing more accurate and precise information on the last occurrences of extinct species, have provided a better data base for studying extinction and its causes.

The contextual information from the related studies of pollen, spores, molluscs, sediments and soils enables a much clearer picture of past environments to be constructed and allows some inferences to be drawn. The local extinction of the northern lynx is suspected to be related to early forest burning or clearance. On the other hand, the beaver is now known to have survived much longer than previously believed. Even Creswell Crags lake appears to have survived notable quantities of waste sediment and coal detritus being deposited within its feeder catchment during the mid- and early-twentieth century. The recent rehabilitation of the lake marks one stage in a major change in attitudes to the wildlife, scenery and archaeological resources of the Crags: a change from an eagerness to exploit to the healthier ideals of enjoyment, recreation, conservation and study.

REFERENCES

Anon 1862 Pleasley Vale. In *Sherwood Forest* Nottingham. White, F.

Armstrong A.L. 1923 Report of Committee for the Archaeological Explanation of Derbyshire Caves. Interim Report 2. *Report of the British Association for the Advancement of Science*. Unpaged.

Armstrong A.L. 1926 Excavations in the Pin Hole Cave, Creswell Crags. *Reports of the British Association for the Advancement of Science*. Pp. 392.

Armstrong A.L. 1928 Excavations at the Pin Hole Cave, Creswell Crags, Derbyshire. *Proceedings of the Prehistoric Society of East Anglia* 6:330–4.

Armstrong A.L. 1929 Excavations at Creswell Crags, the Pin Hole Cave. *Transactions of the Hunter Archaeological Society* III:116–22.

Armstrong, A.L. 1940 Dog Hole Cave excavation. *Creswell Crags Centre photographic archive* No. B35. Creswell Crags Visitor Centre, Welbeck, Worksop, Notts.

Aspinall A. and Pickard K. 1971 A direct earth resistance meter. *Prospezioni Archaeologiche* 6:21–4.

Aspinall A. and Lynam J.T. 1970 An induced polarization instrument for the detection of near surface features. *Prospezioni Archeologiche* 5:67–75.

Avery B.W. and Bascombe C.L. 1974 *Soil Survey Laboratory Methods*. Technical Monograph No. 6. Harpenden, U.K.

Baillie M. 1982 *Tree Ring Dating*. London: Croom Helm.

Ball D.F. 1964 Loss-on-ignition as an estimate of organic carbon in non-calcareous soils. *Journal of Soil Science* 15:84–92.

Ballman P. 1973 Die fossilen Vogel sus dem jungpleistozan Hohle Marie-Jeanne bie Hastiere, Belgien. *Le Gerfaut* 63:3–16.

Ballmann P. 1980 Molluscs, fish and birds from the Late Palaeolithic sites in Wadi Kubbaniya. In *Loaves and Fishes: the Prehistory of Wadi Kubbaniya*. A.E. Close (ed). Dallas: Southern Methodist University. Pp. 281–93.

Baronovskaya N.T. 1935 Food habits of the fox *Vulpes vulpes*. *Zoologica Zeitschrift* 14:523–50.

Bate D. 1915–16 *Aves*. In Site fauna and industry of La Cotte de la St. Brelade, Jersey. Marrett. *Archaeologia* 67:75–118.

Bate D. 1928 *Aves*. In Excavation of a Mousterian rock-shelter at Devil's Tower, Gibraltar. D.A.E. Garrod *et al*. *Journal of the Royal Anthropological Institute* 58:104–9.

Blanc G.A. 1920 Grotta Romanelli. *Archivio per l'Anthropologie et Ethnologie* 50:65–103.

Bliss L.C. (ed) 1977 *Truelove Lowland, Devon. Island Canada—A High Arctic Ecosystem*. Edmonton: University of Alberta Press.

Blore J.D. 1981 *Lynx Cave Excavations, Clwyd* 23. Private publication.

Bouchud J. 1952 Les oeseaux d'Isturitz. *Bulletin Societie Prehistoric Francaise* 49:450–7.

Boycott A.E. 1934 The habitats of land Mollusca in Britain. *Journal of Ecology* 22:1–38.

Bramwell D. 1960 Some research into bird distribution in Britain during the Late Glacial and Post Glacial Periods. *Bird Report 1959–60. Merseyside Naturalists Association* 51–8.

Bramwell D. 1973 *Archaeology in the Peak District*. Moorland.

Briggs D.J. 1977 *Sources and Methods in Geography: Sediments*. London: Butterworth.

Burcak-Abramovich N.I. 1975 Die Pleistozäne Vogelfauna der USSR *Quartärtpaläontologie* 1:87–105.

Burr W.T.G. 1910 Creswell Crags. *East Derbyshire Field Club Transactions* 5–7.

Campbell J. 1969 Excavations at Creswell Crags. *Derbyshire Archaeological Journal* 89:47–58.

Campbell J.B. 1977 *The Upper Palaeolithic in Britain* 2 vols. Oxford: Oxford University Press.

Capek W. 1910 Uber Funde diluvialer Vogelknochen aus Mahren. *V. Internan. Ornitholishe Kongross* (Berlin) 936–42.

Cassoli P.F. 1980 L'avifauna del pleistocene superiore delle Arene Candide (Liguria). *Memorie dell'Instituto di Palaeontologia Umana* NS 3:155–234.

Christiani A. 1929 Om nogle jordfunde Knogler fra Vardo i Norge. *Danske Ornith. For. Tidskr*. 23:79–83.

Clapham A.R., Tutin T.G. and Warburg E.F. 1962 *Flora of the British Isles*. London: Cambridge University Press.

Clark G. 1948 Fowling in prehistoric Europe. *Antiquity* 22:116–30.

Collcutt S.N. 1975 *The Stratigraphy of Creswell Crags*. Unpublished M.A. Thesis University of Edinburgh, Department of Archaeology.

Coope G.R., Morgan A. and Osborne P.J. 1971 Fossil Coleoptera as indicators of climatic fluctuations during the last Glaciation in Britain. *Palaeogeography, Palaeoclimatology, Palaeoecology* 10:87–101.

Corbet G.B. and Southern H.N. 1977 *Handbook of British Mammals*. London: Blackwells.

Croizet J.B. and Jobert A.C.G. 1828 *Recherches sur les ossemens fossiles du department du Puy-de-Dome*. Paris.

Cullingford R.A., Casedine C.J. and Gotts P.E. 1980 Early Flandrian land and sea level changes in Lower Strathearn. *Nature* 284:159–61.

Curry-Lindahl K. 1981 *Bird Migration in Africa*. London: Academic Press.

Davies G. and Turner J. 1979 Pollen diagrams from Northumberland. *New Phytologist* 82:783–804.

Davies J.A. 1922 Aveline's Hole, Burrington Coombe. *Proceeding University of Bristol Speleological Society* 2:268–70.

Dawkins W. Boyd 1866 *Felis lynx*. British Pleistocene Felidae, British Pleistocene Mammalia. Vol. 1. *Palaeontographical Society*. London.

Dawkins W. Boyd 1875 Recent Discoveries in Derbyshire *Pall Mall Magazine* unnumbered.

Dawkins W. Boyd 1876 On the mammalia and traces of Man in Robin Hood's Cave. *Quarterly Journal Geological Society London* 32:240–259.

Dawkins W. Boyd 1878 The Creswell Caves Exploration 1876. *Nature*: 106–7.

Dawkins W. Boyd 1910 The arrival of man in Britain in the Pleistocene Age. *Journal Anthropological Institute* 40:233–63.

Dawkins W. Boyd 1924 Correspondence with Sollas and Woodward. *Derbyshire County Records Office* Matlock (unpublished).

Dawkins W. Boyd and Sandford W.A. 1866 British Pleistocene Mammalia; *Felidae*. *Palaeontographical Society Monographs* 1:1194.

Dawkins W. Boyd and Sandford W.A. 1872 British Pleistocene Mammalia. Vol. 1. *Palaeontographical Society Monographs*. London.

Dick W.A. and Tabatabai M.A. 1977 An alkaline oxidation method for determination of total phosphorus in soils. *Journal of Soil Science Society America* 41:511–14.

Duckworth W.L.H. and Swainson F.E. 1895 A new ossiferous fissure in Creswell Crags. *Quarterly Journal Geological Society London* 51:232.

Eden R.A., Stevenson I.P. and Edwards W. 1957 *Geology of the Country Around Sheffield*. Memoirs of the Geological Survey of Great Britain. London: H.M.S.O.

Egerton J. 1978 *British Sporting and Animal Paintings 1500–1850*. The Paul Mellon Collection.

Evans J.G. 1972 *Land Snails in Archaeology*. London: Seminar Press.

Evans J.G. and Jones H. 1973 Subfossil and modern land-snail faunas from rock rubble habitats. *Journal of Conchology, London* 28:103–130.

Gale S.J. and Hunt C.O. 1984 in press Kirkhead Cave: new evidence for colonisation of Britain after the last glaciation. *Archaeometry* 26(2).

Garrod D.A.E. 1926 *The Upper Palaeolithic of Britain*. Oxford: Clarendon Press.

Godwin H. 1975 *The History of the British Flora*. London: Cambridge University Press.

Grubert C. 1976 *Uncovering the Past at Steetley Cave*. Worksop: Steetley News.

Gruson E.S. 1976 *A Checklist of the Birds of the World*. London: Collins.

Guggisberg C.A.W. 1975 *Wild Cats of the World*. Newton Abbot: David and Charles.

Harrison C.J.O. 1977 Non-passerine birds of the Ipswichian interglacial from the Gower Caves. *Trans. British Cave Research Association* 4(4):441–442.

Harrison C.J.O. 1979 Pleistocene birds from Swanscombe, Kent. *The London Naturalist* 58:6–8.

Harrison C.J.O. 1980 A re-examination of British Devensian and earlier Holocene bird bones in the British Museum. *Journal of Archaeological Science* 7:53–68.

Harrison C.J.O. and Walker C.A. 1977 A re-examination of the fossil birds from the Upper Pleistocene in the London Basin. *The London Naturalist* 56:6–9.

Hawkioja E. and Hakala T. 1975 Herbivore cycles and periodic outbreaks, formulation of a general hypothesis. *Reports of the Kevo Subarctic Research Studies*, Vol. 12.

Heath T. 1880 *Creswell Crags v. Professor Boyd Dawkins*. Derby: Clulow Press. 40pp.

Heinrich W.-D. 1977 Untersuchungen an Vogel Resten aus dem fossilen Tierbantsystem von Pisede bei Malchin. Teil 1. Taxonomische und biometrische kennzeichung des Fundgates. *Wiss. Zeit der Humboldt-Universitat zu Berlin, Math, R.* 26:329–345.

Howitt R.C.L. and Howitt B.M. 1963 *A Flora of Nottinghamshire*. Nottingham: privately published.

Hunt C.O. 1984 Recent advances in pollen extraction techniques: a brief review. In *Palaeoenvironmental Investigations*. N.R.J. Fieller, D.D. Gilbertson and N.G.A. Ralph (eds). Oxford: British Archaeological Reports.

Ives J.D. and Barry R.G. 1974 *Arctic and Alpine Environments*. London: Methuen.

Jackson J.W. 1926 The vertebrate and molluscan fauna of Chelm's Combe, Cheddar. *Transactions of the Somerset Archaeological and Natural History Society* 72:115–123.

Jackson J.W. 1931 Lynx remains from Yorkshire Caves. *Naturalist* :115–6.

Jackson J.W. 1932 A cave on Giggleswick Scars, Near Settle, Yorkshire. *Naturalist* :5–9.

Jackson J.W. 1936 The Upper Pleistocene fauna and its relation to the Ice Age. *Proceeding Liverpool Geological Society* 19(4):165–182.

Jackson J.W. 1938 Schedule of Cave Finds. *Caves and Caving* 1(1):18–21.

Jackson J.W. 1962 Archaeology and palaeontology. In *British Caving: an Introduction to Speleology* Cullingford (ed). London. Pp.252–346.

Jacobi R. 1980 The Upper Palaeolithic of Britain with special reference to Wales. In *Culture and Environment in Prehistoric Wales*. J.A. Taylor (ed). British Archaeological Reports. British Series 76:15–96.

Janossy D. 1979 Plio-pleistocene bird remains from the Carpathian Basin V. Anseriformes, Gruiformes, Charadriiformes, Passeriformes. *Aquila* 85:11–39.

Jenkinson R.D.S. 1978 Archaeological caves and rock shelters in the Creswell Crags area. *Creswell Crags Visitor Centre Research Report No. 1*. Nottinghamshire County Council.

Jenkinson R.D.S. 1984 *Creswell Crags: Late Pleistocene Sites in the East Midlands*. Oxford: British Archaeological Reports. British Series 122.

Jenkinson R.D.S., Bramwell D., Briggs D.J., Gilbertson D.D., Griffin, C.M., Stebbings, R.E., Watts, C.J. and Wilkinson M. 1982 *Death of a Wolf. Creswell Crags Visitor Centre, Research Report No. 3.*

Kaddah M.T. 1974 The hydrometer method for detailed particle size analysis 1. Graphical interpretation of hydrometer readings and test of method. *Soil Science* 118(2):102–7.

Kerney M.P. 1976a *Atlas of the Non-marine Mollusca of the British Isles*. Cambridge: Conchology Society of Great Britain and Northern Ireland N.E.R.C.

Kerney M.P. 1976b A list of fresh and brackish water Mollusca of the British Isles. *Journal of Conchology* (London) 29:26–8.

Kerney M.P. 1976c Two Post-glacial Molluscan faunas from south-west England. *Journal of Conchology* (London) 29:71–3.

Kerney M.P. 1977a British Quaternary non-marine Mollusca: a brief review. In *British Quaternary Studies: Recent Advances*. F.W. Shotton (ed). Oxford: Clarendon Press. Pp. 31–42.

Kerney M.P. 1977b A proposed zonation scheme for Late-glacial and Post-glacial deposits using land Mollusca. *Journal of Archaeological Science* 4:387–90.

Kerney M.P. and Cameron R.A.D. 1979 *A Field Guide to the Land Snails of Britain and North West Europe*. London: Collins.

Kerney M.P., Preece R.C. and Turner C. 1980 Molluscan and plant biostratigraphy of some Late Devensian and Flandrian deposits in Kent. *Philosophical Transactions of the Royal Society of London* B 291:1–43.

Kitching J. 1963 *Bone, Tooth and Horn Tools of Palaeolithic Man: an account of the Osteodontokeratic Discoveries in Pin Hole, Derbyshire*. Manchester: Manchester University Press.

Kurten B. 1968 *Pleistocene Mammals of Europe*. London: Weidenfeld and Nicholson.

Kurten B. 1978 The Lynx from Etouaiers, *Lynx issiodorensis* Croizet and Jobert late Pliocene. *Annals Zoologica Fennica* 15:314–332.

Laing R. 1889 On the Bone Caves of Creswell and discovery of an extinct Pliocene Feline *(Felis brevirostris)* new to Great Britain. *British Association Advance Science*:582–4.

Laird R. 1821 *Description of the County of Nottinghamshire*. Nottingham.

Lambrecht K. 1933 *Hardbuch der Palaoornithologie*. Berlin: Borntraeger, édit.

Lloyd O.C. 1977 Ferns in cave entrances. *Proceedings International Speleological Congress* 7:228.

Martin P.S. 1967 Pleistocene overkill. In *Pleistocene Extinctions—The Search For A Cause*. P.S. Martin and H.E. Wright (eds). Connecticut: Yale University Press. Pp. 75–120.

Mayhew D.F. 1977 Avian predators as accumulators of fossil mammal material. *Boreas* 6:25–31.
Mayr E. and Meise W. 1980 Theoretische zur Geschichte des Vogelzuges. *Der Vogelzug* Berling 1:149–72.
McBurney C.B.M. 1962 Correspondence with Welbeck Estates Limited. *Welbeck Estates Limited.* (unpublished).
Mellars P.A. 1969 Radiocarbon dates for a new Creswellian site. *Antiquity* :308–10.
Mellet J.S. 1974 Scatological origin of microvertebrate fossil assemblages. *Science* 185.
Mello J.M. 1875 On some bone caves in Creswell Crags. *Quarterly Journal Society of London* 31:679–91.
Mello J.M. 1876 On the bone caves of Creswell. *Quarterly Journal of the Geological Society London* 32:240–59.
Milne-Edwards A. 1867–71 *Recherches anatomiques et palaeontologiques pour servir à la histoire des oiseaux fossiles de la France.* Paris: Victor Messon et fils édit.
Mitchell G.F. 1976 *The Irish Landscape.* London: Collins.
Moreau R.E. 1954 The main vicissitudes of the European avifauna since the Pliocene. *Ibis* 96:411-31.
Mourer-Chauviré C. 1975 Les oiseaux du Pleistocene Moyen et Supérieur de France. *Documents des Laboratoires de Geologie de la Faculte des Sciences de Lyon* 64.
Mullins E.H. 1913 The Ossiferous Cave at Langwith. *Derbyshire Archaeological and Natural History Journal* 35:137–58.
Munsell Soil Colour Charts 1975. Baltimore.
Murphy J. and Riley J.P. 1962 A modified single solution method for the determination of phosphate in natural waters. *Annual Chemical Acta* 27:31–6.
Peach B.N. and Horne J. 1917 The bone cave in the Valley of Allt nan Blamh (Burn of Caves) near Inchnadamff, Assynt, Sutherlandshire. *Proceedings of the Royal Society Edinburgh* 37:327–49.
Pennington W. 1974 *The History of British Vegetation.* London: English Universities Press.
Powers M. 1953 A new roundness scale for sedimentary particles. *Journal Sedimentary Petrology* 25:117–9.
Ransom W.H. 1866 On the occurrence of *Felis lynx* as a British fossil. *Reports British Association Advancement Science* (Nottingham): 66–7.
Regalia E. 1907 Avifauna fossili Italianea. *Avicula* XI:49–54, 78–84.
Remmert H. 1980 *Arctic Animal Ecology.* Berlin: Springer-Verlag.
Saint-Perier R. de 1927 La grotte de Gouerris a Lespugue. *L'Anthropologie* 37:263–76.
Samson C. 1979 *The location of subterranean cavities in the region of Creswell Crags, Derbyshire, by means of geophysical prospection.* Unpublished M.Sc. Thesis. University of Bradford.
Samson C. and Jenkinson R.D.S. 1979 *On the Discovery and Geophysical Survey of New Archaeological Caves in Creswell Crags.* Nottinghamshire and Derbyshire County Council. Creswell Crags Research Report No. 2.
Savage R.J.G. 1966 Irish Pleistocene Mammals. *Irish Naturalist's Journal* 15:117–30.
Scott J.E. and Hughes E.W. 1981 Chondroitin sulphate from fossilized antlers. *Nature* 291:580–1.
Shovkoplyas I.G. 1965 *The Merzin Site.* Kiev: Naukova Dum (in Russian).
Smith-Woodward A. 1924 Correspondence with Sollas and Woodward. In Dawkins W.B. (1924) *op cit.* Derbyshire County Record Office, Matlock (unpublished manuscripts).
Soergel E. 1961 III. Die Vogelreste. In Ein Mittel-Steinzeitlicher Wohnplatz in Mecklenburg. E. Schuldt and Hohen Viecheln (eds). *Deutsche Akademie der Wissenschaften, Berlin. Schrifturn Sektion for Vor-und Frügeschichte* 10:64–9.
Soergel E. 1966 Die Tuefels—oder Fuchsenlucken bei Eggenberg (NÖ). *Österr. Akad. Wissenschaften, wein Mathematisch-Naturwissenschafliche Klasse* 112:93–107.
Sollas W.J. 1915 *Ancient Hunters and their Modern Representatives.* London.
South R. 1961 *The Moths of the British Isles.* 2 vols. London: Warne.
Stehlin H.G. and Studer, Th. 1918 Saugetiere und Vögel. In Die Steinzeitlichen Stationen des Birstales, wischen Basel und Delsberg. F. Sarasin (ed). *Neue Denkschrift der Schweizelschen Naturforschenden Gesellschaft* 54. Zürich.
Stressmann A.P. 1948 Die Wanderungen des Pirols. *Ornis Berlin* (Heidelberg) 1:126–42.
Stuart A.J. 1977 British Quaternary Vertebrates. In *British Quaternary Studies: Recent Advances.* F.W. Shotton (ed). Oxford: Clarendon Press.
Stuart A.J. 1980 The vertebrate fauna from interglacial deposits at Sugworth near Oxford. *Philosophical Transactions Royal Society* B 289:87–97.
Stuart A.J. 1983 *Pleistocene vertebrates in the British Isles.* London: Longman.
Stubbs G. 1767 *Two Gentlemen Going Shooting with a view of Creswell Crags taken on the spots.* Oil on canvas. Yale Centre for British Art. Paul Mellon Collection No. B1976.7.85. Painted on the spot.
Swinton W.E. 1964 The avifauna of Barnfield Pit. In *The Swanscombe Skull.* C.D. Ovey (ed). London: Royal Anthropological Society.
Thompson A.H. 1938 *The Praemonstratension Abbey of Welbeck.* London: published privately.
Tierzen L.L. 1978 Vegetation and productive ecology of an Alaskan Arctic Tundra. *Ecology Studies* 29:1–686.
Tuberville A.S. 1938 *History of Welbeck Abbey and its owners 1539–1755.* London: Faber and Faber.
Vandel A. 1965 *Biospeleology: The Biology of Cavernicolous Animals.* Oxford: Pergamon Press.
Villalta J.F. 1964 Datos para un catalogo de las aves fosiles del cuaternario Espanol. *Speleon. Esp.* Oviedo 11:79–102.
Walden H.W. 1976 A nomenclatural list of the land Mollusca of the British Isles. *Journal Conchology London* 29:21–5.
Wiijnagaarden-Bakker L.H. van 1974 The animal remains from the Beaker settlement at Newgrange, Co. Meath. First report. *Proceedings of the Royal Irish Academy* 74C:313–83.
Williams P.W. and Williams R.B.G. 1966 The deposits at Ballymihill Cave, Co. Clare, Ireland with particular references to non-marine Mollusca. *Proceedings Speleological Society* 11:71–82.
Winge H. 1903 Om jordfunde Fugle fra Danmark. *Vidensk. Meddel. Naturh. Foren. Copenhagen* 6:61–110.
White G. 1970 *Dead Man's Cave, North Anston.* Worksop Museum.
Wishart D. 1978 *Clustan User Manual.* (3rd ed). Programme Library Unit, Edinburgh University.
Yalden D. 1982 When did the mammal fauna of the British Isles arrive? *Mammal Review* 12(1):1–57.